Small Scale Enterprises in Industrial Development

Editorial Advisory Committee

Small Scale Enterprises in Industrial Development: The Indian Experience

Edited by
K.B. SURI

SAGE PUBLICATIONS
New Delhi/Newbury Park/London

This publication has been jointly sponsored by the Institute of Economic Growth, Delhi and the World Bank.

First published in 1988 by

Sage Publications India Pvt Ltd
32 M–Block Market, Greater Kailash I
New Delhi 110 048

Sage Publications Inc
2111 West Hillcrest Drive
Newbury Park
California 91320

Sage Publications Ltd
28 Banner Street
London EC1Y 8QE
England

Published by Tejeshwar Singh for Sage Publications India Pvt Ltd, phototypeset at South End Typographics, Pondicherry, and printed at Chaman Offset Printers, New Delhi.

Library of Congress Cataloging-in-Publication Data

Small Scale enterprises in industrial development.

    1. Small business—India—Congresses.
I. Suri, K. B., 1932
HD2346.I5S547   1988   338.6'42'0954   87-23221

ISBN 0-8039-9539-3 (U.S.-hbk.) ISBN 81-7036-060-9 (India-hbk.)
ISBN 0-8039-9543-1 (U.S.-pbk.) ISBN 81-7036-061-7 (India-pbk.)

Contents

Foreword

Supply side interventions in favour of small firms became popular in the 1970s, especially among the industrialised countries. In the case of developing countries, the World Bank enthusiastically promoted loans to small firms through the medium of Development Finance Corporations, as part of its efforts to obtain a more labour-demanding industrialisation. This policy was itself part of the Bank's efforts, dear to McNamara, to achieve growth with greater equity than in the past.

However, on the research side of the Bank, it seemed to some that the idea that the supply side promotion of small firms would contribute significantly to a more labour-demanding development rested on very insecure empirical foundations. As I was at the time (1976) a special adviser in the Development Economics Department I instigated some research into the subject. India was the main basis for the new 'shop-floor' enquiries that concentrated—though not exclusively—on the relation between factor use and size (some surveys were also made in Colombia). Dipak Mazumdar and John Page had primary responsibility for this work in India. For various reasons, not their fault, progress was extremely slow. It was only in early 1985 that a draft of the forthcoming book *Small Manufacturing Enterprises: A Comparative Study of India and Other Countries*, by I.M.D. Little, D. Mazumdar and J. Page, was available. In line with the Bank's aim of disseminating research findings of policy relevance, a three-day conference on small scale industry development in India was organised jointly by the World Bank and the Institute of Economic Growth, Delhi. Dr Mazumdar and I were thus able to present the findings included here, and benefit from the observations of a critical audience. Many Indian and other scholars participated and made wide-ranging and important contributions, as this volume of papers and proceedings, edited by Professor K.B. Suri, makes clear. I believe this volume can contribute to the evolution of a more informed and sound industrial policy in India.

December 1987

I.M.D. LITTLE
Nuffield College
Oxford

Acknowledgements

The proceedings of the Conference on Small Scale Industry Development, held in New Delhi during 22–24 March 1985 under the joint auspices of the Institute of Economic Growth and the World Bank, form the basis of this volume.

The initiative for the Conference came from Professor I.M.D. Little, Dr Dipak Mazumdar and Dr John M. Page, Jr., who had organised and completed at the World Bank, Washington D.C., researches in the economics of small scale industries in India and in a few other developing countries. I express my gratitude to them for their keen and sustained interest in the Conference. I am thankful to Professor K. Krishnamurty, Director, Institute of Economic Growth, and Dr E. Bevan Waide, Chief of the World Bank's Resident Mission in India, for their fruitful collaboration to organise the Conference in New Delhi.

The Steering Committee, with Professor K. Krishnamurty, IEG, and Roger Grawe, Senior Economist at the World Bank as Co-Chairmen, Professor K.L. Krishna, Head of the Department of Economics, Delhi School of Economics, Professors D.U. Sastry and Devendra B. Gupta, IEG, Dr Y.K. Alagh, Chairman, Bureau of Industrial Costs and Prices as Members and Professor K.B. Suri, School of Planning and Architecture, as Member-Secretary, played an important part in working out the details of the Conference. I am grateful to the members of the Steering Committee for their individual and collective help and wise counsel in designing the academic frame of the Conference.

I sincerely thank the authors of the research papers and those who made oral presentations, the chairmen, discussants and rapporteurs for the working sessions and all others who took part in the Conference. The authors of the papers readily agreed to revise their respective papers on the basis of the discussions at the Conference and also the specific comments made by the Editorial Advisory Committee. I am indebted to them.

The Editorial Advisory Committee consisted of Professors K. Krishnamurty, D.U. Sastry and Devendra B. Gupta of the Institute of Economic Growth, Professors K.L. Krishna and Suresh D. Tendulkar of the Delhi School of Economics, Dr Y.K. Alagh of the Bureau of Industrial Costs and Prices and Dr G. Pursell of the World Bank. I am obliged to the members of the EAC for their invaluable help. Professors Krishna, Tendulkar, Sastry, Gupta, and Dr K. Sundaram (Delhi School of Economics) read through the papers and gave their comments and suggestions for their revision; I am thankful to all of them. I express my deep gratitude to Professor Gupta for his generous help and guidance in the detailed editing of many of the original and revised papers.

I have found the statements of the discussants for the working sessions, namely Dr K. Sundaram (Session I—Data Base), Professor K.L. Krishna and Dr Bishwanath Goldar (Session II—Relative Efficiency), Professor D.U. Sastry (Session III—Entrepreneurship Development), Professors Suresh D. Tendulkar, J.C. Sandesara and Lalit K. Deshpande (Session IV—Factor and Product Markets and Linkages) and Dr Isher J. Ahluwalia (Session V—Government Policy), very useful in the preparation of my Introduction. I am thankful to them.

I have immensely benefited from the detailed critical comments on an earlier draft of the Introduction by Dr G. Pursell and Dr John R. Hansen of the World Bank and Professor Devendra B. Gupta, currently of the Faculty of Management Studies, Delhi University.

The Resident Mission of the World Bank in India—the co-sponsors of the Conference—have provided generous financial and infrastructural support for the Conference as well as for the preparation and the publication of this volume. I am grateful to Dr E. Bevan Waide, the Chief of the Resident Mission.

Ashok Kapoor rendered able secretarial assistance for the Conference and V. Subramanian has patiently typed and retyped this volume. I thank both of them.

I must stress in the end that the views and interpretations in this document are those of the authors and other contributors and should not be attributed to the institutions or organisations where they happen to work.

July 1987   K.B. SURI
                                                                          New Delhi

1 K.B. Suri

Introduction

Small scale industries, including traditional village industries, small workshops and modern small enterprises, have been given an important place in the framework of Indian economic planning for ideological and economic reasons. The small industries sector has been imbued with a multiplicity of objectives, important among these being (*i*) the generation of immediate employment opportunities with relatively low investment, (*ii*) the promotion of more equitable distribution of national income, (*iii*) effective mobilisation of untapped capital and human skills, and (*iv*) dispersal of manufacturing activities all over the country, leading to growth of villages, small towns and economically lagging regions.[1]

The village and small scale industries have found their economic rationale in the Mahalanobis model, which forms the theoretical basis of India's Second and subsequent Five Year Plans. The Mahalanobis industrialisation strategy, with its focus on the development of the highly capital-intensive large-scale basic and heavy industries, underlined the development of the village and small industries sector as a means to promote large-scale employment and also meet the increased demand for consumer goods. While the Second Five Year Plan was being formulated, an international team of experts sponsored by the Ford Foundation visited India in 1954 and recommended the development of the urban oriented and relatively modern small scale industries through a massive multidimensional programme of government assistance. The programme

See P.N. Dhar (1979), pp. 178–79. See also Government of India, Development Commissioner, Small Scale Industries (1982), pp. 6–7.

included market research, technology upgradation, improvement in organisation and management, financial assistance, formation of cooperatives, and so on.

India has earned the rare distinction among the developing countries of having ardently supported the village and small scale industries (VSSIs) throughout the post-Independence period. The VSSIs have been protected from the unequal competition of large scale industries through physical controls on the product range and the growth of the large industries, discriminatory fiscal levies on the large sector and direct financial aid and assistance and other promotional programmes for the VSSIs.

Government agencies have claimed impressive growth of small enterprises, specially in the modern small scale sector which for developmental purposes has been under the purview of the GOI's Small Industries Development Organisation (SIDO). The sector is reported to have made, in the recent past, substantial gains in terms of the number of units, value of output and exports, though its contribution to employment generation has been found to belie the expectations. The official claims, based as these were on deficient data premise and suffering from several methodological weaknesses, have been questioned. Doubts have been raised from time to time about the long-held beliefs in the economic viability and social merit of the traditional village industries as well as the modern small sector and also in the role assigned to the VSSIs in the process of Indian industrial and economic development.[2] The government policies and programmes to protect and promote the small scale sector have been found to be wanting in effective pursuit of the expressed objectives. In some instances the policies seem to have even hurt the interests of the small scale enterprises.[3]

The debate on the place of small enterprises in the evolving industrial and economic structure and their role in the socio-economic transformation of India and other less developed countries has gathered momentum in the recent past. Many individuals, institutions and organisations in India and in other countries have made significant contributions to research on small industries. The Research Department of the World Bank also conducted in India

[2] V.N. Balasubramanyam (1984), pp. 115–18 and 131–35. See also P.N. Dhar and H.F. Lydall (1961), J.C. Sandesara (1966), and Nirmala Banerjee (1981), pp. 277–96.

[3] J.N. Bhagwati and P. Desai (1970).

and in a few other developing countries field studies of selected product-specific industries, focusing on the comparative economics of small and large manufacturing establishments. The Institute of Economic Growth, Delhi and the World Bank jointly sponsored a conference on 'Small Scale Industry Development' in New Delhi during March 1985 to discuss and deliberate over the results of the researches on the positive and normative aspects of small scale enterprises, completed by the World Bank[4] as well as by other scholars and researchers.

This volume contains the revised version of some of the papers presented at the Conference.[5] The papers have been divided in five parts, namely, Data Base, Relative Efficiency, Industry Studies, Factor and Product Markets and Linkages, and Government Policy. What follows is a review of the papers.

Data Base

The small scale sector, as commonly understood in India, includes a wide range of manufacturing units which vary in the size of employment, capital investment and value of output as well as in the level of organisation, technology, source of power, type and quality of products, and so on. The sector is very heterogeneous as it covers manually operated tiny household units widely dispersed all over the country as well as urban based relatively large establishments using modern technology. The small units, thus, belong to three sub-sectors: (*a*) traditional village industries including handicrafts, (*b*) small unregistered household and non-household units not covered by the Factories Act of 1948, and (*c*) registered factories.

The official definition of 'small scale industries' (SSIs), which are under the protective umbrella of the Indian government's Small Industries Development Organisation (SIDO), is based on the initial investment in plant and machinery. The SSIs, so defined, are heavily concentrated in and around large urban centres as this sector excludes traditional village industries. The limit for the in-

---

The results of the research studies organised by the World Bank during the year 1978–83 have been published. See Little, Mazumdar and Page (forthcoming).

[5] The paper 'Technology, Firm Size and Product Quality: A Study of Laundry Soap in India' by K.B. Suri, which could not be completed in time for the Conference, has been included in this volume.

clusion of a unit in the SSI has been revised upwards several times in the recent past.

In the face of the diversities of the Indian small manufacturing enterprises, it would be an uphill task for any organisation to build a data inventory covering the entire VSSI sector with details of principal economic parameters. Unfortunately, several government agencies have been involved in the collection of data for different segments of the VSSIs. Because of ineffective central direction and coordination, the concepts and the definitions employed by these agencies lack uniformity and the data collected for some segments suffers from serious gaps. This has vitiated comparability of the data over time as well as between the various segments. Further, there have been unduly long time lags between the collection and the publication of the data mainly on account of limited resources at the disposal of the data producing agencies.

Three specialists have contributed to Part I. In the first paper G. Ramachandran focuses on the data base for the 'Small Scale Industries' (SSIs) which comprise all the unregistered units—non-household and household—also known as the unregistered or unorganised industries, and the registered factories in which the investment in plant and machinery is within the prescribed limits.

The author points to the unsatisfactory state of available data for the SSI sector, particularly relating to the non-factory or unregistered units. The SIDO's in-house data, collected from the SSI units registered with the State Directorates of Industries (SDI), suffer from grossly incomplete coverage, specially of smaller non-factory units, since the registration of the units for assistance is voluntary. The dependence on the Central Statistical Organisation (CSO) for the data on the factory sector collected through the Annual Survey of Industries (ASI) has also not been of much help as these data stop at the three-digit level and further, the number of 'unspecified' units, constituting the 'miscellaneous' category, has in the course of time increased to alarming proportions. It is, in fact, hard to find reliable estimates of total production in specific lines in the SSI sector for the factory and non-factory units.

M.R. Saluja makes a detailed appraisal of the various sources of data relating to the unregistered sector. He highlights the conceptual and methodological inconsistencies which have resulted in (a) incomplete coverage of various segments of the sector, (b) overlapping between the coverage by different sources, and (c) distortions in chronological comparison of data from the same source. More recent efforts by the CSO and its sister organisation, the National Sample Survey Organisation (NSSO), to conduct censuses and surveys of the unregistered sector, consisting of the household and the non-household enterprises would meet a vital informational need. These efforts, if freed from the above weaknesses, can generate more reliable and useful data in the future.

The above contributions underline some serious flaws in the methods used by the CSO to estimate the contribution of the unregistered sector to the national product. These inconsistencies have resulted in the use of indices of production and growth of organised large scale establishments for estimating the production and the growth of the unregistered sector.

K. Sundaram and Suresh Tendulkar have, perhaps, been the first to systematically work out an approximation of the size structure of manufacturing industry in India, covering the entire range from tiny household units to the large factory establishments. By collecting data available from different sources, the authors have estimated the size distributions at the two-digit level of disaggregation. The paper distinguishes five segments within each two-digit industry, viz. (*i*) census sector of the ASI, (*ii*) sample sector of the ASI, (*iii*) unorganised workshops with five or more workers, (*iv*) rural household manufacturing, and (*v*) urban household manufacturing. They have worked out for each industry the percentage value added and employment shares for the five segments and assessed their relative 'significance' or 'dominance'.

The authors find the size structure of the Indian manufacturing enterprises to be highly polarised with concentration of value added in the ASI census segment and of employment in the segment of rural household manufacturing. Further, they derive the upper bound estimates of the value added for the modern small scale sector (SSI) by pooling together the sample segment of the ASI and the segment of unregistered workshops with five or more workers. On the basis of these estimates they have identified seven industries in which the SSI sector is 'significant' in its share of value added. The SSI sector is found to be 'dominant' only in one industry, viz. metal products and parts.

The authors have also found large inter-segment differentials in labour productivity which they attribute to differences in capital intensity per worker, the latter representing different technology regimes. The large productivity differentials, according to the authors, call for explanation of the co-existence of different segments with wide variations in the level of technology. Some of the issues relating to the co-existence of manufacturing units of varying sizes and using different technologies are examined in Part III on 'Industry Studies'.

Relative Efficiency

Fact-finding researches in the relative efficiency, in terms of factor productivities, factor intensities and technical efficiency, of the small manufacturing enterprises assume significance in view of the widely prevalent belief that small units as compared with large establishments possess, besides other virtues, employment creating and capital saving characteristics. The two papers included in Part II review the relevant international experience and present results of the studies of the Indian industries which merit the attention of researchers, planners and policy makers.

Bishwanath Goldar in his paper compares for thirty-seven Indian industries at the three-digit level the technical efficiency of small scale and large scale industries for the year 1976–77. The data for the small scale industries relate to the aggregates for the units assisted by commercial banks while the data for the large scale establishments relate to the ASI census sector. The author presents estimates of relative labour productivity, relative capital productivity and relative total factor productivity (relative efficiency) of the modern SSIs. The author finds that the SSIs (compared to the large scale establishments) generally have low labour productivity, high capital productivity, low capital intensity (measured as capital per employee) and low total factor productivity. He infers that the modern small scale sector is inefficient relative to the large sector in a large number of industries. He also finds that the relative efficiency of the SSIs varies directly with capital intensity, so that the SSIs cannot be relied upon as a source of efficient employment generation.

The author attempts to explain the inter-industry differences in relative efficiency with the help of multiple regression analysis. The relative efficiency index is found to be positively related to relative size and the proportion of units using power, and negatively related to the ratio of short-term bank borrowings to inventories. The latter relationship, according to the author, perhaps indicates that the availability of bank credit exerts an adverse effect on the efficiency of SSIs. This inference of the author is in line with J.C. Sandesara's conclusion (Part V) that bank-assisted small scale units have not performed as well as non-assisted units.

In the second paper, Ian Little presents a summary of Chapters 7 through 12 of the World Bank Study by Little, Mazumdar and Page. The examination of relevant international experience of Japan and of India, Colombia, Korea and Taiwan among the LDCs, based on the census material, shows that the hypothesised relationship between factor productivities and intensities and employment size of the firm (the larger the size the greater is the capital intensity and labour productivity and lower the capital productivity), by and large, holds for manufacturing in the aggregate, though there are exceptions in that the smallest size class is not always the most labour intensive or with the highest capital productivity. Capital productivity generally shows an inverted U pattern. These results, though not generally favourable to smaller size, are of little policy relevance because the comparison of the economic ratios across size classes assumes that firms of different sizes in an industry produce goods of comparable quality and that all industries have the same production function.

When the analysis is undertaken at the disaggregated level, the hypothesised relationships between unit size and factor productivities/ intensities fail. The smallest size class is quite often not the most labour intensive; nor does it have the highest capital productivity. Also, it is not the best size class in terms of total factor productivity. There is considerable evidence from most of the countries that in many industries the medium class—50–500 workers—is the 'most beautiful'.

Next, the author presents the results of the IBRD sample surveys of five narrowly defined industries carried out in India, namely, printing, machine tools, laundry soap, shoes and iron castings. The surveys generally support the above results obtained from the cross-country evidence. In none of the five industries examined is there a monotonic progression of average capital intensity with size. Also, for capital intensity as well as for capital productivity, the variations *within* size groups are so great that the variations *between* size groups appear to be of little consequence. On the basis of the above analyses, the author notes that (*a*) inter-industry variations in capital intensity are far greater than intra-industry variations by size group, and (b) enterprises with very low capital productivity and capital intensity are generally manually-operated units using traditional methods of production. These inferences tally with the findings of Goldar.

The econometric analysis of the IBRD survey sample, carried out by John Page, gives the estimates of translog production functions, both of the average and the frontier kind, with capital, skilled labour and unskilled labour as inputs. The estimates indicate substantial substitution possibilities between inputs, except between capital and unskilled labour in which case these appear to be somewhat limited. Estimates of frontier translog function show that technical efficiency (and total productivity) does not vary systematically or significantly with firm size, except in the machine tools industry where the inefficiency of the small size group is significant compared to larger establishments. For shoes and soap also, the smallest size is the least efficient and the largest size the most efficient, though the variations across size are not statistically significant. Further, the analysis does not indicate significant scale economies or diseconomies across the entire size range. Workers' firm-specific experience and the newness of equipment are found to exert significant favourable effect on productivity, but there is little systematic variation in the vintage of capital or workers' experience with size. It may, however, be pointed out that newness of equipment does not necessarily indicate a higher level of technology. The hypothesis that smaller firms employ a lower level of technology resulting in lower productivity, therefore, remains to be invalidated.

The foregoing analyses, which form a part of the World Bank study, are very valuable from the methodological point of view. The results as summarised here have important policy implications which are examined in the last section on 'Government Policy'.

Industry Studies

The examination of the relative efficiency of small scale enterprises and related issues continues in Part III. We have seen in Part II that the aggregative approach to the comparative analysis of the small and large scale industries using the material from the censuses and surveys and even disaggregation of the data at the four- or five-digit level may not completely ensure product homogeneity which is a necessary condition for a meaningful analysis of factor productivities, factor intensities and efficiency. The studies included in this part, like the World Bank studies of narrowly-defined industries in India, are based on intensive field surveys of small and large enterprises engaged in the processing of specific products and an in-depth examination of their distinguishing economic features.

Four papers are included in Part III. The first paper by George Waardenburg examines the factor intensities (including employment effects), efficiency and other socio-economic aspects of small scale leather shoe-manufacturing units in Agra, differentiated according to marketing channels and the size of production. In the second paper, Harry de Haan compares two major cane-processing technologies employed in the sugar industry on the basis of his field-work in western Uttar Pradesh. The last two papers by Nirmala Banerjee and K.B. Suri, which are sample studies of the electric fan industry in Calcutta and the laundry soap units in and around Delhi, respectively, probe into the simultaneous functioning of firms of varying sizes, and employing (in some cases) different technologies but producing items which appear to be the same. Each study takes up a unique case and attempts to identify a specific set of factors in order to explain the phenomenon of co-existence in that particular industry.

Waardenburg's study of small leather shoe-making units shows that with an increase in size, labour intensity decreases very sharply without any significant increase in capital intensity. These patterns, according to the author, strongly suggest economies of scale. They also suggest that without adequate protection, smaller units may be wiped out by larger units. Comparison across marketing channels reveals that the small local suppliers and suppliers to the Uttar Pradesh Leather Development and Marketing Corporation (UPLDMC) are most labour intensive and least capital intensive whereas the exporters and the ancillaries to large shoe companies are the least labour intensive and most capital intensive. It follows that the former mentioned categories (i.e., the local suppliers and the suppliers to the UPLDMC) have the highest labour-capital ratios while the latter categories of exporters and ancillaries have the least labour-capital ratios. The author attributes the wide variations in the factor proportions to a considerable range of technological choice in the small scale shoe making sector. Direct evidence about different technologies used by the small firms appears to be necessary in support of the above-mentioned surmise of the author.

The author makes estimates of a Cobb-Douglas production function in order to compare the technical efficiency of the various categories. The 'local suppliers large' and 'local suppliers small' are found to be the least efficient and the 'ancillaries' and perhaps the 'exporters,' the most efficient. Efficiency is also found to generally increase with size.

Implicit in Waardenburg's analysis is the question of co-existence of the shoe-making units varying over size, employment structure, type of organisation including marketing arrangements, production techniques to the extent of mechanisation effecting various sub-processes, etc. Among the factors aiding the co-existence of different types of units, variation in factor proportions, cost of production, quality and price of the product and the caste factor (which acts as a powerful non-economic constraint on occupational mobility, especially in small scale units or small local suppliers and suppliers to the UPLDMC) might be playing an important role. Waardenburg shows concern for the small units (or the local suppliers) which have been stagnating in the recent past. These units employ very poor people from the scheduled castes and account for a substantial proportion of the total working force engaged in shoe-making. Government support is necessary to protect the poor people who are trying to eke out a meagre living. Any attempt to upgrade their technology, according to the author, might displace labour and hurt the people.

In the next paper, de Haan attempts an economic evaluation of modern technology of the large scale mill sector and recently developed intermediate technology—an improved version of the Khandsari process—of small factories in the sugar industry in India. The modern process, known as the vacuum pan sulphitation (VPS) method—as compared with the intermediate technology, known as the open pan sulphitation (OPS) method—has considerably higher capital-labour ratio and produces sugar of superior quality which commands better prices in the free market. The OPS method has considerably lower capital costs and generates more employment per unit of physical output than the VPS method, though it suffers from lower crushing and boiling efficiency which leads to higher cane cost and lower sugar recovery and lower quality of the output.

The evaluation of the two technologies is made against the backdrop of (*a*) recent rapid growth of small units using the OPS process at the expense of the mill sector on account of deliberate government policy, and (*b*) international debate on appropriate sugar technology which has led to the hypothesis that though the OPS as currently practised is not a viable alternative, technological improvements can make it 'sufficiently cost effective to withstand competition from the VPS under equal conditions'.

De Haan uses the benefit-cost technique based on the principles proposed by Hansen and presents the evaluation of the two technologies at economic prices which reflect the real scarcities of the outputs and the inputs of the production processes. The results of the analysis establish the clear superiority of the VPS under the assumption of free market prices and even under partial decontrol. The author examines at length the possibility of increasing the rate of recovery by introducing technical improvements in the expeller and the furnace and of improving the quality of sugar to get higher prices in the case of the OPS. He concludes that the possibilities are quite remote and that under the current and future technological environment, the OPS cannot be improved to the extent necessary to outweigh the advantages of the VPS process. Even with the maximum possible improvement in the recovery rate and the price ratio, the OPS process is not found to be viable.

De Haan's comparative evaluation of the two technologies raises two important questions. First, why has the OPS, the less efficient technology, grown so rapidly in the face of the overwhelmingly large mill sector? This question is closely related to the issue of the co-existence of firms of different sizes using different technologies. The answer to this question can be found in the author's reference to the quality and price differentials in the products of the two types of firms and, more importantly, to the discriminatory government policies against the mill sector. Second, how far can economic evaluation be a complete answer to the choice between the two technologies? During the discussion at the Conference, the author identified some of the beneficiaries and the victims of the rapid growth of the OPS process at the cost of the mill sector. This points to the need to take into consideration the effects of income redistribution, including the social valuation of larger employment at lower wage rates of the OPS against less employment at higher wage rates of the VPS within the analytical framework of social benefit-cost analysis.

The other two papers have their focus on issues relating to the co-existence of small and large units in a given industry. Banerjee, in her study of Calcutta's electric fan industry, examines the co-existence of very small artisan-type units and very large industrial establishments, the former operating as ancillaries to the large firms for certain specified sub-processes. The author compares the efficiency of small and large firms in terms of the unit cost of the piece-work carried out by the small units and of the same work done by the large units. The results show that the small units have higher unit costs even when their cost disadvantages (in respect of material inputs and borrowed capital) are not taken into account. The payment received by the small units for the piece-work is less than their estimated cost and the small units, therefore, suffer losses.

The author investigates the economic rationale of the ancillary relationship which has been continuing in spite of the apparent losses of the small units. The large firms, in the face of uncertain demand from the domestic and foreign markets, use the small unorganised units to meet the sporadic excess demand without investing in additional capacity which they cannot use continuously over long intervals. In this way the large firms transmit the uncertainty of their demand to the small units. They make meagre payment to the small units which does not even cover their production costs. The small units, on their part, pay subsistence wages to the hired workers when they have work and retrench them when there is no work. They use crude techniques, save on inputs, use inferior quality materials and avoid certain operations if they can, thus lowering the quality of the final product. The main objective of the small units is not to maximise profits but to find some employment for a living for as long as possible. These units, thus, subsist by resorting to unfair practices. The large firms knowingly compromise on the quality of their products. As a consequence they may suffer further shrinkage of their markets. The ancillary arrangement in this case, according to the author, instead of being complementary and mutually beneficial, has turned into a low level trap for all concerned, specially for a poor and vulnerable section of the population, resulting in the exploitation of poor people with inadequate information and knowledge and a very weak resource base.

In this case the functional tie-up between the large scale oligopolistic industry and the relatively inefficient small artisan shops, which are the two extremes of the size spectrum, entails an unequal exploitative relationship which adversely affects the overall efficiency of the industry and the quality of the final product. What has prompted the evolution of the relationship? Is it the absence of a long-term development perspective and an over-emphasis on making quick gains on the part of the oligopolistic electric fan industry, or the pressure from the highly competitive foreign markets, highly elastic labour supply at subsistence wage rates, or the depressing general industrial and economic environment which is, perhaps, indirectly influenced by government policies? How can the ancillary arrangement of the above type be uplifted so as to improve the level of efficiency, assure the quality of the product and protect the economic interests of the entrepreneurs and workers in the un-organised small sector? These questions, as in the case of Waardenburg's study of small scale shoe makers in Agra, do not have easy answers.

In his study of the laundry soap industry, Suri examines the co-existence of the large firms using power-based modern technology and the small manually-operated units using traditional technology. In this case not only the organised (power using) sector and the decentralised (manual or non-power) sector have functioned side by side, but the non-power sector has grown very substantially at the expense of the power sector in the last two decades. The author attributes the rapid expansion of the non-power sector, to some extent, to government policy.

He explains the co-existence of the two sectors in terms of (*i*) differentials in the quality of the product, the non-power sector—particularly the small manually operated units—producing low quality sub-standard soap on account of crude methods of production and also poor quality and composition of the raw materials used; (*ii*) differentiated factor markets facing the two sectors, as reflected by large differentials in the wage rates and the shortage of institutional finance for the small manually operated units; (*iii*) large differences in the level and the structure of costs of soap produced in the two sectors, the costs being significantly higher in the power sector, mainly on account of markedly higher selling costs, including publicity and distribution costs, higher costs of packing materials, excise taxes and costlier raw materials; (*iv*) highly structured product markets, the soap produced by the power sector commanding higher prices from affluent sections *largely* on account of its superior quality while the sub-standard soap made by small scale manually-operated units finding outlets among lower income groups in localised markets. The power sector firms and the larger manually operated units also have a monopolistic hold over the market by artificially differentiating their products through brand names and intensive publicity campaigns, as well as by segmenting the market spatially and on the basis of socio-economic and cultural traits of the clientele; and (v) government's fiscal and other regulatory policies which have discriminated against the power sector.

Suri brings out the major effects of the co-existence of the two technologies—distinguished by the use or non-use of electric power—which has been strongly aided by discriminatory government policies. The power sector, with its licensed capacity for the manufacture of laundry soap frozen at levels far below its installed or rated capacity and the burden of excise taxes, has reacted by specialising in the manufacture of superior quality high priced soap, searching for new distant markets and, most important, by diverting its capacity to manufacture toilet soap and synthetic detergents which are highly priced items. Further, toilet soap is not within the manufacturing capability of the non-power sector. The author concludes that the growth of the non-power sector has resulted in (i) substitution of better quality soap by sub-standard varieties, (ii) low wages to labour and (iii) loss of excise tax revenue to the government.

Factor and Product Markets and Linkages

The working of factor markets and the resulting factor prices which face firms of different sizes in an industry is likely to exert a strong influence on the factor proportions and the choice of technology. In the preceding section, large wage differentials have been observed between small and large establishments, which in some instances use different technologies (see papers by Banerjee, Suri and de Haan). It is also believed that small scale enterprises have poor access to organised capital markets and institutional finance and, therefore, largely depend on informal or unorganised sources of credit. Apart from factor prices, product markets may also vary over firm size and technology, particularly when the products manufactured by different units in the industry lack homogeneity due to real or perceived differences in the quality and composition of raw materials and also packaging, brand names and publicity campaigns. These differences are likely to be reflected in production and related costs as well as in the price levels.

The papers included in this part examine important issues relating to the factor and product markets as well as the development linkages of small scale enterprises. Dipak Mazumdar, in his paper, first examines the labour market issue of the wage differential between small and large units and assesses the relative importance of institutional factors, i.e., 'distortion' and economic factors, to explain the differential. The author uses the Bombay labour market study to bring out large wage differentials between small (10–99 workers) and large (100 + workers) factories. He also examines the ASI aggregative data relating to the Indian registered factories classified into census (large) and sample (small) sectors across six major Indian states along with the corresponding NSSO data for unregistered small scale units for urban and rural areas. He finds huge differentials between the census and the sample sectors and relatively small differentials between the sample sector and the unregistered urban sector.

Mazumdar looks into the historical evidence pertaining to the period before the Second World War and also the data of the survey of small scale industries conducted in Bombay city during the late fifties and infers that compared to economic factors, the institutional factors have been quite weak, though their importance has grown in the post-Independence period. He claims that in spite of unionisation of labour and state intervention, the larger factories paid markedly higher wages mainly for economic reasons.

Mazumdar suggests a hypothesis to explain the earnings differentials, which comprises: (*i*) supply price is higher for permanent than for temporary migrants and the former, being more stable and more productive, are preferred in the large factories while the latter find employment mostly in small factories; (*ii*) the wage-efficiency relationship perceived in the larger factories results in a preference for a firm-specific stable work force which belongs to the set of permanent migrants; and (*iii*) large firms have an internal labour market where the entry is through recruitment at the bottom of the ladder and the vacancies at the higher levels are filled through internal promotion. This arrangement reduces the training costs and develops a system of incentives to go up the ladder through 'on the job' learning and performance.

Two main comments are in order. First, this hypothesis has inadequate empirical support and second, it rests entirely on the concept of migrant labour. The implied assumptions that rural-urban migrants form an important part of the entrants to the labour force for the manufacturing sector, that family migrants are more stable than lone migrants and the former have a higher supply price, and that stable migrants are stable workers need to be empirically verified.

The second part of the paper is devoted to product markets for small and large establishments. The author addresses himself to the question whether heterogeneity of products can produce differences in capital intensity by size *even in the absence of factor price differences*. He argues that larger firms produce qualitatively better products (which cost more per unit of physical output) meant for the higher income segment of the market, that the larger firms use more capital and much less labour per unit of value added and spend substantial amounts on advertising in order to reap scale economies. As the small and large establishments sell in different parts of the market, they co-exist with different price levels.

The argument that *empirically* higher quality products tend to be more capital-intensive raises some doubts. For instance, high quality products in the handicraft and handloom sector are typically more labour and skill intensive. Further, large units may produce artificial differentiation in their products through advertising without effecting qualitative improvements. Subcontracting by large units where the articles are manufactured by small labour-intensive units but marketed by the former under their own brand names proclaiming high quality also contradicts the relationship between product quality and capital intensity. Detailed statistical analyses by Banerjee, Suri and de Haan of the close association between larger size, modern capital-intensive technology and product quality, however, support the author's argument.

The last part of the paper brings out some welfare implications of the analysis of the labour and product markets. In view of the finding that the wage differential between large and small firms is not due to 'distortion' but largely for economic reasons, it is inferred that the choice between small and large firms which involves technological choices rests on the issue of distribution of income—that is, between a large volume of employment at low wages and a small volume of employment at high wages. About product markets which are segmented on account of differences in the quality of products, the case for the protection and subsidisation of less mechanised processes depends on the welfare effects of promoting the consumption of lower quality goods. The author argues that there may be economic reasons for levying differential excise taxes on 'superior' products. But, given these taxes, there seems to be no ground for continuing restrictions on the productive capacity of the large mechanised units.

On capital markets, V.S. Patvardhan in his paper focuses on the access of the small scale industries, which are under the purview of the SIDO, to institutional finance. Patvardhan examines financial assistance to the SSI by the Industrial Development Bank of India (IDBI) through the State Financial Corporations (SFCs) for long-term loans and by the commercial banks mainly for short-term loans. He also uses the results of the RBI survey of small scale assisted units and his own field survey of an industrially developed and a backward centre in Maharashtra.

The author finds that in spite of the increasing role of the SFCs to assist the SSI by way of re-finance from the IDBI, the term loan assistance has reached only about a fifth of the registered SSI units and that the smaller SSIs have not benefited at all. The beneficiaries from the re-finance have been concentrated in relatively developed states. The commercial banks, after their nationalisation in 1969, have gradually expanded their assistance to the SSIs (specially of short term loans) to meet working capital needs. The penetration of the commercial banks has been much deeper than that of the SFCs on account of their very wide branch network. But the share of the SSI sector in aggregate assistance disbursed by all of the financial institutions has just been around 10 per cent. He also shows that the amount of assistance per unit has been much smaller in backward districts than in the relatively developed districts and, further, that even the non-institutional credit has been more restricted in the undeveloped areas. The author infers that the long-term financial requirements of small units have not been adequately met.

While Patvardhan expresses concern over the inadequate financial assistance to small firms by institutional and non-institutional sources, Little doubts the economic justification for providing con-cessional credit to the small sector through the government-sponsored institutional network. This is perhaps because of the imperfections in the working of capital markets, the inherent weaknesses of small firms, including the high rate of mortality among them, lack of information required for appraisal of their viability and credit worthiness, and their exaggerated role in the economy.[6]

One may agree that easy access to institutional finance at concessional rates for small firms generally results in various kinds of waste of scarce capital resources. It would, however, hurt the interests of the new starts, should financial institutions stop completely or even partially financial help to them. J.C. Sandesara in his paper has, in fact, shown that small firms attach considerable importance to institutional credit and its timely availability. Financial institutions, obviously, have to exercise caution in selecting new start-ups for assistance.

The above contributions on capital market focus on the poor accessibility of the small sector to institutional credit which result in their heavy dependence on non-institutional sources usually bearing higher costs of credit. A pertinent question in this context is whether the limited access of small firms to credit and its high cost lead to the choice of relatively labour-intensive techniques by the small sector. Clearly, this would require firm evidence on the comparative cost of finance and wage cost for small and large firms, and also the relative access of small firms to alternative technologies.

S.R. Hashim in his paper highlights the developmental role of the small scale sector as an instrument of regional dispersal and diffusion of ownership and entrepreneurship rather than as a source of employment generation. The author, on the basis of technology and organisation, classifies small scale industries into (*a*) traditional— art and craft, (*b*) traditional—consumer goods; and (*c*) modern small scale units. He finds that from the viewpoint of growth potential, the first two categories of industries are of little consequence in the small sector and asserts that it is only the third category (viz., small scale industries based on modern technology) which has considerable growth potential and which also has an important developmental role through spatial linkages and marketing channels.

Another interesting point made by the author is that the scale economies tend to decline as the order of process becomes higher— that is, as the processes are closer to the finished or final products. He further argues that industries involving production technologies

[6] This is based on the recording of Ian Little's oral presentation on capital markets at the Conference.

and processes which are neutral to scale can be better organised on a smaller scale so as to subserve the stated developmental objectives. But small firms, according to the author, need government support 'for quite some time' in order to (*i*) compensate them for financial and commercial disadvantages, and (*ii*) fill infrastructural gaps in the rural areas.

On the basis of a comparative field study of modern (power operated) small scale units in an urbanised district and a district with highly developed agriculture in Gujarat, Hashim finds a dispersed pattern of industrial growth in the latter district. He also finds that modern small firms in both the districts have been set up by first generation entrepreneurs, are formally organised with hired workers, and have access to wider markets through well-established marketing channels. The survey results, according to the author, bring out the developmental role of the modern small sector of diffusing and dispersing industry in semi-urbanised and rural areas involving numerous small entrepreneurs and workers who otherwise cannot benefit from large scale industries.

It needs to be pointed out that the available empirical evidence suggests the prevalence of a U-shaped cost curve in a large number of industries. Also, the first least cost point in many instances is found to correspond to large levels of output, which can hardly be achieved by the small scale industries as currently defined by the government. Therefore, further empirical evidence is required in support of Hashim's proposition that the industries closer to manufacturing final products are neutral to scale. One may also question the claim that small firms can generate wider dispersal of industrial activity over space. The known evidence suggests that small industries cannot be spread too thinly because their viability depends on the existence of industrial clusters and the provision of economic and social infrastructure.

Government Policy

Three papers on government policy are included in the last part. J.C. Sandesara in his paper evaluated the government programmes of support for the SSI sector, specifically relating to long term finance, the reservation policy, other incentive schemes and industrial estates. The author makes extensive use of his studies of SSI units at Bombay, Hyderabad and Jaipur conducted during the late seventies. In the next paper Arun Ghosh traces at length the evolution of government policy for the development of small scale industries, gives his assessment of the growth of small scale and village industries during the seventies and, finally, raises certain policy-related issues. In the third paper, Dipak Mazumdar examines the government policy on textiles, a major Indian industry. The paper is based on a larger study of the Indian textile industry completed by the author for the World Bank in 1984.

Sandesara evaluated the performance of sample units in terms of ratios of profitability, productivity and capital intensity. He finds that, by and large, the units assisted with long term finance did not perform as well as the non-assisted units and also that the former registered lower growth rates than the non-assisted units. The assisted units generally showed higher capital-output ratios. Easily available financial assistance at concessional rates, without rigorous scrutiny, according to the author, tends to be 'wasted' as it is excessively used, even as a substitute for labour, leading to excess capacity and high capital intensity which runs counter to the objective of employment generation.

Next, the author compares the 'reserve' and the 'non-reserve' industries in terms of the same economic ratios and infers that the performance of the reserve industries does not outshine that of other industries. He attributes the poor performance of financially assisted units as well as those in the 'reserve' industries to 'easy' entry into the SSI sector, which has intensified competition within the sector, and resulted in excess supply and a fall in profitability.

So far as the perception of the assisted units with regard to various incentive schemes is concerned, credit and land (including built sheds) are found to be high priority items. The need for streamlining procedures for providing financial assistance (including its timely availability) is also strongly emphasised.

A surprising finding by Sandesara on the basis of a review of the existing studies is the better performance of small scale units outside the industrial estates as compared to similar units inside the estates This is despite better access to institutional finance and many other facilities and incentives to the units in the industrial estates.

Despite some shortcomings of the small scale sector, the author emphasises the need to promote this sector through preferential treatment. He, however, favours discriminatory assistance to 'growth prone and viable' units.

About Sandesara's explanation that the increase in the competition within the small scale sector has adversely affected the performance of the 'reserve' industries, it may be pointed out that the objective of the reservation policy and other assistance programmes has been to insulate the small sector from unequal competition of large industrial establishments, so that the sector can grow through expansion of existing units and the entry of new firms. This should have improved the performance of the sector through a reduction in production costs and improvement in the quality of products!

It needs to be realised that the reservation policy over the years has restricted new capacity installation in the medium and large scale sectors in industries on the reserved list. The policy has been used in the latter stages to disallow capacity expansion under various schemes—such as, re-endorsement and regularisation of capacity. The licensed capacity in many instances has been pegged to levels far below the installed or rated capacity, giving rise to situations in which the turnover of small firms with extended definitional limits exceeds the licensed capacity of some medium and large establishments. Indeed, the reservation policy may require some rationalisation so that it does not inhibit the growth of the medium and large scale sector, *particularly* those industries with some export potential.

In the next paper, Arun Ghosh begins by tracing the historical evolution of government policies on small scale industries. An analysis of the trends in the performance of the small sector registered under the SIDO shows a phenomenal growth during the seventies in the number of units, investment and output in the modern small scale sector. The analysis also shows the concentration of small scale industries in metropolitan areas with considerable under-utilisation of capacity and sickness in this sector.

Finally, the author raises a number of policy-related issues. *First*, steady industrial growth along with a commensurate increase in employment requires sustained demand for industrial products which depends on the improvement of rural incomes. *Second*, the policy of reservation of industries for small scale units has stunted their size. The urge of the small units to expand has resulted in their horizontal and vertical splitting, so that the units remain within the officially prescribed limits of small scale industry and continue to enjoy the protection and support of the government. *Third*, the growth of the small scale sector with massive official support has not satisfactorily subserved the objective of employment generation. *Fourth*, cottage and village industries deserve better attention in order to help in the rapid growth of employment in the decentralised sector.

About the author's inference on the sickness and capacity under-utilisation in the small scale sector, it would, perhaps, be more instructive to carry out some comparisons of the small units with the large establishments. So far as the issue of the splitting of small scale units is concerned, the author does not provide any empirical evidence. His conclusion implies that a part of the growth of the modern small scale sector, as presented by the author himself, might be illusory, resulting from the splitting of the establishments which might have otherwise grown and graduated into the medium and large sectors.

Regarding policy issues, Ghosh seems to lay excessive emphasis on inadequate demand as a factor constraining the growth of the small sector. On the author's plea for infrastructural support to cottage and village industries, it may be observed that if rural industrialisation is accepted as a means to generate employment and improve incomes of the poor, questions about factor intensities and efficiency become somewhat redundant.

Dipak Mazumdar in his examination of the government policy towards the textile industry brings out the lack of coherence and coordination in the official policies which have adversely affected the growth of the industry with unforeseen consequences. The government's protection of the traditional handloom sector, which began in the early fifties, was secured through physical controls on the growth of the mill sector and restricted growth allowed for the 'decentralised' powerloom sector. The mill sector was also heavily burdened with discriminatory excise taxes. The outcome was totally different from what was intended. Over the years, mill cotton cloth production fell markedly, while the output of the powerlooms recorded a very large increase.

Explaining the phenomenal but unanticipated growth of power-looms, the author points out the advantages of the powerloom sector over the mills mainly in lower labour costs and preferential government policies. A crude cost-benefit analysis attempted by the author suggests that the private profitability of the powerloom sector has been enormous. But the social profitability of the power-looms (ignoring distributional considerations) based on the use of shadow wage rates for the mill sector is found to be considerably reduced. Mazumdar infers that the large expansion of powerlooms has been a social loss, whereas the expansion of either handlooms or the mills would have been socially profitable.

In view of the high private profitability of the powerlooms, the other two sectors, according to the author, have co-existed with specialisation by product lines.

The effect of the government policy, in addition to the socially undesirable growth of powerlooms, was an increase in employment (in the powerloom sector) and stagnation in the total textile output. On account of another set of policies unrelated to the protection of handlooms, the Indian textile industy could not take advantage of the world-wide revolution in man-made fabrics. The restrictive and discriminatory policies raised the domestic cost of synthetic fibre to exorbitant levels. Due to the cost disadvantage India also missed the opportunity to exploit the rapidly expanding export markets in man-made textiles. Mazumdar concludes that the rapid growth of powerlooms, which has been initiated by an entirely new entrepre-neurial class comprising the rich landlords and traders, has not in any way benefited the handlooms.

With regard to the comparative social profitability of the three sectors of the textile industry, it may be observed that the heavy social cost of the powerloom sector, as worked out by Mazumdar, may decrease when the effects of income redistribution, dispersal of industry and diffusion of ownership and development of new entre-preneurship are considered. Also, it may be argued that the relative social profitability of the handloom sector may improve further if the opportunity cost of labour (i.e., the shadow wage for handloom workers) is assumed to approach zero and if some consideration is given to the fact that handlooms save on power which is still a scarce resource.

Several effects of income redistribution may be taking place, such as (*a*) from the highly-paid smaller work force in the mill sector to the low paid larger number of workers in powerlooms; (*b*) from the government and the mill sector to the powerloom entrepreneurs on account of non-payment of direct and indirect taxes by the latter; (*c*) from the consumers of man-made fibres to cotton growers on account of a shift of demand to cotton cloth, due to high costs and prices of synthetic fabrics; and (d) from the consumers of cotton cloth to the workers and entrepreneurs in the powerloom sector on account of high prices of cotton cloth resulting from slow growth of the textile industry. Most redistribution effects do not seem to favour the powerloom sector.

The Indian textile policy has indeed been revised since the Conference was held. *First*, the physical controls on the capacity expansion of the existing units and capacity creation by new units in the mill sector have been lifted. The mills (and also the powerlooms and handlooms) have been provided with full flexibility in the use of cotton and man-made fibres. *Second*, the powerloom and the mills are to be treated *at par* with respect to the incidence of excise taxes and other regulatory measures. The powerlooms sector is brought within a more effective regulatory network through compulsory registration. *Third*, fiscal levies on man-made fibres/yarn are to be progressively reduced. *Fourth*, domestic capacity to produce man-made fibres is permitted to expand and new capacity created so as to realise scale economies in order to reduce the cost of production. *Fifth*, the responsibility for the entire production of controlled cloth is to be gradually transferred from the mills to the handloom sector. It may be pointed out that the mill sector has been under obligation to manufacture a certain quantity of coarse cloth to sell at subsidised prices. This has been acting as a drag on the already sagging economic capacity of the mills, causing widespread industrial sickness.[7]

It seems appropriate to conclude this overview with the main observations on government policy made by Ian Little.[8] He first outlines some of the major policy conclusions on the basis of the World Bank study. The examination of efficiency-related issues in Part II has shown that, though employment size is a poor indicator of capital intensity and productivity and of technical efficiency for narrowly defined industries, the very small enterprises with less than 10 workers are rarely found to be the most labour-intensive or with the highest capital productivity and efficiency. Evidence from India and many other countries shows that firms in the medium size range of 50–200 workers have the highest economic and social merit. Small enterprises should not, therefore, be looked to for efficient

[7] Government of India (Ministry of Supply and Textiles, Department of Textiles), *Statement on Textile Policy*, New Delhi, June 1985.

[8] This is based on a recording of Ian Little's oral presentation on government policy at the Conference.

use of factors of production. Where small enterprises are labour-intensive they are often inefficient and use traditional technology.

The analyses further show that inter-industry differences in factor intensity dwarf the differences within the industries when enterprises are classified by employment size. It follows that the supply side intervention in favour of small scale may not generate a more labour demanding development and better income distribution. These objectives, according to Little, can be better met by changing the pattern of demand in favour of labour-intensive industries.

These shifts in demand require policy measures that either promote exports through opening up the economy or support agricultural development and improve income distribution. Recent experience of the Far-Eastern export-oriented economies has shown without doubt that exports are more labour-intensive than import substitution. These economies have been the most labour-demanding among the developing countries and have at the same time recorded heavy declines in the relative share of small firms.

Next, he makes two observations on Indian policies: first, regarding the financial assistance to new and very small firms and second, on the reservation policy. He does not regret the poor access of very small firms to institutional finance. The government's drive to make commercial banks lend to the very small is of doubtful social value. World-wide evidence shows that many attempts on the part of the formal institutions to lend to the very small have had an appalling record. Little holds the view that the very small and the new starts get more efficient financial support from informal lending institutions (such as, friends and relatives). There is nothing wrong in the 'benign neglect' of the very small and the new starts. Enough new small firms have been springing up without assistance to act as a seedbed for healthy organic industrial growth.

The policy of reserving a large number of products for the small sector has serious disadvantages. As has also been emphasised by Sandesara and Ghosh, these policies tend to inhibit the natural growth of firms and also of exports because, in general, small firms are poor exporters.

Finally, while making it clear that he would not favour intervention for small firms through subsidised credit or other supply-related policies, Little appears to be equally opposed to discrimination against the small scale. He considers it necessary to remove artificial obstacles in the growth of small enterprises which may arise out of the regulatory policies of the government.

I   Data Base

2 G. Ramachandran

Data Base for Small Scale Industries: An Appraisal

The Small Scale Industries Sector

For purposes of development, industry in India has been broadly divided into two sectors, small scale and large scale, the former comprising today all units having investment in plant and machinery (gross value) not exceeding Rs. 2 million.[1]

The small scale sector, which is termed 'Village and Small Industries' by the Planning Commission, can further be broadly subdivided into traditional industries and non-traditional industries. Traditional industries are mostly carried on in households/cottages using traditional skills (such as, pottery, hand-pounding of paddy, basket making, hand-spinning and hand-weaving, hand-made paper, carpet, toys and dolls, embroidered articles, etc.). Industries

[1] Rs. 2.5 million in the case of ancillary industries which

   (a) manufacture parts, components, sub-assemblies, toolings, intermediates, or
   (b) render services, or
   (c) supply or render or propose to supply or render 50 per cent of the production or services to other units for production or services to other units for production of other articles.

provided that the unit shall not be a subsidiary or owned or controlled by any other unit.

Since March 1985 the ceiling for small scale industry has been raised to Rs. 3.5 million (for ancillary units—Rs. 4.5 million).

producing leather and plastic products, ready-made garments, chemical and engineering products are examples of non-traditional industries. The latter-mentioned group also includes sophisticated electrical and electronic items, precision components, automobile parts, etc.

In view of the heterogeneous nature of industries in the sector and the variety of developmental problems, the small scale sector has been sub-divided into seven braod groups: handicrafts, handlooms, Khadi and Village Industries, coir, sericulture, powerlooms, and small scale industries (residual).

The first five fall under the category 'traditional,' whereas the last two are non-traditional. While development of small scale industries is a state subject, co-ordination of the development programmes at the Central level is effected through specialised agencies (such as, the Handlooms and Handicrafts Board, and the Khadi and Village Industries Commission (KVIC)). The KVIC, which is also called 'modern small scale industries,' is under the purview of the Small Industries Development Organisation (SIDO) at the Centre. In this paper we shall confine our attention to the development of data base for modern small scale industries.

From its very inception, the SIDO has been providing extension service— advice and assistance— to small scale units under its purview. Due to limitations of staff resources, such extension service has, however, been provided only to those who seek assistance. We have, thus, within the small scale sector, two sub-sectors— assisted and not assisted. During the period the small scale unit is under the extension service umbrella, the SIDO is in a position to obtain any information about the unit. The unit is also helped, where necessary, by the SIDO officers in maintaining proper accounts and in compiling essential statistical information. Several of these units continue to supply data even later but cases are not rare where the unit forgets the SIDO once it is on its own legs. The SIDO also does not have enough staff resources to continue its contact with these units through field visits.

Agencies responsible for collecting industrial statistics on a regular basis have divided the sector into three broad groups— factory (registered sector), non-factory non-household and non-factory household. The main consideration behind such a division of the sector is the state of availability of a frame. In respect of units registered under the Factories Act, a list is regularly available and, as such, the factory sector is covered every year for data collection. The other two non-factory sectors are covered only infrequently.

Data Needs

The industrial policy in the country seeks to harmonise the development of the small scale sector with that of the large scale sector. This can be ensured only if basic information on the current status of different industry lines in the small scale sector—for instance, number of units, their size distribution, spatial distribution, level of production and capacity utilisation, availability of skills and resources (material as well as financial) and economies of scale—is available at regular intervals. Particularly to ensure the success of the policies on reservation (under which product lines are earmarked for future exclusive development in the small scale sector) and import substitution, item-wise data on capacity and production should be available at regular intervals

In the absence of comprehensive data to facilitate effective administration and coordination of industrial policy, the SIDO has had to plan and implement its programmes on the basis of whatever scanty information is readily available on these aspects. Committees and working groups evaluating the impact of implementation of different policy measures do go by the informed and objective assessment of trends available in research studies by the academic and independent scholars in different parts of the country. The utility of these studies is also limited by the non-availability of comprehensive information at regular intervals.

The Central Statistical Organisation (CSO) computes the contribution to national income from the manufacturing sector separately for the registered factories and the unregistered sector. While in the former, the data available through the Annual Survey of Industries are utilised, the methodology adopted for the unregistered sector is unsatisfactory due to the non-availability of similar comprehensive data. The bench-mark data for the sector through the 29th round (1973–74) of the National Sample Survey is even now the starting point. The estimates are brought forward year after year with the help of indicators of growth at the two-digit level of the National Industrial Classification (NIC). Such indicators of growth in the sector are available only for some industry groups. For chemical and engineering industry groups, which are essentially modern small scale industries, the index of production in the large scale sector is used as the indicator. Bench-mark data for a more recent year and indicators of growth at a more disaggregated level are necessary for computing meaningful estimates for the sector.

Data Availability and Limitations

In the initial few years of planning, the SIDO leaned heavily on results of area and industry studies of a diagnostic nature conducted by its staff in different parts of the country. Since 1959, however, data collecting agencies such as the Census Organisation and the CSO/National Sample Survey Organisation (NSSO) have been trying to accommodate the data requirements of the SIDO in their data collection programmes. There has been a steady improvement in the availability of data in terms of quantity as well as quality. But the position even today cannot be considered satisfactory from the point of view of development planning.

Since 1961, at the time of house-listing operations preceding the population census, the Census Organisation has been collecting basic information helpful in building up a frame of all industrial units in the country. The information collected from every census house used as a workshop pertained to the nature of activity, type of power used and the number employed. This information, tabulated industry-wise, provided a fairly good idea about the magnitude of the sector, regional distribution of units in different industry lines, the progress in the last one decade and the employment provided. More than this cannot be expected through a massive operation like the population census. One limitation of the frame thus built up is that it goes out of date unless a follow-up sample survey for detailed information is planned and conducted immediately. Several units either go out of existence or change the products/industry line every year. Units which avail of assistance and advice right from the formative stages have been found to be comparatively stable.

Comprehensive data on the registered factory sector have been collected since 1959 through the Annual Survey of Industries (ASI) under the provisions of the Collection of Statistics Act. The coverage of the survey has been restricted to the factory sector since its inception as the location particulars of the units required to serve notice by post have been regularly available only for this sector. Factories employing 50 or more workers when working with power and 100 or more workers when working without power are covered in the ASI on a census basis (called the census sector) and the rest of the factories, on a sample basis (sample sector/non-census sector). Keeping in view the SIDO's pressing demands for detailed industry/ product level information separately for the small scale factories (more than 90 per cent of the factories are small scale), the coverage in the sample sector has since 1973–74 been progressively increased over the years to 50 per cent. The pattern of coverage is such that over a period of two years data would be collected from every factory in the sample sector. Information on the gross value of plant and machinery is also collected on the survey schedule to facilitate separate tabulation of results for small scale factories.

The census sector data used to be tabulated in detail at the ultimate level of industry classification and the data relating to production and raw material consumption presented item-wise. The latest year for which such detailed tables have been brought out is 1973–74. It has not been possible to bring out such tables for subsequent years due to the limitations of the resources available for the ASI tabulation. Naturally, detailed tables are not available for small scale factories also in the census sector.

Information on the total production of a particular item, whether manufactured as a main product, subsidiary product or by-product, has not been available through the detailed tables presented till 1973–74. This is due to the fact that unique product codes were not available. The main data requirement of the SIDO could not thus have been met even if detailed tables as presented for the census sector were made available for the small scale factories in the census sector. The limitation may, perhaps, be overcome when the common product nomenclature is finalised by the CSO. The data collected in the ASI census sector have been of little use to the SIDO.

The question of bringing out detailed tables out of the data collected in the sample sector does not arise when such tables are not published for the census sector. These tabulations could have been taken up by some agency outside the Department of Statistics since the entire ASI data have been put on computer tapes. Section 7 of the Collection of Statistics Act, however, stipulates that none other than those engaged in the collection of statistics shall be permitted to see information relating to an industrial concern. The tapes cannot, therefore, be used by any office/department other than the Department of Statistics for a detailed tabulation of data.

Integration of data collected from the sample sector factories over a period of two years for bringing out detailed tables may not be quite meaningful since (*a*) the frame cannot remain unchanged over the period, and (*b*) there may be natural growth in existing units as well as price variation from year to year. However, keeping in view the fact that even in the census sector the reference year (which is the accounting year of the unit closed during the survey year) is not uniform and also that the frame is updated in the ASI only once in two years, the detailed industry/product level information, if brought out on the basis of the coverage over two years of sample sector factories, can be considered good enough for administrative/developmental as well as policy purposes. At best, what may be needed is only a correction factor for natural growth as well as price variation. Such tables would also provide information for a time series at the ultimate level of the NIC, as from 1973–74 for the small scale factories as well as for all factories. Prior to 1973–74, the classification used in the ASI was different from the NIC and a one-to-one correspondence with the NIC may not be possible beyond the three-digit level for several industries. Moreover, the sample design adopted prior to 1973–74 may not permit disaggregation beyond the three-digit level.

The ASI summary results for the census sector and the factory sector each include one table which is of some use to the SIDO. The table presents the principal characteristics at the All-India-all-industries level for factories in different capital ranges (capital means gross value of plant and machinery) and helps in segregating the data relating to small scale factories. This table, however, includes several factories classified as 'unspecified,' information on the gross value of plant and machinery being not available in these cases as the factory has either not provided the information or has no plant and machinery. The number of factories in this category has been steadily increasing— 4,660 out of 64,000 in 1973–74 and 20,940 out of 96,500 in 1980–81— though one should actually expect the contrary. The same factory is being covered every year in the census sector and once in two years in the sample sector and there should not be any difficulty in collecting this information in a subsequent round, even if it is missed once. The average investment in fixed assets in the factories in this category is seen to be only

Rs. 20,000, but this by itself cannot lead one to the conclusion that all of them may be small scale.

As stated earlier, the index of production in the large scale sector is used to bring forward the estimates of national income for some industry groups in the unregistered sector. Such industry groups contribute nearly 40 per cent to the total national income from the unregistered sector. The National Accounts Statistics being the only source providing a time series for the unregistered sector, the rate of growth as reflected in this series is taken to indicate the progress in this sector. One is, thus, led to the misleading conclusion that growth in the unregistered SIDO sector is the same as in the large scale sector.

The coverage in the ASI had to be restricted to the registered factories due to non-availability of a frame for the non-factory sector. The first organised effort to build up a frame for the non-factory sector was made in 1960 by the Ministry of Industry when a scheme for voluntary registration of small scale units with the State Directorates of Industries (SDI) was introduced. The application form for registration provided for basic information about the unit. After getting registered with the SDI, the unit was expected to submit a quarterly production return, which could help assess the progress in the sector from time to time. 36,000 units were registered in the first year itself and an overall 160 per cent growth was witnessed in the next three years. When the rate slowed down in subsequent years, an element of compulsion was brought in making such registration and the submission of quarterly returns as a pre-condition for assistance. While this had the desired effect, it also encouraged bogus registrations in order to avail of scarce raw materials. In some states, an interpretation seems to have been given that only such units as could be assisted need to be registered. In some other states, forgetting the fact that registration was parimarily meant to build up a complete frame for statistical purposes, de-registration was resorted to as a penal measure in case of mis-utilisation of facilities or non-submission of returns. In short, the registration scheme did not achieve the desired results in several states.

Very few of the units registered with the SDI were seen to be submitting quarterly returns, making it impossible for the SIDO to estimate the contribution of the sector as well as to assess its progress. The SIDO, therefore, decided to conduct sample surveys taking up a few industries at a time. Two rounds of such surveys were conducted by 1971. On the basis of the results of these surveys, it was possible to make a rough assessment of the rate of growth of SIDO industries.

The Ministry of Industry, in collaboration with the CSO, decided to conduct a survey of the village and small industries in the un-organised sector. Utilising the 1971 population census house-list, a list of manufacturing units in urban areas employing five or more workers was drawn up and a sample survey was undertaken in 1971 utilising the staff resources available with the State Statistical Bureaux/SDI. This survey, however, did not throw up information on production in individual product lines as needed by the SIDO.

Towards the close of 1972, the SIDO was asked whether it could conduct a comprehensive survey of the small scale units under its purview by utilising funds which could be provided under the scheme 'Half a million jobs for the educated unemployed'. A census survey of the small scale units was, therefore, organised by the SIDO in 1973–74, through the SDI. Being basically an employment-generation scheme, the collection of data was entrusted to 3,500 newly-appointed enumerators drawn from unemployed graduates/engineers who were given three months intensive training in techniques of data collection from small scale units of different sizes. The census was planned as a one year time-bound project, with three months for training, six months for the collection of data in the field and three months for the processing of data on the computer. On the advice of an expert committee, the coverage was restricted to the units on the rolls of the SDI since this massive exercise was being undertaken by the SIDO for the first time. Through a massive publicity drive preceding the survey, several unregistered units got registered. The main theme of the publicity drive was that a small scale unit may need assistance any time and that such assistance can be extended only to the units which have been surveyed and registered.

The field-work started with a frame of 260,000 units; the data could be collected from about 140,000 units. The reference period for the census survey was 1972 for units not maintaining accounts and the accounting year closed during the period 1 April 1972 to 31 March 1973 for those maintaining proper accounts. The data were collected through the survey on (*i*) employment, (*ii*) capital, (*iii*) outstanding loans, (*iv*) capacity (item-wise), (*v*) production/job production—item-wise/job work (three years), (*vi*) consumption of fuels, lubricants, electricity, raw materials and industrial components—imported as well as indigenous, and (*vii*) exports. The data were tabulated district-wise at the NIC four-digit level. The data on production and raw material consumption were presented item-wise using unique codes.

The census revealed that only about 17,500 out of about 40,000 SIDO units in the factory sector had got registered with the SDI and these 17,500 factories accounted for 53 per cent of the output in the 140,000 units covered in the census. About 38 per cent of the units in the frame were seen to be either closed or not traceable and these were weeded out from the state-level records.

The census brought to light several lacunae in the procedure for registration of small scale units followed by the different states. The procedure was streamlined after the completion of the census in order to get the frame perfected for future surveys. The format of the registration number was brought in line with the census identification number to facilitate the integration of information to be collected in future with the census data on the computer. Codes were introduced in the registration number to facilitate identification of SIDO units. A decision was taken to update the census data every five years through a repeat census/sample survey and to prepare estimates in the intervening period through production returns to be collected from a sample of units in important product lines and the information supplied by newly registered units. Staff resources were provided to facilitate computation of an annual index by using the production returns from a 20 per cent sample to be drawn from the product frame built up through the census. A subsequent decision to compute the index on a monthly basis with the sanctioned staff resources, however, necessitated a reduction of the sample size to 2 per cent, permitting indices only at the two-digit NIC level.

The first economic census covering the non-agricultural sector was conducted by the CSO in 1977. After initial listing, the frame for units employing one or more hired workers was prepared in two segments: (*a*) establishments having six or more hired workers and/or having an annual turnover exceeding Rs. one lakh, and (*b*) the rest. Follow-up surveys were conducted in 1978–79 separately for (*i*) the first category of establishment, called directory establishments, and (*ii*) non-directory establishments and own account enterprises. The concepts used in the surveys were the same as in the ASI. The report on the survey covering the directory establishments has been finalised and is under print. The report presents detailed tables for rural and urban areas separately at the NIC four-digit level for handicrafts and village industries but only at the NIC three-digit level for other industries (including the SIDO industries). One has, however, to wait for the results of the second survey covering the non-directory establishments and own account enterprises in order to have a comprehensive picture of the unregistered sector. The second economic census was undertaken along with the house-listing operations of the 1981 population census. The detailed follow-up survey based on this frame has recently been taken up.

As stated earlier, it has not been possible so far to meet the data requirements for development planning through the increased coverage in the ASI sample sector. The economic census and follow-up surveys have also not provided data in as much detail as needed for administrative/development purposes. The SIDO, therefore, decided to take up a repeat census-cum-sample survey of small scale units under its purview. The survey was planned for 1978–79, but due to the administrative delay in several states the survey could be taken up only in 1983–84 with 1982–83 as the reference year. The next round of the survey is also now in progress with 1984–85 as the reference year.

The repeat surveys are taken up in two stages. The perfection of the frame (comprising the existing units out of those covered in the earlier census/survey and those registered subsequently) is undertaken in the first stage when the data in the registration records are updated, if need be, by reference to the unit, rectifying omissions and discrepancies. A sample survey covering 20 per cent of the units is then undertaken for the collection of detailed information. The proforma for the sample survey makes provision for all the items of information covered in the 1974 census proforma. The significant additions are (a) sales (item-wise), (b) supplies made by ancillaries, and (c) supplies made under the Central/state government purchase programme. The data relating to production were collected item-wise for three years, 1980–81 to 1982–83, in the first round and are being collected for two years (namely, 1983–84 and 1984–85) in the second round now in progress. The data collected in the first round are now being processed on computer. Estimates will be provided at the NIC four-digit level for each state and at the two-digit level for each district. Estimates of production will also be provided at the state level for each of the important product lines among reserved items and mass consumption items. Besides facilitating the assessment of growth in different industries, the survey results will help in providing an insight into the efficacy of the programmes implemented to develop reserved and mass consumption items.

One limitation in the approach adopted by the SIDO (namely, the coverage of only the units registered with the SDI) is that a good part of the contribution of the SIDO units in the factory sector is missed in these surveys. The fact that several of the small scale units in the factory sector do not get registered with the SDI was not known at the time of the 1974 census and, as stated earlier, only 17,500 out of about 40,000 SIDO units in the factory sector got covered in the census. Particularly since (a) detailed product level information is not yet available through the ASI, (b) big factories with substantial contribution to output get included in the small scale sector every time the investment ceiling for the small scale sector is raised, (c) such units may not get registered with the SDI as they have the option to draw raw material from the allocation made by the Directorate General of Technical Development, and (d) the frame for the factory sector is readily available, it will not be desirable to leave out these units from the repeat surveys just because they have not completed the formality of voluntary registration.

The Reserve Bank of India conducted a sample survey in 1977 covering the small scale units which had availed of assistance under the Credit Guarantee Scheme. Data were collected on capital structure, investment expenditure, source of funds, value of output, pattern of sales, and so on. The units covered in the survey belonged to the factory as well as the non-factory sectors. The report on the survey was brought out in two volumes in 1979.[2] Since the coverage is limited to units availing of institutional credit, the estimate would not provide a comprehensive picture of the small scale sector. The results should be useful for studies on comparative performance.

Outlook for the Future

The analysis in the foregoing paragraphs would show that several agencies have attempted to collect as much data on small scale

---

[2] Reserve Bank of India (1979).

industries as is possible with the resources available with them. The mass of data collected, however, has been of limited utility since (*a*) the coverage has been limited in every case, (*b*) the data collected remain for months in the proformae or on computer tapes but are not processed and presented in a form useful for planning and policy purposes, and (*c*) even the limited information tabulated has been available with considerable time-lag either due to a delayed response from the respondent units or due to inconsistencies/omissions in the filled-in proforma or due to the limitations of tabulation resources. When the data are available after a considerable time-lag, they are of little utility to the administrator.

It would appear, thus, that the administrator should rather depend on quick estimates worked out on the basis of reasonably good indicators. These estimates can be corrected as and when data through a comprehensive survey become available. The indicators of growth provided by the SIDO's 2 per cent sample (monthly production returns) are not good enough for this purpose as these are worked out at the NIC two-digit level and their behaviour over a period of time is quite erratic. One has to think of ways and means of improving the coverage of this index in terms of the number of responding units.

In 1979, the Ministry of Industry notified rules under Section 30 of the Industries (Development and Regulation) Act requiring all small scale units engaged in scheduled industries and registered with the SDI to submit a monthly production return on a prescribed proforma. One copy each of the return was to be sent to the SDI, the State Small Industries Service Institute and the Office of the Development Commissioner (Small Scale Industries)— the last two are part of the SIDO. A concerted effort backed by the above-mentioned notification and the penal provisions available in regard to non-submission of the returns should have resulted in the flow of a substantial number of production returns and an improvement of coverage for the monthly index computed by the SIDO. In the absence of such efforts even the units, which get transferred to the small scale sector with every revision of the investment ceiling, discontinue the returns which they were submitting to the DGTD earlier.

On behalf of the industrial units, it has to be stated that they are required to furnish the same information over and over again to different agencies either in the form of statutory/survey returns or in applications for assistance/facilities. Since, in the latter case, they have something to gain and since, as stated earlier, legal provisions are not being enforced, the industrial units naturally assign the lowest priority to the statutory/survey returns. They also often plead that they do not have competent hands to fill in the 'complicated' returns. This attitude results in a delay in submission of returns as well as in inconsistencies which lead to correspondence or repeated visits of the field staff.

As stated earlier, the format of the SDI registration number was made uniform after the 1974 SSI census and every registered unit has today a unique registration number. The registration number also provides for distinction as the SIDO or non-SIDO unit. If this unique registration number is quoted in every application for assistance/facility and in the statutory returns, integration of the data supplied to the different agencies by the same unit should be possible since more and more agencies (including the SIDO) now have computer facilities or terminals provided by the National Informatics Centre. Once the stage is reached when the basic information required for processing an application can be tapped from the statutory return itself, the industrial unit will give top-most priority to the statutory return.

The question, however, arises: How much completeness of information will an approach ensure, at least for the SIDO sector? Since the economic census will be providing a complete frame for the non-factory sector every five years and a frame is available for the factory sector every year, what is required is the allotment of a (unique) SDI registration number to every unit. In short, the present voluntary registration scheme is to be converted into a compulsory registration scheme.

Every small scale unit registered with the SDI (the list of scheduled industries gives almost complete coverage of the SIDO industries) is to submit a monthly production return under the notified rules. Since the frame provided by the economic census is maintained at the block/district level, it should not be difficult to update the frame, even in the inter-censal years, through identification of new units during field visits of the development staff. What is needed for the success of the scheme is, of course, the will to enforce the enabling legal provisions and a good understanding between the agencies in the field of small industry development.

3 M.R. Saluja

Data Base of the Unorganised Manufacturing Industry: An Appraisal

Introduction

The unorganised sector of the manufacturing industry has been featuring in every major industrial policy statement since 1948 because of its labour-using and decentralised character. However, systematic data covering this entire sector on a uniform basis with regard to gross output, value added, employment and input-output relations are hard to find. The basic difficulties appear to be the following:

(i) Because of its decentralised and geographically diffused character, combined with a high mortality rate for individual units, the cost of collecting information may have been high relative to its importance in gross output and value added;

(ii) Two different forms of organisation predominate in this sector.

Acknowledgements: Grateful acknowledgements are due to K. Sundaram and S.D. Tendulkar for offering valuable comments and suggestions.

These are: (*a*) family enterprise carrying on productive activity in the household helped mainly by family members, (*b*) unregistered workshop with mostly single proprietorship, and (sometimes) partnership where the productive activity is carried on by own-account workers with the help of hired labour, and also public and corporate establishments, cooperative societies, trusts, and so on, which are not registered under the Factories Act. The problems of data collection differ for these forms. The sampling frames can have either household or non-registered manufacturing enterprise as the ultimate stage unit. In the first type of frame, the household enterprises are fairly covered, while the non-household ones are not likely to be fully captured, and vice versa if the second type of frame is used. It may be mentioned here that the definition of the household enterprise varied from one source of data to another. Sometimes it varied even for the same source of data over time. Secondly, in the case of household enterprises, the household members have a loose connection with the productive activity, depending on the demand pressures, so that there are problems in distinguishing between 'gainful' and 'non-gainful' activity. Similarly, the prevalence of part-time unemployment or underemployment necessitates going beyond the customary measure of number of workers as an indicator of labour input;

(*iii*) The criteria used for specifying this sector have varied according to the policy regulations and concessions covering the various individual industries in this sector. The fragmentary data collected during the administration of these policies, which themselves changed over time, have been subject to inadequate as well as varying coverage, under-enumeration as well as overlap with other sources. As a result, a complete and systematic coverage of various industries on a uniform basis with respect to the items included and for the same bench-mark year(s) is difficult to find.

The focus of this paper is to highlight the difficulties that are confronted in the process of getting the *total* picture for the manufacturing industry as a whole in an attempt to (*i*) gauge the importance of the unorganised sector in gross output, value added and employment, and (*ii*) assess the performance of the manufacturing industry and its major sub-sectors over time. As the available data do not directly give the estimates of value added from the un-

registered sector, the Central Statistical Organisation (CSO) pre-
pares the estimates by using a variety of indirect calculations. A
brief account of the method employed to prepare the estimates
along with the shortcomings is given in the last section.

The employment criterion has been used in differentiating the
factories registered under the Factories Act 1948 from the non-
registered units. The criterion of registration covers those factories
employing 10 or more workers if using power, and those employing
20 or more workers if not using power. By definition, the complement of this would cover the unregistered and, hence, the unorganised manufacturing sector. The Annual Survey of Industries (ASI)
covers the registered part of the industrial sector on two bases: (*i*)
factories employing 50 or more workers if using power and 100 or
more if not using power are covered on a census basis; (*ii*) factories
employing 10 to 49 workers if using power and 20 to 99 workers if
not using power are covered on a 50 per cent sample basis. The
scope of the ASI is fairly complete, except for the variation in
coverage from year to year due to non-response. In other words,
even if the data relating to a given industry may cover the same
number of units in two years, there is no guarantee that the data
would refer to the identical set of units in those two years because of
varying non-responding units. An important point in the present
context relates to the borderline cases at the registration cut-off
point. Because registration under the Factories Act brings the units
under certain regulations, there has been a tendency to evade it so
that the unorganised sector would contain units which should have
been registered as factories.

We now turn to the various sources of data on the unorganised
sector so as to assess the overlap as well as inadequate coverage.
Our critical appraisal of various sources has to be viewed in the
context of the aforesaid objectives.

The National Sample Survey Organisation (NSSO)

The NSSO is the main agency collecting data on the unregistered
manufacturing industries. During the 14th, 23rd and 29th round
covering the periods 1958–59, 1968–69 and 1974–75, respectively,
it collected information on the unregistered enterprises regarding
inputs, employment, capital, value of output and value added,

which is tabulated at the two-digit level of the industrial classification.[1] For these surveys, the household was the ultimate stage unit of observation. For the 14th round, the data were collected only from household enterprises. For the 23rd round, the data were collected from household as well as non-household unregistered enterprises but were tabulated only for household enterprises, as the coverage for the non-household part was reported to be very unsatisfactory. One possible reason for this may have been the adoption of the household as the ultimate unit and its possible inability to adequately cover unregistered workshops. The results for the 29th round also relate only to the household units. According to the NSSO, all non-institutional unregistered enterprises are defined as household enterprises. As no data was available on the basis of the NSSO surveys regarding institutional unregistered enterprises, a complete picture of the unorganised sector could not be obtained.[2]

According to the definition adopted in the 23rd and 29th rounds, if any member of a household is engaged in activities of manufacturing or handicrafts for 30 days during the 365 days preceding the date of the survey of non-seasonal enterprises, or 15 days in the case of seasonal enterprises, the household is regarded as a manufacturing household. During the 14th round, all households which were engaged in manufacturing (at least in the secondary capacity) for one day during the last 365 days were considered for the survey. Consequently, the results of the 14th round cannot be compared with those of the latter rounds. One would expect the estimated number of enterprises as well as employment to go down with the stricter definition adopted in the 23rd and 29th rounds. This is roughly confirmed in Table 1.

While comparing the results of the 23rd and 29th rounds, one may also note that in rural areas the number of enterprises is less in the 29th round than in the 23rd round, while employment is more for the 29th round. This may possibly be because of high mortality, particularly among the self-employed units and the seasonal variation in the number of such units.

A person is considered as a worker on the basis of participation in

[1] Surveys on this subject were also conducted during the 7th to 10th rounds. These rounds were, however, of a shorter duration. Also, according to the NSSO, the unregistered units for these rounds were called small scale units.

[2] Estimates of value added per person, as obtained from the NSSO surveys, were used by the CSO for estimating the contribution to national product from the household unregistered establishments.

Table 1
*NSSO Estimates of Number of Enterprises and
Employment in Different Rounds (in thousands)*

	14th	23rd	29th
Number of enterprises			
Rural	n.a.	6,569	6,492
Urban	n.a.	1,691	2,318
Total	n.a.	8,560	8,810
Employment			
Rural	12,911	9,986	11,556
Urban	4,407	3,930	4,751
Total	17,318	13,916	16,307

Source: NSSO, Government of India, Report No. 205, *Twenty-third
Round*, July 1968–June 1969, Also, *Sarvekshna*, April 1980

the work rather than the time he spends on the activity. The intensity
of work is not captured in the employement estimates which are
inflated, and labour-output ratios based on these data are also
over-estimated. The intensity dimension is attempted to be captured
in the quinquennial surveys by the NSSO on employment and
unemployment, where daily status participation is recorded in terms
of half-day units. This, however, does not give us any idea about
industry-wise employment in terms of man-days worked corresponding to the output produced.

As far as the coverage of the unregistered household enterprises
is concerned, the NSSO appears to be the only reliable source.
However, the borderline cases between the household and non-
household enterprises may overlap. For non-household enterprises,
surveys can be carried out by using the establishment frame for
sampling either by the NSSO or by some other independent authority.

The Population Census

The population census provides some useful economic data on the
decennial basis. In the 1961 census, information in respect of manufacturing and processing establishments was collected through the
household list/schedule regarding (*i*) The product, repair or service
undertaken, (*ii*) average number of persons employed, (*iii*) kind of
fuel or power, if machinery is used, and so on. In the 1971 census, a

separate schedule (known as the establishment schedule) was canvassed along with the household schedule. The information collected related to the type of establishment, average number of workers, whether household or non-household or registered under the Factories Act, description of the product manufactured or processed, type of power used, and so on. The results are tabulated separately for the rural and urban areas of each district at the two-digit level industry groups. These tables attempt to cover the number of establishments along with the employment aspects of the entire industrial sector. The data are tabulated separately for the registered factories, unregistered workshops and the household units.

The definition of the household industry used in the 1971 census differs from that adopted by the NSSO. According to the census, a *household industry* is defined as

an industry conducted by the head of the household himself/herself and/or mainly by the members of the household at home or within the village in rural areas, and only within the premises of the house where the household lives in urban areas. The industry should not be run as a registered factory.

It may be noted that as compared to the definition adopted by the NSSO, there is no specific reference period mentioned in the definition adopted by the census. Also, according to the definition applied by the NSSO, the restriction of location of the enterprise in the same village in case of rural areas, or in the same premises where the household resides in urban areas, is not there. The definition of a *registered factory* in the census is the same as that adopted by the ASI. The *unregistered workshop* is defined as 'a place where some kind of "production," processing, servicing, repairing or making of goods for sale, is going on'. It should neither be a registered factory nor a household industry.

Despite the identical definition, there are discrepancies between the census and the ASI 1970 with respect to registered factories:

	Number of Factories	Employment (in thousands)
1971 Establishment Census	89,238	5,604
ASI 1970–71	64,565	5,216

Source: For ASI data, Government of India, CSO *Annual Survey of Industries, 1973–74— Summary Results for Factory Sector*, New Delhi.

These discrepancies in the number of factories are hard to explain although the employment figures are not so way out, considering minor differences in measuring employment as well as the period covered.

In the case of household industries, there are much wider discrepancies as compared to the NSSO 23rd round (1968–69):

	Number of Units	Employment
	(in thousands)	
1971 Establishment Census	2,080	3,804
NSSO 23rd Round (1968–69)	8,574	13,916

Even after allowing for the differences in the definition of household industry and also the different time period to which the two estimates relate, the number of units as well as employment from the 1971 census appear to be extremely low.[3] It is possible that since, the establishment schedule, which was canvassed separately, could have proved inadequate to cover the household industries and, therefore, many household industrial units might have escaped enumeration. It may, however, be mentioned here that a good part of the non-household units would have been enumerated as household enterprises, if the census had used the NSSO definition of the household unit.

For the 1981 census, the establishment schedule was canvassed in the form of an economic census along with house-listing operations (to be described in a later section).

The Small Industries Development Organisation

Though the SIDO deals mainly with modern small industries and covers a substantial part of the registered factories as well, the CSO[4]

---

[3] The CSO used the 1971 census figures to estimate the industrywise work-force for the bench-mark year (1970–71) for the household unregistered manufacturing sector.

[4] For estimating the value added for persons from the non-household, non-registered manufacturing industries, the CSO also used the results of a survey conducted under the centrally-sponsored scheme on Survey of Small Scale Industries by the Ministry of Industrial Development, with 1970–71 as the reference year. This survey covered units employing five or more workers and in the urban areas only. It was a one-time effort and the results were not published.

widely used the results of the census carried out by the former during 1973–74 with 1972 as a reference year for estimating the value added per person for the non-household part of the unorganised industries for the bench mark year 1970–71. It seems appropriate to give a brief review of the SIDO census data.

Over the period, the SIDO have made efforts to collect comprehensive data for the small scale industries under its purview and evolve a system whereby the required data are available on a regular and continuing basis. The above-mentioned census is the first major effort in this direction.[5]

The definition of a small scale unit for this census was in terms of investment in plant and machinery (original value) of Rs. 0.75 million and less and Rs. 1.0 million and less in the case of small scale ancillary units.[6]

The coverage 'related to the modern small scale sector' and hence it 'excluded a large category of industries which came within the purview of different specialised boards, committees or agencies'. The Report brought out by the SIDO lists twenty-two categories of small scale industries outside the purview of the census covering mainly handlooms and powerlooms, industries covered by the Khadi and Village Industries Commission as well as handicrafts and certain other miscellaneous industries. Some idea about the data being collected by these agencies is given in the next section. Of the industries falling within the purview of the census, only the units registered with the State Directorates of Industries (SDI) were covered. Of the 258,000 units registered with the SDI, after allowing for non-traceable as well as non-responding units, the data could be finally tabulated only for 140,000 units. A summary picture is given in Table 2.

The extent of overlap of the census of small scale industrial units with the registered sector can be roughly estimated from the fact that at least 11 per cent of the units accounting for 55 per cent of the

[5] The results of this census are published in Government of India (Development Commissioner, Small Scale Industries, Ministry of Industry), *Report on Census of Small Scale Industrial Units*, New Delhi, January, 1977, Volumes 1 & 2. Details about this census and further work carried out by the SIDO are given in a paper by G. Ramachandran in this volume.

[6] The limits have been raised many times. Recent limits are Rs. 3.5 million and Rs. 4.5 million for industries producing main products and those producing ancillaries, respectively. (See the Budget Speech of the Finance Minister Part A, 16 March 1985.)

Table 2
Number of Units and Gross Output According to Employment Criterion
from the Census of Small Scale Industrial Units
(Gross value of output in Rs. million)

No. of workers	No. of Units	%	Gross Output	%
1–9	98,181	70.4	5,282	20.3
10–19	26,138	18.7	6,326	24.3
20 and above	15,258	10.9	14,409	55.4
Total	139,577	100.0	26,017	100.0

Source: Government of India, Development Commissioner, Small Scale Industries, Ministry of Industry, *Report on Census of Small Scale Industrial Units*, New Delhi, January 1977.

gross output and employing 20 or more workers form a part of the registered sector and, hence, are covered by the ASI. This is a lower bound of the overlap since of the units employing 10–19 workers and those using power have to be added. But this cannot be done for lack of appropriate cross-classification.

An upper bound of the extent of overlap of small scale units (invested capital criterion) with the registered factories is available from the ASI 1973–74. According to this source, 83 per cent of the registered factories accounting for 25.5 per cent of the gross output and 33 per cent of total employment had the (original) value of invested capital in plant and machinery not exceeding Rs. 0.75 million. This is exclusive of ancillary producing units with invested capital exceeding Rs. 0.75 million and up to Rs. 1.0 million. Of course, within the universe of registered factories, the coverage as well as the representative character of the ASI data are expected to be better than those of the census of small scale industrial units.

The data provided by the census relate to the number of units, employment, fixed capital, borrowings, inputs, output, capacity and exports at the four-digit level of the National Industrial Classification. Information on the number of units, capacity and production of about 2,400 industrial items under various industry groups is also available.

The census covers only those units which are registered with the State Directorates of Industries. Since registration is not compulsory, there are a large number of units which are not registered but, according to the definition of small industry, come under this sector. These units are left out of the survey. To cover the entire small manufacturing sector, these units should also be brought under the survey. Also, since a major part of the small units are covered by the ASI, the SIDO should concentrate on those units which are not covered by the ASI. The ASI should supply the required data in respect of the units coming under the purview of the SIDO. Further, the data should be cross-classified according to employment so that it can be used to cover non-household enterprises— mostly urban based—though one cannot be sure of their representative character.

Traditional Small Industries

Some data on the unorganised traditional industries are being collected by their respective commissions/boards. The following are the main agencies: (*a*) Khadi and Village Industries Commission (KVIC), (*b*) Development Commissioner, Handlooms, (*c*) Development Commissioner, Handicrafts, (*d*) Central Silk Board, and (*e*) Coir Board.

The data collected by these agencies is a by-product of the administrative needs. The available data are neither comprehensive in coverage nor reliable and suffer from severe limitations.

The data in respect of the KVIC are confined only to aided units/institutions and do not cover the entire sector. The data relate to the production and sale of khadi and village industries, distribution of equipment and implements, employment and earnings, and so on. The employment figures are separately given for full and part-time employees but, for the final analysis, these are simply added to get the total employment. In the case of handlooms, most of the information (like number of looms, production and employment) is derived from the statistics relating to the quantum of hank yarn delivered by spinning mills,[7] which is not methodologically correct. Some states have conducted censuses/sample surveys of handlooms. The results of these censuses/surveys are yet to be aggregated and cross-checked. For many handicrafts, the major sources of data are the export statistics. Sericulture is generally

---

[7] Similar data on powerlooms are released by the Textile Commissioner. The methodology of getting these data is similar to that for handlooms.

carried on as a subsidiary activity, which makes it even more difficult to collect reliable data. Due to the peculiar character of the coir industry—its various stages of production and the production practices—it becomes difficult to collect information on production, labour employed, and so on. However, the Coir Board makes a yearly assessment of production based on data on internal consumption and exports. All these agencies publish the data in their annual reports or bulletins.

Economic Censuses of Non-Agricultural Enterprises

In order to fill the gap in the data available for the unorganised sectors of the economy, the Department of Statistics has embarked upon a massive programme of conducting periodic economic censuses and follow-up surveys.

The first economic census was conducted during October–December 1977 by the CSO in collaboration with the State Directorates of Economics and Statistics. The census was confined to the listing of addresses of the establishments along with certain basic characteristics—such as type of ownership, type of power used, number of persons usually working, and so on. It adopted the complete house-listing approach in the urban areas and in villages with a 1971 census population of more than 5,000. However, in smaller villages, a village level enquiry approach was adopted in which the enumerator would list the likely establishments from one or more knowledgeable informants in the village. For the purpose of this census, 'an establishment is defined as a unit or a household which undertakes non-agricultural activities and employs at least one hired worker on a fairly regular basis'. Thus it did not cover the own-account enterprises utilising family labour. The census covered all the unorganised sectors of the economy, including, besides manufacturing, trade, transport and services. The All India Report on Economic Census 1977 has been released by the CSO (January 1985). According to this census, there existed 3.037 million non-agricultural enterprises employing one or more hired workers in which the number usually working was 25.86 million, including 23.519 million hired workers. The corresponding figures for the manufacturing sector are 0.735 million, 9.122 million and 8.154 million, respectively. The establishments covered by the census were classified into two categories: (*a*) directory establishments, having six or more workers and/or an annual output of Rs. 0.1 million or more; (*b*) non-directory establishments— where the total number of workers is less than six and the annual output is less than Rs. 0.1 million.

This census was utilised as a frame for conducting follow-up surveys for different unorganised sectors of the economy. The non-factory manufacturing sector was covered during 1978–79 and the sectors of trade, transport and services were surveyed during 1979–80. The non-directory establishments and own-account or self employed enterprises of the manufacturing sectors were surveyed by the NSSO as part of their normal 33rd round, while the larger establishments— called Directory Manufacturing Establishments (DME)— were surveyed during the year 1978–79 by the special staff appointed by both the Centre and the states, under the supervision of the CSO.

The main differences between the NSSO 33rd round survey and its previous rounds (14th, 23rd and 29th) are that for the former the establishment approach in place of the household approach is used for the sampling frame. The definition of the household enterprises adopted was in line with that used for the 1971 population census establishment survey. Also, the design of this round was such that the estimate covering important items would be available at the district level separately for the rural and urban areas. The data for seventy-three industries associated with handicrafts, handlooms and khadi are being tabulated for individual industries. The results of this round of the survey are not yet available.

For the DME, the CSO has brought out a report. The first part of this report deals with the principal characteristics, such as, type of establishments, type of organisation, size of employment, size of capital, and so on. The second part gives basic tables at the three-digit industry level for the rural, urban and combined sectors. The results are based on the summary block of the schedules, and, for some major characteristics, are separately given for the household and the non-household segments. The data relate to the capital, employees, emoluments, value of output, gross and net value added and outstanding loans. The data are separately given for handicrafts, handlooms, and other industries under the purview of various commissions/boards.

The results, when available, for the NSSO 33rd round survey and the detailed results of the DME will fill a long-standing gap in the data for the unorganised manufacturing sector. In the absence of detailed results, a few comments are offered:

(*i*) The estimated number of DME, according to the report by the CSO, are 335,000. While going through their employment-wise figures, one finds that 17,000 are in the employment range of 0–5. This could include enterprises employing less than six persons but having a value output of Rs. 0.1 million or more. The number of establishments employing more than 20 workers is 25,000 (8 per cent of total establishments). It is not clear how these establishments (supposed to be registered factories) could form part of the DME. In addition, some of the 104,000 establishments in the employment range of 10–19, which use power, should also be registered factories. This points to an overlap between the registered factories and the DME. As mentioned earlier, some establishments eligible for registration actually do not get themselves registered to save themselves from the regulations of the Factories Act.

(*ii*) Though the results of the 33rd round survey are not yet tabulated, the provisional results are available with the NSSO. According to a recent study using the provisional results,[8] the number of establishments during 1978–79 for the entire unregistered manufacturing sector is 9.005 million (6.901 million in the rural areas and 2.104 million in the urban areas), which is just about 0.2 million more than for the year 1974–75. In the urban areas, there was a decline in the number of establishments from 2.318 to 2.104 million. This looks implausible. It has already been pointed out that as the 1974–75 survey included only the household enterprises, there might have been an underestimation of the units surveyed. In 1978–79, as the establishment was the final unit of observation, the underestimation may be from own-account enterprises. This underestimation can be avoided if the establishment approach is applied for the directory establishments and the household approach for relatively small units.

[8] Government of India, Department of Statistics, NSSO, 'Performance of Non-Factory Manufacturing Industries and Pattern of Rural Industrialisation', Paper presented at the Seminar on Rural Industrialisation, New Delhi, 21–22, October 1984 (mimeograph).

Economic Census, 1980

The second economic census was carried out in 1980 along with the house-listing operations for the 1981 population census. This census included own-account enterprises also. Besides non-agricultural enterprises, agricultural enterprises, excluding crop production and plantations, were also covered. Follow-up surveys, on the lines of those for the first census, are being conducted for this census also. A survey of the non-factory manufacturing sector was carried out in 1984–85 on the lines of the 1978–79 survey. There have been slight changes in the concepts used. The directory establishments are now defined only on the basis of employment, irrespective of the value of output. The definition of the household enterprise during the 40th round of NSSO (1984–85) is the same as applied up to the 29th rounds. The changes in concepts may not cause distortions as far as the entire unorganised sector is concerned but will affect the comparison between different types of enterprises. According to the press release issued by the CSO on 17 February, 1985, the total number of enterprises and employment in the manufacturing and repairing services are as given in Table 3.

Table 3
Number of Enterprises and Employment in
Unorganised Manufacturing— 1980 Census (in million)

	Own-Account Enterprises		Establishments		Total	
	Number	Employment	Number	Employment	Number	Employment
Rural	2.978	5.162	0.460	3.548	3.438	8.710
Urban	1.298	2.291	0.724	7.393	2.022	9.684
Total	4.276	7.453	1.184	10.941	5.460	18.394

Note: Figures are exclusive of the data from Assam, Bihar, Kerala and Lakshadweep.

The total number of establishments according to the 1977 census was 0.735 million employing 9.122 million persons. The data only on the establishments can be compared for the two censuses, because the own-account enterprises were not covered by the 1977 census. According to these data, there has been a 61 per cent increase in the number of establishments, while employment has increased by only 20 per cent. The marked increase, particularly in the number of establishments, seems implausible.[9]

Methods Followed by the CSO for Estimating the National Product from the Unregistered Manufacturing Sector

The estimates of the gross domestic product are worked out by the CSO by preparing the estimates for the bench-mark year 1970–71 and carrying these forward to other years on the basis of indicators of physical output/input.

To prepare the estimates for the bench-mark year, the industry is divided into household manufacturing and non-household manufacturing. The estimates of value added in the two sub-sectors are prepared separately. Broadly speaking, the estimate of value added in either of the sub-sectors is worked out by using the estimates of value added per worker and of the working force, separately for rural and urban areas.

For household industries, the estimates of the value added per person for different groups of industries are based on the results of the NSSO sample surveys carried out in the 23rd and 29th rounds. The estimates based on the 23rd round (i.e., 1968–69) are moved forward to obtain the corresponding estimates for 1970–71 and 1974–75. The indices used for the purpose are the index of wages of the rural skilled workers (specially prepared by the CSO) and of the urban factory workers (published by the Labour Bureau). The figures so obtained are compared with the 1974–75 figures available from the results of the 1974–75 (29th round) survey, in order to obtain adjustment factors. The estimates for different years are adjusted on a prorata basis for the difference between the projected and the actual figures (based on the 29th round survey) so as to obtain a set of estimates compatible with the results of both of the NSSO rounds. The estimates of the working force are based on the 1971 population census, with some adjustments due to different time periods and also due to the addition of secondary workers. Estimates of secondary workers are made by using the published

[9] The increase will be more when the results for excluded states are added.

results of the NSSO 23rd round. The estimates are separately prepared for the rural and urban areas.

For the non-household unregistered industries, the estimates of the value added per worker are based on the Survey of Small Scale Industries which was conducted by the Ministry of Industrial Development to collect data in the urban non-household sub-sector with 1970–71 as the reference period and also on the All-India Report on the census of Small Scale Industrial Units in 1972. As the census results were for the year 1972, the value added per worker was brought back to 1970 with the help of an index of earnings of factory workers with monthly earnings up to Rs. 400. The estimates at the industry group level for the urban areas are obtained by combining the corresponding estimates from the two sources. There are no such surveys for the rural areas and the value added per worker is estimated by using the rural-urban differentials of value added per person, as observed in the NSSO 23rd round.

The estimates of the work-force are obtained by subtracting the number of workers in the registered manufacturing sector from the number of workers engaged in non-household manufacturing units, as available from the population census. The rural-urban break-up of employment is obtained with the help of rural-urban employment ratios derived from the Establishment Tables of 1971 population census.

The estimates provided are not very reliable. The data on value added per worker are based on the surveys with incomplete coverage. Also, as the definitions of the household enterprises adopted by the population census and the NSSO are different, the use of the value added per worker from the NSSO and the working force from the population census creates some error. The estimates of the working force for the household sector should also be based on the NSSO results and the corresponding estimates for the non-household sector should be suitably adjusted.

The use of the 1972 census of small scale industries for estimating the value added per worker may also produce an error. As mentioned in an earlier section, at least 11 per cent of the units in this census covering 55 per cent of the production belonged to the registered sector.

Again, to obtain the total work-force in household enterprises, the use of the ratio of secondary to main workers based on the NSSO data is not proper because of the different definitions of household enterprises used by the NSSO and the population census.

Estimates for Other Years

The estimation of gross value added for other years is made first at the base year prices by carrying forward the bench-mark estimates with the help of suitable physical indicators of output/input. The corresponding estimates at current prices are obtained from the constant price estimates by superimposing the relevant price changes for each industry group separately. For this purpose, the index numbers of wholesale prices are used. Incidently, for the organised sector, the value added estimates are first prepared at current prices and then changed to constant price estimates by using relevant wholesale price index numbers.

The value added figures for the unregistered sector are given for sixteen industry groups. For nine out of the sixteen groups the indices of industrial production, which are based on large industries, are used. For other sectors also the indices used cannot be considered satisfactory.

Conclusion

A few suggestions emerging from the foregoing examination of the various sources of data concerning the unorganised manufacturing sector are given below:

(*i*) An appropriate cross-classification based on the twin criteria of employment size and investment in plant and machinery may be undertaken both for the organised and the unorganised manu-facturing sectors. This would enable the estimation and elimination of the existing overlap across the categories. The same applies to the future surveys to be conducted by the NSSO, CSO, or other special-ised agencies.

(*ii*) The overlap in the coverage of the manufacturing enterprises under the surveys of the ASI and the SIDO should be avoided. The ASI should make available to the SIDO the required data regarding the small scale factory units with minimum delay. The SIDO should at best cover all the units outside the purview of the ASI. In fact, the data for the unregistered part may also be made available from the follow-up surveys of the economic censuses relating to the non-factory manufacturing sector. In that case, the SIDO should concentrate its resources on monitoring the progress and impact of the reservation policy.

(*iii*) The data available from the economic censuses regarding number of units, location, and so on, could be cross-checked by the supporting organisations/commissions/boards established for the specific segments of the industrial sector. In this connection, efforts should be made to adequately explain the discrepancies in the information available from various sources.

(*iv*) In future surveys of the unorganised sector, the distinction between household and non-household units may be incorporated and separate tabulations attempted. To ensure comparability over time, the concepts and definitions should be kept uniform, as far as possible.

(*v*) There has been considerable delay in the availability of data after the surveys have been conducted. While the ASI brings out the summary results reasonably promptly, similar arrangements would be desirable for other surveys of the unorganised sector.

(*vi*) As the technology of industries using power is completely different from that of the units not using power, it is necessary to have a detailed tabulation programme separately for these two segments at an appropriate level.

(*vii*) As for follow-up surveys, going from past experience, it will be preferable to have household industries surveyed by using the household approach and non-household industries by using the establishment approach.

4

K. Sundaram
S.D. Tendulkar

An Approximation to the Size-Structure of Indian Manufacturing Industry

Introduction

In any analytical enquiry, a description of the complex reality is a first step towards arriving at certain stylised facts. The stylised facts, in turn, provide an empirical base for a possible analytical explanation of the phenomenon under consideration. The modest objective of this paper is to provide the first step in such an analytical enquiry, namely, a description of the size structure of the manufacturing

Acknowledgements: We are indebted to the Office of the Development Commissioner for making available unpublished tabulations relating to the Census of Small Scale Industrial Units. Useful comments on an earlier draft by K.L. Krishna and other participants at the 'IEG-World Bank Conference on Small Scale Industry Development' (New Delhi, 22–24 March 1985) are gratefully acknowledged. We accept full responsibility for the views and interpretations as also for the errors that may remain.

industry in India in the early 1970s covering the *entire* range— from the tiny household sector to the large scale factory sector. This has not been done so far in a comprehensive manner possibly because of the lack of readily available and comparable data. We venture to do this despite these difficulties because we firmly believe that it is a small but still indispensable first step in the analytical enquiry.

We attempt to approximate the size-structure of the manufacturing sector at the all-India level and at the two-digit level of disaggregation, combining several data sources which are discussed in the next section. The third section defines the different segments of the manufacturing sector distinguished in this paper, discusses the problems of overlap, comparability and choices among alternative data sources and, finally, identifies the major industry-groups falling in each segment using value-added shares and employment shares as criteria. The following section attempts to locate the industry groups where modern small scale industry could be regarded as significant. The fifth section takes up for examination relative differentials in value added per worker across different segments. Concluding observations appear in the last section.

It may be mentioned straight away that we are compelled to confine ourselves to the two-digit level disaggregation because of the non-availability of data relating to the household sector at a more disaggregated level. It is obvious that we cannot examine the extent of competition in the product market at this level of aggregation. Our focus, therefore, is on highlighting the segment-specific concentrations in terms of value added and employment within each industry group and on bringing out differentials across segments in the productivity per worker. Since the fixed capital equipment available to the worker is the major determinant of productivity per worker, we attribute the productivity differentials mainly to differentials in fixed capital per worker. If this argument is accepted, we can characterise segments differing substantially in productivity per worker as representing different technology regimes. Consequently, wide differentials in productivity per worker can also be taken to be indicative of the lack of continuum in technology regimes.

Data Base

There is, to our knowledge, no single data source (or complementary data sources) which adequately covers (in a non-overlapping fashion) different segments of the manufacturing sector. The data sources used by us for the early 1970s are as follows:

The Industrial Statistics Wing of the Central Statistical Organisation brings out the Annual Survey of Industry (ASI for short) on an annual basis for the factory sector, separately for (*a*) the census sector, and (*b*) the sample sector. The information is available on all major economic characteristics. However, no rural-urban break-up has been provided uptil now. We use the report for 1974–75.

The National Sample Survey Organisation (NSSO) carried out for 1974–75 (29th round) a survey of self-employed households in non-agricultural enterprises. The report of this survey provides data on major economic characteristics of the enterprises covered in the survey separately for the rural and urban areas.

The Establishment Tables of the 1971 population census provide information on the number of enterprises and the number of workers by employment size-groups for the three segments of the manufacturing sector: household, unregistered workshops and factories. This information is available separately for rural and urban areas.

An *ad-hoc* Census of Small Scale Industrial Units (CSSIU for short) for the year 1972 was carried out by the Development Commissioner's Office of the Ministry of Industrial Development. The census covered units registered with the Development Commissioner for Small Scale Industries (DCSSI) and falling under the category of modern small scale industry where 'small scale' is defined by reference to the value of plant and equipment. The CSSIU report gives information on all major economic characteristics by detailed industry groups but without a rural-urban breakdown.

In addition, more detailed information on the CSSIU provided by the DCSSI enabled us to eliminate the overlap between the CSSIU and the factory sector and distinguish two size groups of one-four workers and five and above.

Our effort has been to use these data sources in order to present a synthesised picture of the size-structure of the manufacturing sector for the early 1970s. Admittedly, not all data sources relate to the same reference year, nor have we been able to completely eliminate overlaps amongst the different segments identified in this paper. However, in our judgement, the synthesised picture nevertheless substantially represents the facts on the ground in the early 1970s.

Role of Different Segments in Indian Manufacturing

In this section, we identify at the all-India level the two-digit industry groups where different segments representing employment size are significantly present. The segments distinguished for this purpose are: (*i*) the census sector of the ASI; (*ii*) the sample sector of the ASI; (*iii*) unregistered workshops with five or more workers; (*iv*) household sector: urban; (*v*) household sector: rural.

Five comments are warranted on the sources and the processing of data. The 29th round survey of the NSSO (Constituting the data source for segments (*iv*) and (*v*) had as an explicit objective the provision of data on the unorganised manufacturing sector fully complementing the registered factory segment covered by the ASI. However, our examination of the 29th round data suggested that, in practice, the coverage in the survey of units with five or more workers was inadequate. This might possibly be due to the survey being canvassed on the household frame leading to a possible under-estimation of non-factory establishments with five or more workers organised outside the household. It is for this reason that we have used the data on unregistered workshops with five or more workers from the Establishment Tables of the 1971 population census [segment (*iii*) above] to complement the data on the other four segments, even though we recognise that there would be some overlap between categories (*iii*), (*iv*) and (*v*). This overlap will have the effect of over-stating the relative importance of unregistered workshops.

Secondly, the Establishment Tables of the 1971 population census provide information on the number of workers but not on the value added. Consequently, we have used the price-adjusted value added per worker at the two-digit level from the CSSIU in deriving an estimate of the value added contributed by unregistered workshops. Since the coverage of the CSSIU was stated to be mostly urban, our procedure of multiplying the value added per worker by the number of workers in both the rural and urban unregistered workshops would probably overstate the value added originating in unregistered workshops.

Third, the time reference for the Establishment Tables was 1971, whereas it was 1974–75 for both the ASI and the NSS 29th round. Our preliminary examination showed that the number of workers in unregistered workshops with five or more workers was generally higher than the figure given in the CSSIU. By preferring the higher figures from the Establishment Tables, we may be biasing our estimates in favour of the modern small scale sector.

Fourth, we have chosen to ignore the data on the household sector from the Establishment Tables, preferring instead the information provided by the 29th round of the NSS. Apart from the time reference of the Establishment Tables differing from 1974–75, our choice was based on the judgement that the establishment as a basis of enumeration would not adequately capture small scale household enterprises.

Finally, we recognise that the nature of participation differs in different segments of the manufacturing industry noted earlier. Workers in the factory sector would be mostly on a hired basis, have more or less regular employment and have high productivity because of the relatively high fixed capital per unit of labour. At the other end, those working in the household sector would be mostly own-account workers or self-employed, have irregular and/or part-time attachment to the industry and have low productivity because of the relatively low fixed capital per worker. Unregistered workshops would represent an intermediate situation between these two polar cases. Consequently, when we are pooling the number of workers or value added across different segments, our aim is to get the total picture across the full range of the manufacturing sector at a two-digit industry level. The range represented in the five segments noted earlier in this section would approximate the successive technology regimes according to a descending order of capital-labour ratios.

With these background comments, we now note for each segment the industry groups where that segment is relatively significant. The significance is judged primarily in terms of share in total value added across segments for each two-digit level industry. We also note the following indicators for each industry group.

VS : value added share across segments (i) to (v)
ES : employment share across segments (i) to (v)
VS*: value added share across segments (i), (ii), (iv), (v)
ES*: employment share across segments (i), (ii), (iv), (v)

In view of our earlier comments, we use VS and ES when we wish to deliberately overstate the importance of unregistered workshops with five or more workers in order to highlight the scope of the modern small scale industry in relation to the factory/sector which gets correspondingly understated.

While judging the relative importance of the household sector which also gets understated in VS and ES, we use VS* and ES* as corrected indicators. Complete details of these indicators are given in the Appendix Tables A.1 and A.2.

The major findings emerging from Tables 1–5 should be noted.

(*i*) There are four industry groups (code numbers 25, 33, 36 and 37) where the census sector is dominant with its value added share exceeding 87 per cent and employment share exceeding 70 per cent.

Table 1
Industry Groups where the Census Sector is Dominant

Two-Digit Code	Industry Description	VS	ES
25*	Jute, hemp, & mesta textiles	96.74	80.33
33	Basic metals & alloys	91.73	71.90
36	Electrical machinery & parts	87.27	74.89
37	Transport equipment & parts	87.27	79.48
31	Chemicals and chemical products	82.17	49.97
30	Rubber, plastic, petroleum & coal products	68.46	34.20
23	Manufacture of cotton textiles	66.81	29.53
35	Non-electrical machinery & parts	66.36	32.30
28	Paper & paper products	66.01	44.10
24*	Wool, silk & synthetic fibres	65.16	20.83

Note: *For these groups, value added per worker is not given in the CSSIU and hence VS = VS* and ES = ES*.

Table 2
Industry Groups Where the Sample Sector is Significant

Two-Digit Code	Industry Description	VS	ES	VS*	ES*
34	Metal products & parts	14.44	11.69	18.72	13.53
36	Electrical machinery & parts	13.24	12.27	13.77	12.79
35	Non-electrical machinery & parts	10.95	10.27	12.26	10.89

Table 3
Industry Groups where Unregistered Workshops are Significant

Two-Digit Code	Industry Description	VS	ES
26	Textile products	33.92	5.46
22	Beverages, tobacco & tobacco products	24.87	9.55
29	Leather & leather products	24.68	6.10
34	Metal products & parts	22.90	13.56
38	Miscellaneous manufacturers	21.76	6.39

Table 4
Industry Groups where the Urban Household Sector is Significant

Two-Digit Code	Industry Description	VS	ES	VS*	ES*
39	Repair services	47.47	37.48	54.08	40.31
38	Miscellaneous manufactures	41.74	36.80	53.35	39.52
26	Textile products	30.00	30.92	45.40	32.70
27	Wood, wood products, furniture & fixtures	26.05	18.37	32.10	19.08
29	Leather & leather products	21.70	29.13	28.81	31.02
24	Wood, silk, synthetic fibre, textiles	N.A.	N.A.	22.56	45.69
34	Metal products & parts	15.75	29.86	20.42	28.75

There are five other industry groups where the value added share of the census sector exceeds two-thirds (Table 1).

(*ii*) The sample sector of the ASI is not dominant in any industry group (Table 2).

(*iii*) Unregistered workshops were not dominant in any industry either in terms of value added share or employment share. There were 5 industry groups (26, 22, 29, 34 and 38) where value added shares ranged between 22 and 34 per cent with the employment share exceeding 10 per cent in only one industry group, namely, 34 (Table 3).

(*iv*) There were three industry groups (namely, 39, 38 and 26) where shares of the urban household sector exceeded 45 per cent in

Table 5
Industry Groups where the Rural Household Sector is Significant

Two-Digit Code	Industry Description	VS	ES	VS*	ES*
27	Wood, wood products, furniture & fixtures	43.41	74.62	53.50	77.54
26	Textile products	24.21	60.47	36.63	63.96
29	Leather & leather products	21.53	54.69	28.59	58.24
20–21	Food products	21.38	51.56	26.30	54.35
22	Beverages, tobacco & tobacco products	17.53	53.16	23.33	58.77
32	Manufacture of non-metallic mineral products	18.40	65.89	20.34	68.05
38	Miscellaneous manufacturing	14.39	48.33	18.40	51.90
39	Repair services	15.53	43.10	17.69	46.36
23	Cotton textiles	7.35	41.04	8.78	43.11

Note: We have adopted an ES exceeding 40 per cent as a criterion for inclusion in view of the employment concentration in this sector.

terms of value added and 32 per cent in terms of employment. In four other industry groups (27, 29, 24, 34), shares in value added (and often in employment as well) exceeded 20 per cent (Table 4).

The rural household sector dominates in terms of employment shares in six industry groups (namely, 27, 26, 29, 20–21, 22 and 32). It has significant employment— shares between 40 to 50 per cent— in three other industry groups (38, 39, 23) (Table 5).

(*v*) Wood, wood products, furniture and fixtures (group 27) is the only sector where the rural household sector has the highest share in value added and in employment among different segments. This group, along with textile products (group 26), are the only ones where the share of the census sector is less than 10 per cent in value added as well as in employment.

(*vi*) Thus, we have at one end nine industry groups in the census sector (Table 1) whose value added shares exceeds 65 per cent. At the other end, we have six other industry groups in the rural household sector (Table 5) whose employment shares exceeds 50 per cent. The role of the 'middle' sector is dominant at best in only one industry group— namely, miscellaneous manufacturing.

Modern Small Scale Industry

Modern small scale industry coming under the jurisdiction of the Development Commissioner for Small Scale Industry (DCSSI) covers units operating with the value of plant and equipment less than a prespecified limit (Rs. 0.75 million for a unit producing the main product and Rs. 1.0 million for ancillary units, in 1974–75) which has varied over time. It also excludes certain traditional industries. Some of these units would also fulfil the criterion defining a factory under the Factories Act and, as such, would be covered under the ASI, probably in the sample segment. However, not all units in the sample segment of the ASI would satisfy the capital employed criterion laid down by the DCSSI. The factory component of the modern small scale industry would thus largely be a subset of the sample segment of the ASI. As regards the non-factory units falling under the rubric of the modern small scale industry under the DCSSI, one would expect these to be covered adequately under the category 'unregistered workshops with five or more workers' (UR 5 + for short) in the Establishment Tables of the 1971 census. As we had noted earlier, in almost all cases, the number of workers in unregistered workshops with five or more workers (rural *plus* urban) exceed the number of workers reported in the Census of Small Scale Industrial Units (CSSIU) of the DCSSI. Further, by using the CSSIU estimates of value added per worker in units with five or more workers together with the estimate of the number of workers in UR 5 + in both rural and urban areas, we are deliberately overstating the role of non-factory modern small scale industry in the Indian manufacturing sector.

One singular exception to this general rule that the estimate of workers in UR 5 + exceed that reported in the CSSIU is provided by industry group 34—metal products and parts—where the CSSIU estimate of 210,000 substantially exceeds the estimate of UR 5 + of 85,000 from the Establishment Tables of the 1971 census. In this case, we have substituted the CSSIU estimate of workers in place of UR 5 +. In this case too, the value added estimate in the modern small scale segment has been obtained as a product of the estimated number of workers (from the CSSIU) and the price-adjusted value added per worker for units with five or more workers.

Taking the factory and non-factory units together, the total modern small scale industry can be approximated by pooling together the sample segment of ASI and UR 5 +. This would involve an over-estimate of the share of modern small scale industry to the extent that the sample segment may include units which may fall outside the capital-employed criterion used by the DCSSI. This source of over-estimation is independent of and additional to the over-estimation arising in respect of UR 5 + noted earlier. It would, thus, be obvious that pooling these two segments (namely, the sample segment of the ASI and UR 5 +) would provide an upper bound estimate of the contribution of the modern small scale sector.

Table 6 shows seven industry groups for which the upper bound estimates of the share of the modern small scale sector in value added exceeded 20 per cent. It is apparent that only one industry group (namely, metal products and parts) could claim dominant status in terms of value added. For textile products, the value added share was between 30 and 40 per cent. For the rest of the industries, the upper bound estimate of shares was between 20 and 30 per cent. The share in employment was significant in only two industry groups (namely, 34 and 28).

Table 6
Industry Groups where Modern Small Scale Sector is Significant

Two-Digit Code	Industry Description	VS	ES
34	Metal products and parts*	61.08	44.62
26	Textile products	38.07	6.74
22	Beverages, tobacco & tobacco products	29.52	13.16
38	Miscellaneous manufacturing	29.16	9.71
20–21	Food products	27.97	12.47
28	Paper, paper products, printing & publishing	25.95	29.06
27	Wood, wood products, furniture & fixtures	23.41	5.46

Note: *Adjusted share as discussed in the text.

Differentials in Value Added Per Worker

In this section, we propose to examine differentials in value added per worker across segments within each two-digit industry group. These are taken to be reflective of differences in fixed capital per worker which lead to differences in productivity per worker and, consequently, to differences in potential earnings to be derived from attachment to different segments for each industry group. Clearly, potential earning differentials would be lower than differences in value added per worker because of the preponderance of wage employment in the sample and census segments in particular but also, to some extent, in the unregistered workshops with five or more workers.

Table 7 presents the indices of differentials in value added per worker for five segments within each of the nineteen two-digit industry groups. In order to focus attention on meaningful comparisons, it is necessary to ensure that the segments being compared have some pre-specified minimum share (or higher) in value added, employment or both. We have (somewhat arbitrarily) chosen this minimum share to be 10 per cent. Accordingly, each index in columns (3) to (7) in Table 7 has been given an asterisk on the right if the share of that segment in the aggregate value added in the industry group is 10 per cent or higher and an asterisk on the left if the share of the segment in the aggregate employment in the industry group is 10 per cent or higher. For this analysis, we have used Appendix Table A.2 for all the industry groups (except industry groups 24 and 25 for which we have relied on Table A.1). Using the 10 per cent cut-off point, we consider the comparison to be 'meaningful' among segments whose indices carry at least one asterisk. Applying this criterion, we have further classified the nineteen industry groups into five categories 1–5 in Table 7 depending on the number of segments relevant for meaningful comparison.

By way of general observations on Table 7, notice that at one end of the spectrum stands the census sector of the ASI which makes itself eligible for comparison on the basis of the value added share (VS for short) in seventeen industries; of these, thirteen also make it on the basis of the employment share (ES for short). At the other end of the spectrum lie the rural and urban segments of the household industry which qualify themselves for comparison, mainly on the basis of the ES, in fifteen different industries; of these, nine also make it on the basis of the VS. In between, the unregistered workshops with five or more workers enter the comparison in twelve industries mainly on the basis of the VS whereas the sample sector of the ASI makes it mainly on the basis of the ES—but only in seven industries.

We turn now to the discussion of the five categories distinguished in Table 7.

In category 1 with two industry groups—metal products and parts (34) and non-electrical machinery and parts (35)—all the five segments are relevant for comparison. The unregistered workshops with five or more workers and the sample sector of the ASI can be clubbed together because they have more or less the same value added per worker. The relative differentials in the value added per worker among these two segments together and the rest can be seen to be very substantial.

The second category with comparison across four segments contains ten industry groups. These include three major consumer goods [food products (20–21), beverages and products (22) and cotton textiles (23)] and five mainly intermediates [paper and products (28), leather and products (29), rubber, plastic, petroleum and coal products (30), chemicals and products (31) and non-metallic mineral products (32)], along with miscellaneous manufacturing (38) and repair services (39). The urban segment of the household industry and the census sector of the ASI appear in all the comparisons, the differential ranging between nearly 1:2 (industry group 39) and nearly 1:12 (industry group 22) but mostly around 1:5. The rural-urban differentials within the household industry are nearly 1:2 or higher in seven of the nine meaningful comparisons. The unregistered workshops with five or more workers lie close to the census sector of the ASI in terms of value added per worker and away from the urban segment of the household industry in six of the eight meaningful comparisons.

Category 3 with comparison across three segments contains three industry groups. Of these, wool, silk and synthetic fibre textiles (24) has extremely wide differentials in value added per worker across the rural segment, the urban segment (both of the household industry) and the census sector of the ASI in the proportion of 1:4:25. In the remaining two industries [textile products (26) and wood products (27)], the differentials, though wide (1:2.5:6) are not as extreme with comparisons among the rural and urban segments of the household industry and the unregistered workshops with five or more workers.

Category 4, with comparisons across two segments, consists of three industry groups. In one case—namely, jute, hemp and mesta textiles (25)—the comparison is between the two ends of the spectrum involving the rural segment of the household industry and the census sector of the ASI with 1:18 differential in value added per worker. In the remaining two cases, the comparison is between the sample and census sector of the ASI with differential in value added per worker exceeding 1:3 in basic metals and parts (33) and negligible in electrical machinery and parts (36).

Finally, category 5 contains the unique case of transport equipment and parts (37) where the census sector of the ASI overwhelms all other segments with no other meaningfully comparable segment.

Concluding Observations

The size structure of the manufacturing industry in India at the two-digit level has been found to be very concentrated. At one end, we have the very large scale census sector of the ASI whose value added shares in as many as ten industry groups exceed 65 per cent (Table 1). At the other extreme, the rural segment of the household industry accounts for more than half the employment in six other industry groups. The unregistered workshops (with five or more workers) and the sample sector of the ASI are not found to be dominant in any industry group (Tables 2, 3). The urban segment of the household industry accounts for more than half the employment, only if we omit from comparison the unregistered workshops with five or more workers and that too only in two industry groups (Table 4). The intermediate segments between the rural household industry and the census sector of the ASI are thus found to be non-dominant. We could locate only one industry group (i.e., metal products and parts) where the upper bound on the share of the modern small scale industry was found to be dominant (Table 6).

The differentials in value added per worker across segments for the two-digit industry groups were examined in the last section. While sharp differentials between the two extremes—namely, the rural household industry and the census sector of the ASI—are only to be expected, they have been found to be empirically relevant in thirteen industry groups with differentials ranging between 1:4 and 1:25. Even the differential between the rural and the urban segments of the household industry have been found to be nearly 1:2 or higher in twelve of the fourteen meaningful comparisons. The unregistered workshops with five or more workers and the sample sector of the ASI were found to be similar in terms of value added per worker and both of these appear closer to the census sector of the ASI than the urban household industry (Table 7).

These findings give rise to the question: How does one explain the co-existence of different segments, each with a sizeable share in value added and/or employment, in the *same* two-digit industry group despite the presence of such large productivity differentials. We have not been able to examine these questions in detail. We only mention briefly possible factors which could lead to the stylised facts noted earlier.

To start with, our analysis has been carried out at the two-digit level. This was forced on us because of the non-availability of more detailed data from the 29th round for the household sector. It is possible that different segments may be specialising in different product lines at the three-digit or higher level of disaggregation. For example, bidi-making may be concentrated in the household sector whereas cigarettes may be produced in the large scale census segments, although both may come under tobacco products. This would also hold for the heterogeneous machinery industry (groups 35, 36, 37), metal products and parts (34) as also the miscellaneous group (38).

Secondly, even though the product group may remain the same at the three-digit or higher level, there may be product differentiation across different segments. Leather footwear, ready-made garments and wear apparel are illustrations of this possibility.

Third, there is also a strong possibility of geographical segmentation of the product market in a large country like India where, in the absence of a rural-urban continuum, large transport cost differentials may provide a sheltered local market for a small scale segment in certain specific pockets. A similar effect would also be produced in a situation of excess demand, by an effective ceiling being imposed by policy on the production of the large scale factory sector. Different brands of edible oils being sold in local markets, where standard brands are not available, is an illustration of this possibility. Confectionery products also fall in the same category.

Finally, government policy may explicitly favour a small scale decentralised sector by controlling the raw material supplies (e.g., yarn for weaving) to different segments, by imposing differential excise duty on products produced in different segments, by making available scarce imported or domestically produced inputs at premium-exclusive prices, by subsidising the output price, and so on. All these policies would make the competing products produced in the decentralised sector cheaper than those in the large scale factory.

More detailed investigation of these factors in specific cases is clearly needed. This has not, however, been undertaken in this paper.

Table 7

Differential in Value Added Per Worker Across Segments and Two-Digit Industry Groups

Industry Group Code	Value Added Per Worker in Rural Household Industry (Rupees)	Index of Differential in Value Added Per Worker				
		R	U	UR5+	S	C
(1)	(2)	(3)	(4)	(5)	(6)	(7)
1. Industry groups with comparison across 5 segments:						
34	1,053	*1.00	*3.25*	*6.28*	*6.33*	*13.01*
35	1,022	*1.00	*4.69	9.54*	*8.13*	*15.66*
2. Industry groups with comparison across 4 segments:						
20–21	1,380	*1.00*	*2.40*	4.12*	3.06	*4.20*
22	806	*1.00*	*1.23	6.70*	3.91	14.21*
23	725	*1.00	*1.82	9.72*	4.22	*12.62*
28	2,235	1.00	*1.48	*3.71*	*3.11	*7.11*
29	1,030	*1.00*	*1.89*	6.47*	5.42	9.18*
30	5,424	*1.00*	*1.08	1.69	*1.71	*5.60*
31	2,314	*1.00	*2.24	4.12	*4.84	*13.89*
32	776	*1.00*	*5.41*	4.27*	6.46	*10.61*
38	1,069	*1.00*	*3.81*	7.07*	8.82	9.56*
39	1,176	*1.00*	*3.52*	4.93*	5.57	5.88*

(continued)

Industry Group Code	Value Added Per Worker in Rural Household Industry (Rupees)	Index of Differential in Value Added Per Worker				
		R	U	UR5+	S	C
(1)	(2)	(3)	(4)	(5)	(6)	(7)
3. Industry groups with comparison across 3 segments:						
24	625	*1.00	*3.92*	N.A.	11.76	*24.80*
26	780	*1.00*	*2.42*	5.80*	8.07	10.33
27	875	*1.00*	*2.44*	6.52*	4.61	7.88
4. Industry groups with comparison across 2 segments:						
25	372	*1.00	7.11	N.A.	15.51	*18.08*
33	1,079	1.00	0.90	9.11	*6.33*	*19.13*
36	1,781	1.00	2.91	5.53	*10.27*	*10.22*
5. Industry group with one dominant segment:						
37	1,114	1.00	6.80	6.64	5.91	*10.52*

Notation: R : household sector, rural; U: household sector, urban
UR5+ : unregistered workshops with five or more workers
S: sample sector of ASI
C: census sector of the ASI

Note: Asterisk on right indicates value added share of 10 per cent or higher.
Asterisk on left indicates employment share of 10 per cent or higher.
Value added shares and employment shares based on Table A.2 for all sectors except groups 24 and 25.

APPENDIX

Table A.1

Value Added and Employment Shares of Different Segments of the Indian Manufacturing Industry At Two-Digit Classification for 1974–75 (Percentages)

Industry Group Code	Value Added Share (VS)				Employment Share (ES)			
	C	S	R	U	C	S	R	U
20–21	42.60	11.41	26.30	19.70	20.96	7.70	54.35	16.99
22	57.22	6.19	23.33	13.26	10.14	3.99	58.77	27.10
23	79.80	3.15	8.78	8.26	31.02	3.67	43.11	22.21
24	65.16	8.81	3.47	22.56	20.83	5.94	27.54	45.69
25	96.74	0.61	1.04	1.61	80.33	0.53	15.68	3.40
26	11.69	6.28	36.63	45.40	1.98	1.36	63.96	32.70
27	8.78	5.62	53.50	32.10	1.61	1.77	77.54	19.08
28	79.22	11.13	0.76	8.89	51.80	16.67	3.53	27.99
29	34.32	8.28	28.59	28.81	7.62	3.12	58.24	31.02
30	73.62	8.90	11.04	6.44	37.16	14.74	31.24	16.86
31	86.65	6.61	1.90	4.84	53.47	11.71	16.27	18.55
32	49.86	10.80	20.84	18.50	15.33	5.45	68.05	11.17
33	93.13	6.04	0.48	0.35	72.79	14.28	7.16	5.77
34	52.25	18.72	8.60	20.42	18.37	13.53	39.35	28.75
35	74.30	12.26	6.01	7.43	34.27	10.89	43.39	11.45

(continued)

Industry Group Code	Value Added Share (VS)				Employment Share (ES)			
	C	S	R	U	C	S	R	U
36	91.05	13.77	0.10	2.76	78.04	12.79	0.86	8.31
37	90.32	5.60	0.39	3.70	82.01	9.05	3.74	5.19
38	18.80	9.46	18.40	53.35	5.55	3.02	51.90	39.52
39	22.27	5.96	17.69	54.08	9.92	3.42	46.36	40.31
All Industries	66.40	7.51	11.75	14.34	21.75	5.52	49.98	22.74

Notation: C: census sector of the ASI
  S: sample sector of the ASI
  R: household sector, rural
  U: household sector, urban

Note: See section on 'Role of Different Segments' for a discussion on data sources.

Table A.2

Value Added and Employment Shares of Different Segments of the Indian Manufacturing Industry At Two-Digit Classification for 1974–75: An Approximation, Including Unregistered Workshops with Five or More Workers (Percentages)

Industry Group Code	Valued Added Share (VS)					Employment Share (ES)					
	C	S	R	U	$R_1 + U_1$	C	S	R	U	R_1	U_1
20–21	34.63	9.27	21.38	16.01	18.70	19.89	7.30	51.56	16.12	2.35	2.78
22	42.99	4.65	17.53	9.97	24.87	9.17	3.61	53.16	24.51	6.70	2.85
23	66.81	2.64	7.35	6.92	16.27	29.53	3.49	41.04	21.14	1.62	3.19
24	N.A.	N.A.	N.A.	N.A.	N.A.	20.16	5.74	26.65	44.22	0.57	2.67
25	N.A.	N.A.	N.A.	N.A.	N.A.	79.75	0.58	15.57	3.37	0.21	0.51
26	7.72	4.15	24.21	30.00	33.92	1.87	1.28	60.47	30.92	1.59	3.87
27	7.13	4.56	43.41	26.05	18.85	1.55	1.70	74.62	18.37	0.94	2.82
28	66.01	9.28	0.63	7.41	16.67	44.10	14.19	3.01	23.83	0.57	14.30
29	25.85	6.24	21.53	21.70	24.68	7.16	2.93	54.69	29.13	0.83	5.25
30	68.46	8.28	10.27	5.99	7.00	34.20	13.56	28.75	15.52	1.01	6.95
31	82.17	6.27	1.80	4.59	5.14	49.97	10.94	15.20	17.33	1.49	5.07
32	44.02	9.53	18.40	16.34	11.70	14.85	5.28	65.89	10.81	1.59	1.58
33	91.73	5.95	0.47	0.34	1.51	71.90	14.10	7.07	5.70	0.06	1.17
34	40.29	14.44	6.63	15.75	22.90	15.89	11.69	34.02	24.86	1.78	11.78
35	66.35	10.95	5.37	6.64	10.70	32.30	10.27	40.89	10.79	0.43	5.33

(continued)

Industry Group Code	Valued Added Share (VS)					Employment Share (ES)					
	C	S	R	U	$R_1 + U_1$	C	S	R	U	R_1	U_1
36	87.27	13.24	0.09	2.65	4.15	74.89	12.27	0.89	7.97*	0.18	3.86
37	87.24	5.41	0.38	3.57	3.41	79.48	8.77	3.63	5.03	0.30	2.79
38	14.71	7.40	14.39	41.74	21.76	5.17	2.82	48.33	36.80	1.14	5.75
39	19.55	5.23	15.53	47.47	12.21	9.22	3.18	43.10	37.48	0.66	6.36
All industries	57.79	6.54	10.23	12.48	12.96	20.53	5.21	47.16	21.46	1.77	3.87

Notation: C: census sector of the ASI, S: sample sector of the ASI.

R: household sector, rural, U: household sector, urban.

R_1: unregistered workshops, rural, U_1: unregistered workshops, urban.

Note: Unregistered workshops with five or more workers are considered in this table.

See section on 'Role of Different Segments' for a discussion on data sources.

While employment figures are available separately for the segments R_1 and U_1, value added figures are not separately available.

Value added figures are not available for segments R_1 and U_1 for the industry groups 24 and 25.

II Relative Efficiency

5 Bishwanath Goldar

Relative Efficiency of Modern Small Scale Industries in India

Introduction

The revival of interest in small scale industry in recent years is largely a result of the recent concern for the problems of unemployment and poverty and realisation that, in the course of industrial development, the growth in industrial employment has lagged far behind the growth in industrial output.[1] It has been claimed that industrial development based on small scale industry is capable of countering simultaneously three important evils of the present industrial strategy (based on heavy industry and big production units), namely, growing unemployment, persisting in-

Acknowledgements: An earlier version of this paper was presented at the Conference on Small Scale Industry Development sponsored by the Institute of Economic Growth and the World Bank in March 1985. I have immensely benefited from the comments of the discussant of the paper, K.L. Krishna, and other participants in the Conference.

[1] D. Morawetz (1974) and L. Squire (1979).

equalities and mass migration to cities. Apart from these, there is also the claim that small scale industry has a potential for tapping substantial new sources of saving and entrepreneurship.[2]

Since a major point of interest in small scale industry lies in its superior ability to absorb labour, it is important to ask how far the differences in labour intensity between small and large scale units are attributable to differences in factor prices. If differences in factor prices explain the differences in labour intensity, and if the relative factor prices faced by small scale units reflect more closely the social opportunity costs of factors, then the expansion of the small scale sector would provide an efficient labour-using increase in output. If, instead, the higher labour intensity in small scale units is due to the adoption of inefficient production methods, then employment generation through small scale industry involves a cost to the society in terms of loss of output; and the higher the degree of inefficiency, the greater is the cost of employment generation.

This paper examines the relative efficiency of modern[3] small scale industries in India compared to their large scale counterparts. This aspect has been examined in a number of earlier studies using partial productivity ratios. In this paper, an index of relative efficiency (based on the concept of total factor productivity) is used. The paper also enquires into inter-industry differences in relative efficiency with the help of correlation/regression analysis.

The paper is organised as follows. The first section presents a brief review of the earlier studies on the relative efficiency of small scale industries in India.[4] Estimates of relative efficiency based on some recent data are presented in the next section. Results of correlation/regression analysis are discussed in the third section. The main findings of this study are summarised in the last section.

Review of Earlier Studies

One of the earliest studies on the relative efficiency of small scale industries in India was undertaken by Dhar and Lydall.[5] They

[2] J. Mellor (1976).

[3] The term 'modern' is used to indicate that this analysis does not cover traditional small scale or cottage industries.

[4] For a survey of the literature on the question of relative efficiency covering studies for other countries, see L.J. White 1978a and J.M. Page (1979).

[5] P.N. Dhar and H.F. Lydall (1961).

compared output-capital ratios for a number of reasonably homogeneous industry groups, each depicting size variation. Two sets of exercises were carried out, one for nine industries using the CMI[6] data for 1956 and the other for fifteen industries using data from studies of the Perspective Planning Division.[7] Comparing the output-capital ratio for units employing 20 or more persons, it was found that the output-capital ratio for units employing 20 or more persons does not fall with size. Rather, in certain cases, it rises with size. For factories employing less than 20 persons, it was found that the output-capital ratio for such units was higher than those immediately above them (20–49 employment range) but not necessarily higher than large scale units. Accordingly, they concluded that small scale units (in the modern sector) are, in general, more capital using than their counterparts in large scale. In the words of Dhar and Lydall, 'The figures suggest that, in general, the *most capital-intensive* type of manufacturing establishment is the small factory using modern machinery, and employing up to 50 workers.'

Similar findings were reported in the studies of Hajra[8] and Sandesara.[9] Hajra used the CMI data for seventeen industries for 1955 and 1958. Comparing partial productivity ratios between large and small scale units, he came to the following two conclusions: (i) both labour and capital productivities are low in small scale industries, and (ii) the ratio of material cost to value added is high in small scale industries (suggesting, thereby, inefficient use of material input).

Using the CMI data for twenty-eight industries for the period 1953–58, Sandesara undertook a comprehensive study of the relationship between size and various important ratios, like the capital-labour ratio and the output-capital ratio. In his work, a positive association was observed between size and the output-capital ratio supporting the conclusion earlier reached by Dhar and Lydall. Sandesara, however, did not find any positive association between size and capital per employee. His findings suggest that, for a given volume of investment, small scale units neither generate

[6] Census of Manufacturing Industries, Directorate of Industrial Statistics, Cabinet Secretariat.

[7] Perspective Planning Decision, Planning Commission, Government of India. 'A Study of Economic Coefficients for Organised Industries in India,' 1959 (mimeo) and 'Capital and Labour Requirements of Small Enterprises,' 1960 (mimeo).

[8] S. Hajra (1965).

[9] J.C. Sandesara (1969) and (1966)

more employment nor produce more output compared to large scale units.

Since the findings of Dhar and Lydall and Hajra and Sandesara are in conflict with the conventional view of small scale industry, an explanation for the observed positive relationship between size and output-capital ratio is called for. To provide an explanation of their findings, Dhar and Lydall pointed out that the modern small scale sector is very different from the traditional small scale sector, which uses family labour and produces traditional products. Modern small scale factories, on the other hand, employ hired labour and use modern machinery to produce modern goods. They are mainly located in urban areas. They get their materials (like steel and chemicals) from far-off places and sell their products widely. They are just like big factories, except that they are small in size and thereby deprive themselves of economies of scale, professional management and multiple shift utilisation.[10] Sandesara also sought the explanation of his results in economies of scale[11] and better managerial ability of the entrepreneurs in large scale units. In his words, 'our results suggest that large units are possibly headed by entrepreneurs who more efficiently combine factors of production—capital and labour. The crucial factor which could explain our results may well be the factor of enterprise.'

In the studies of Dhar and Lydall and Hajra and Sandesara, employment was taken as the size criterion. This was questioned by Mehta,[12] who pointed out that the classification of factories based on employment does not show the productivity level of small scale units properly, since sick or ailing large scale units employing only a skeleton staff or new units undergoing teething troubles may get classified in the small size group. For his analysis, Mehta used the ASI[13] data for thirty-two industries for the period 1960–63. He compared capital-labour, output-labour and output-capital ratios among 'small,' 'medium' and 'large' factories classified according to

[10] P.N. Dhar (1979).

[11] Studies of P.N. Dhar (1958) and National Council of Applied Economic Research (1972) have revealed that the working capital constitutes over 50 per cent of the total productive capital employed by small scale units. Because the scale of operation is low in small scale units, they are at a serious disadvantage in regard to the utilisation of working capital. See T. Thomas (1978).

[12] B.V. Mehta (1969) and J.C. Sandesara (1969).

[13] *Annual Survey of Industries*, Central Statistical Organisation, Department of Statistics, Cabinet Secretariat.

fixed assets and between the census sector and sample sector factories classified according to employment. It was observed in Mehta's study that in almost all cases, the capital-labour ratio rises with size and the output-capital ratio falls with size.

The conflict between the findings of Mehta and those of Dhar-Lydall and Sandesara is somewhat baffling. This cannot be attributed to differences in the time period covered or in the sources of data. The differences in findings may partly be explained by the fact that while Dhar and Lydall, and Sandesara used total productive capital (fixed plus working) for measuring capital input, Mehta used fixed capital. Since the ratio of working capital to fixed capital is high in small scale units, efficiency comparisons based on fixed capital favour small scale units.

A major limitation of the studies based on the CMI/ASI data is that they cover only those small scale units which are registered as 'factories' under the Factories Act, 1948. A large part of the modern small scale industry is, however, outside the purview of the Factories Act. A census of small scale industrial units was conducted in 1973–74 by the Development Commissioner, Small Scale Industries, with 1972 as the reference year.[14] In a recent study, Bhavani[15] examines the relationships between the scale of operation, technology, capital intensity, and relative efficiency, drawing data from the ASI (1973–74) and the Census of Small Scale Industrial Units (CSSI) mentioned earlier. She considers 46 three-digit industries of the National Industrial Classification. She makes a comparison between the census sector of the ASI, the sample sector of the ASI, and the CSSI. She finds that, in most cases, labour productivity (value added-labour ratio) and capital intensity (fixed capital-labour ratio) in the census sector (which includes large scale units) exceeds those in the sample sector and the CSSI. The ratio of value added to fixed capital in the census sector exceeds that in the sample sector for thirty-one industries (out of forty-six) and this pattern holds between the census sector and the CSSI for eighteen industries.[16] Bhavani also notes that the ratio of working capital to fixed capital is relatively high in small scale units,[17] which suggests that the per-

[14] Government of India, Development Commissioner, Small Scale Industries, (1976–77).

[15] A. Bhavani (1980).

[16] *Ibid.*, p. 107.

[17] *Ibid.*, p. 139.

formance of the small scale industry in regard to capital productivity would turn out to be worse if the ratio of value added to productive capital is considered. Clearly, efficiency comparisons between the census and the sample sectors of the ASI in Bhavani's study do not agree with the results of Mehta's study mentioned earlier, and they are more in line with the findings of Dhar-Lydall and Sandesara. A positive relationship between size and capital productivity is, however, not seen when comparisons are made between the census sector and the CSSI. But, even in this case, it is seen from her estimates that in a fairly large number of small scale industries, accounting for nearly 40 per cent of the total value added, both capital and labour productivities are lower than those in large scale units.

A higher output-capital ratio in small scale industry is *necessary but not sufficient* for it to be technically efficient (using Farrell's terminology). This may be seen from Figure 1.

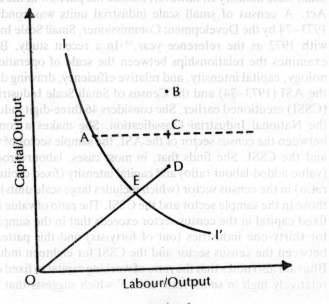

Figure 1

Labour per unit of output and capital per unit of output are shown on the two axes. I I' gives the unit isoquant for the 'best practice' (frontier) production function. Let point A represent the technology being used by large scale units. If the technology of small scale units is represented by point B, then small scale units are technically inefficient because they require both more labour and more capital per unit of output. The same is true, if the technology of small scale units is given by point C, since they use more labour without saving capital. The results of Dhar-Lydall and Sandesara suggest that this pattern holds true for most small scale industries. The results of Mehta suggest, on the other hand, that the capital-output ratio is relatively lower in small scale industry. If the technology of small scale units is represented by point D, the capital-output ratio is lower in small scale units; but they are even then technically inefficient, because the same level of output can be produced using both less labour and less capital if point E on the 'best practice' production frontier is chosen.

It is evident from the foregoing that for a proper assessment of the relative efficiency of small scale industries, simple comparisons of partial productivities are not enough. For the measurement of the relative efficiency of small scale industries, two approaches may be taken— the frontier production function approach and the total factor productivity approach. In the former, a frontier production function is estimated first, and then requirements of labour and capital per unit of output in different size classes are compared to those on the frontier. In the latter, a weighted average of partial productivity indices is taken, the weights being based on income shares of factors. Page[18] has taken the frontier production function approach for four Indian industries. Ho[19] has taken the total factor productivity approach for small scale enterprises in Korea and Taiwan. I[20] have taken both approaches for a study of efficiency variations within the small scale soap industry. In the empirical analysis presented in the third section, the total factor productivity approach is taken.

In the study by Page mentioned earlier, a four-factor translog frontier production function has been estimated from survey data for four industries, namely, shoes, printing, soap and machine tools. The average experience of the labour force within the enterprise, experience of the entrepreneurs, age of the establishment's plant and equipment, and the level of capacity utilisation are found

[18] J.M. Page (1984).

[19] S.P.S. Ho (1980).

[20] B. Goldar (1982).

to be four significant sources of variation in technical efficiency across firms. From a comparison of mean technical efficiency across size groups and from multiple regression analysis, Page finds a significant positive relationship between technical efficiency and firm size in only one case, namely, machine tools.

Considering the available empirical evidence on the question of relative efficiency of small scale industries in India as a whole, it may be concluded that, although small scale industries may not be relatively inefficient in general, there are industries in which small scale units are inefficient compared to large scale units and such industries constitute a sizeable part of the small scale sector. Evidently, why small scale units in one industry are inefficient and in another they are not, is an important question of both intellectual interest and policy significance.

Attention may be drawn here to some empirical problems in the comparison of efficiency between small and large scale units. Ideally, enterprises must be producing the same final product and must be vertically integrated to the same extent. These conditions are, however, rarely met, especially in studies using secondary data. Inasmuch as there are differences in product composition or in the degree of vertical integration, the estimates of relative efficiency are affected. Biases in efficiency estimates are also caused by other factors. Since there is a consumer preference for products manufactured by large units, the buyers of the products of large units generally have a higher capacity to pay, and large units have marketing advantages over small units, it is expected that for the same product small scale units usually get a lower price than large scale units. Further, small scale units generally have to pay a relatively higher price for raw materials, because (*i*) large scale units have the advantage of bulk-purchase, and (*ii*) for raw materials allocated by the government, small scale units are able to get only a small part of their requirements at regulated prices.[21] As against this, small scale units get certain benefits (preferential buying by the government, tax concessions, and so on) which tend to compensate for the disadvantages noted earlier. It is, however, difficult to say whether on balance there is a bias in favour of or against small scale units in the estimates of relative efficiency based on secondary data.

[21] *Development of Small Scale Industries in India: Prospects, Problems and Policies*, Report of The International Perspective Planning Team, sponsored by the Ford Foundation, Ministry of Industry, Government of India, 1963.

Estimates of Relative Efficiency

Data on small scale industry for the present analysis have been drawn from the statistical reports of a sample survey of small scale industrial units undertaken by the Reserve Bank of India (hereafter RBI survey).[22] This survey was confined to small scale industrial units assisted by banks. For the purpose of the survey, the official definition (then obtaining) of small scale industry was adopted, namely, an industrial unit with an initial investment in plant and machinery not exceeding Rs. 1.0 million or an ancillary unit with an initial investment in plant and machinery not exceeding Rs. 1.5 million. The reference period of this survey was the accounting year ending during the period April 1976 to March 1977. The effective sample size was 12,356 units.

Data on large scale industry have been drawn from census sector results of the ASI for 1976–77, which has the same reference period as the RBI survey. The census sector of the ASI covers factories which employ 50 or more workers with the aid of power, or 100 or more workers without the aid of power. There is some marginal overlap between the two sources of data, but this should pose no serious problem in efficiency comparisons.

Efficiency comparisons are made here for thirty-seven three-digit industries of the National Industrial Classification (NIC). These are the industries for which data have been provided in the RBI survey. The choice of the level of disaggregation is, again, dictated by the fact that data are not available at the four-digit or lower level of disaggregation.

Invested capital is taken as the measure of capital input. This is obtained by adding fixed capital and inventories. This is better than taking only fixed capital because inventories involve a real cost per annum to the economy and the ratio of inventories to fixed capital varies between small and large scale units. Clearly, if a technology requires smaller inventories but does not differ in regard to fixed capital, employment and value added, then it is more efficient.

Figures on fixed capital reported in the ASI are book values of fixed assets net of cumulative depreciation. In statistical reports of the RBI survey, on the other hand, net fixed assets, gross fixed

[22] Reserve Bank of India (1977). For some analysis of this data see R. Varma (1980).

assets and replacement value of fixed assets are given. Estimation of the replacement value of fixed assets for all the thirty-seven three-digit industries of the ASI is an enormous task and has not been attempted for this reason. Thus, two measures of capital are used: (*i*) net fixed assets plus inventories (net invested capital), and (*ii*) gross fixed assets plus inventories (gross invested capital). The former is readily available from the data sources. An estimation of gross fixed assets for large scale industries has been done with the help of gross-net ratios computed from 'Finances of Medium and Large Public Limited Companies' brought out regularly by the Reserve Bank of India. The computed gross-net ratios for different industries range from 1.5 to 2.5. In many cases, the gross-net ratio computed for a broad industry group (e.g., electrical machinery) has to be applied to all three-digit industries belonging to that category. For some of the three digit industries, the gross-net ratio could not be obtained. For them the ratio is taken as 2.0, which is the mean gross-net ratio of industries for which such ratios are available.

Table 1 shows relative labour productivity, relative capital productivity and relative efficiency of small scale industries. The gross value added per employee is taken as the measure of labour productivity. The ratio of gross value added to invested capital is taken as the measure of capital productivity. For each industry, relative labour and capital productivities are obtained by dividing labour and capital productivities in small scale units by those in large scale units. Series A in the table is based on gross invested capital and Series B on net invested capital. The relative efficiency index (a ratio of total factor productivities in small and large scale units) is computed as a weighted average of relative labour and capital productivities. Let LP denote labour productivity, KP capital productivity, and a and b the income shares of labour and capital. Also let l and s be the subscripts for large and small scale, respectively. Then the index of relative efficiency, denoted by E, may be computed as

$$\ln E = \bar{a} \ln (LP_S/LP_L) + \bar{b} \ln (KP_S/KP_L)$$

where

$$\bar{a} = \tfrac{1}{2} (a_L + a_S)$$

$$\bar{b} = \tfrac{1}{2} (b_L + b_S)$$

$$\bar{a} + \bar{b} = 1$$

The relative efficiency index has the same form as the one used by Ho in the study mentioned earlier,[23] except that here an average of the income shares in large and small scale units has been taken, which makes it similar to the translog index of total factor productivity.[24] As in the case of capital productivity, two sets of estimates of relative efficiency have been made using gross invested capital (Series A) and net invested capital (Series B).

It is seen from Table 1 that relative labour productivity is less than unity. i.e., labour productivity in small scale units is less than that in large scale units, in all industries, except one. On the other hand, relative capital productivity is greater than unity, i.e., capital productivity in small scale units exceeds that in large scale units, in twenty-two industries (out of thirty-seven) if gross invested capital (Series A) is used and in fifteen industries if net invested capital (Series B) is used. Also, relative capital productivity exceeds relative labour productivity, i.e., capital per employee in large scale units is higher than that in small scale units, in almost all cases. It may be inferred from the estimates of relative productivities that while labour productivity and the capital-labour ratio are generally higher in large scale units, the same is not true about capital productivity. In a large number of industries, capital producitivity is higher in small scale units. These findings accord well with the findings of Bhavani noted earlier.

The relative efficiency index is less than unity in almost all cases. In Series A, based on gross invested capital, the index is less than unity in thirty-four (out of thirty-seven) industries and less than 0.8 in twenty-six. In series B, based on net invested capital, the index is less than unity in thirty-five industries and less than 0.8 in twenty-seven. While these results are quite striking, one must be cautious in drawing inferences from them since the estimates of relative efficiency suffer from a number of defects. First, efficiency comparisons have not been made at a sufficiently disaggregated level. Thus, differences between small and large scale units in regard to product composition and the degree of vertical integration affect efficiency estimates. Secondly, the measures of capital and labour are not very satisfactory. In the measurement of labour, quality differences have not been

---

[23] S.P.S. Ho, *op. cit.*, p. 61.

[24] See S. Star, 'Accounting for the Growth of Output,' *American Economic Review*, March 1974; and J.W. Kendrick and B.N. Vaccara (eds.), *New Developments in Productivity Measurement and Analysis*, NBER, 1980.

Table 1
Relative Labour and Capital Productivities and Relative Efficiency in Small Scale Industries: 1976–77

NIC Code	Description	Relative Labour Productivity	Relative Capital Productivity		Relative Efficiency	
			A	B	A	B
(1)	(2)	(3)	(4)	(5)	(6)	(7)
204	Grain mill products	0.390	0.709	0.477	0.514	0.428
211	Other edible oils & fats (mustard oil, groundnut oil, til oil, etc.)	1.385	1.484	1.172	1.440	1.261
232	Printing, dyeing & bleaching of cotton textiles	0.760	1.425	0.964	1.044	0.857
235	Weaving & finishing of cotton textiles in handlooms, other than khadi	0.338	2.131	1.871	0.693	0.659
236	Weaving & finishing of cotton textiles in powerlooms	0.990	1.707	1.319	1.287	1.137
247	Spinning, weaving & finishing of other textiles, synthetic fibres, rayons, nylons, etc.	0.596	1.180	1.014	0.864	0.795
260	Knitting mills	0.762	1.115	1.138	0.963	0.976
264	All types of textiles, garments (including wearing apparel)	0.602	1.221	1.125	0.837	0.806
271	Sawing & planing of wood (other than plywood)	0.920	0.909	0.743	0.915	0.840

NIC Code (1)	Description (2)	Relative Labour Productivity (3)	Relative Capital Productivity		Relative Efficiency	
			A (4)	B (5)	A (6)	B (7)
272	Wooden & cane boxes, crates, drums, barrels, baskets, etc.	0.249	0.895	0.727	0.482	0.433
276	Wooden furniture & fixtures	0.710	1.469	1.310	0.944	0.903
281	Container & boxes of paper & paper boards	0.433	1.072	0.956	0.738	0.690
285	Printing & publishing of periodicals, books, journals, etc.	0.717	0.684	0.632	0.705	0.685
289	Printing, publishing & allied activities n.e.c.	0.736	0.849	0.798	0.784	0.763
291	Footwear (excluding repair) except vulcanised or moulded rubber or plastic footwear	0.184	0.605	0.551	0.285	0.276
303	Plastic products n.e.c. (except house furnishing)	0.378	0.794	0.734	0.610	0.580
310	Basic industrial organic & inorganic chemicals & gases	0.232	0.997	0.693	0.559	0.449
312	Paints, varnishes & lacquers	0.318	0.787	0.651	0.587	0.517
313	Drugs & medicines	0.280	0.739	0.624	0.516	0.464
314	Perfumes, cosmetics & other toilet preparations	0.170	0.849	0.684	0.516	0.445
320	Structural clay products	0.224	2.054	1.485	0.549	0.481
331	Foundries for casting & forging iron & steel	0.587	1.402	1.347	0.898	0.881

(continued)

NIC Code	Description	Relative Labour Productivity	Relative Capital Productivity		Relative Efficiency	
			A	B	A	B
(1)	(2)	(3)	(4)	(5)	(6)	(7)
340	Fabricated metal products	0.576	0.899	0.842	0.723	0.699
341	Structural metal products	0.407	1.002	0.972	0.688	0.677
343	Handtools & general hardware	0.356	0.650	0.634	0.465	0.460
345	Metal utensils, cutlery & kitchenware	0.447	0.784	0.772	0.621	0.615
350	Agricultural machinery & equipment & parts	0.217	1.102	0.956	0.557	0.513
353	Industrial machinery for food & textile industries	0.551	1.140	1.073	0.834	0.806
354	Industrial machinery for industries other than food & textiles	0.337	2.081	2.050	0.791	0.786
357	Machine tools, their parts & accessories	0.359	1.141	1.008	0.648	0.608
360	Electrical industrial machinery & apparatus & parts	0.299	1.410	1.380	0.677	0.670
363	Electrical apparatus, appliances & their components	0.431	0.883	0.719	0.601	0.547
364	Radio, television, etc.	0.527	1.178	1.004	0.753	0.701
374	Motor vehicles & parts	0.301	1.025	0.854	0.572	0.520
376	Bicycles & cycle rickshaws & parts	0.663	0.929	0.754	0.791	0.709
380	Medical, surgical & scientific equipment	0.680	1.381	1.228	0.907	0.865
973	Repair of motor vehicles & motor cycles	0.693	1.056	0.865	0.789	0.742

Note: Series A is based on gross invested capital; Series B on net invested capital.

taken into account. In the measurement of capital, adjustments have not been made for differences in prices at which fixed assets of different vintages were bought.[25] Third, the relative efficiency index is based on the assumption of competitive equilibrium[26] which is not tenable in Indian factor market conditions. Also, the use of value added as the measure of output and the associated two-factor production model result in biases in the measurement of total factor productivity. And finally, consumer preference for products of large scale units, disadvantages of small scale units regarding procurement of raw materials and promotional measures (like tax concessions, preferential buying, and so on) taken by the government for small scale industry affect the relative efficiency estimates. It is clear from the foregoing that relative efficiency estimates provide only a crude approximation to the true efficiency differences; but there is no strong reason to expect the biases in relative efficiency estimates to be uniformly against small scale industries. Also, efficiency comparisons made here are between large scale units and *assisted* small scale units. Since assisted units are relatively bigger among small scale units,[27] and in some earlier studies[28] a positive relationship has been observed between unit size and efficiency within the small scale industry, it may be argued that the estimates of relative efficiency would have been still lower if non-assisted units were also included. With the above qualifications in mind, it may be inferred from the estimates of relative efficiency that small scale units are relatively inefficient in a fairly large part of the industries covered here, if not in most of them.

This conclusion does not agree with the findings of Page based on a detailed study of four industries. The differences in findings may be attributed, at least in part, to the differences in methodology. In

[25] Another major weakness of the capital measure lies in taking a simple sum of fixed capital and inventories, which implicitly involves the assumption that they are perfectly substitutable. Obviously, a weighted aggregation (using some income shares as weights) would be more appropriate. This could not be done due to difficulties in estimating incomes accruing to these two categories of capital assets.

[26] The bias in relative efficiency estimates caused by the divergence between income shares of labour and capital and the elasticities of output with respect to labour and capital is perhaps not serious. It has been shown in the study by M.M. Dadi (*Income Share of Factory Labour in India*, Shri Ram Centre for Industrial Relations, 1973) that the actual income share of labour is not significantly different from the estimated share based on production function.

[27] Reserve Bank of India, *op. cit.*, Table 3.1.

[28] B. Goldar, *op. cit.*, P.P. Pillai (1978). ·

particular, while Page uses a four-factor frontier production function in which skilled and unskilled labour are separated and material enters as a factor of production, in the present analysis a two-factor model is used in which skilled and unskilled labour are clubbed and material is substracted from output to yield value added. Thus, in the relative efficiency estimates of Page, differences in labour productivity between large and small scale units get a much lower weight.

On the other hand, the findings of Ho (based on a study of small scale enterprises in Korea and Taiwan) are similar to the findings of this analysis. For measuring relative efficiency of small scale units, Ho uses an efficiency index similar to the one used here. For Taiwan, efficiency comparisons have been made for forty-two industries. In twenty industries small plants are found to be equally or more efficient. Ho points out, however, that in Taiwan small scale industries, even when disaggregated to the four-digit level, are not very homogeneous, so that the efficiency measures for Taiwan are not too reliable. Since the Korean data are much more detailed, efficiency comparisons are more revealing and useful. Comparing total factor productivity in establishments of different size classes for two hundred and thirteen four-digit industries, Ho finds that establishments in the size range 5–99 workers are most productive in only a limited number of industries, and in half of these cases, the most productive size is the 'small-medium' category of 50–99 workers.

It has been noted earlier that capital per employee in large scale units is higher than that in small scale units in almost all industries. The difference in capital intensity between large and small scale units varies from industry to industry. For the seven industries in which the relative efficiency index (Series A) is above 0.9, capital intensity in large scale units is, on average, about 1.5 times that in small scale units, implying thereby that the investment required to employ two persons in large scale units will provide employment for three persons in small scale units. On the other hand, for the eleven industries in which the relative efficiency index is below 0.6, capital intensity in large scale units is, on average, about 3.5 times that in small scale units, implying thereby that the investment required to employ two persons in large scale units will provide employment for seven persons in small units. This is suggestive of a relationship between relative efficiency and employment potential in small scale industry. Correlation coefficients between indices of relative efficiency and relative capital intensity (capital-labour ratio in small scale units divided by that in large scale units) is 0.508 using Series A and 0.517 using Series B, both statistically significant at 1 per cent level. It may be inferred from this that small scale units are relatively efficient in those industries in which the difference in capital-labour ratio between small and large scale units is relatively small. Evidently, small scale industries cannot be relied upon to generate a large amount of employment efficiency.[29] Where they have substantial advantage in employment generation, they are relatively inefficient; and where they are efficient, they do not have much advantage in employment generation.

There is an impression that small scale units are wasteful in the use of materials. It is, therefore, important that the material input be incorporated explicitly into the efficiency analysis. Accordingly, a third set of relative efficiency estimates has been worked out, using the gross output version (rather than the value added version) of the production function and taking labour, capital and materials (including power and fuel) as three factors of production. For this purpose, the relative efficiency index has been suitably modified. Gross invested capital has been taken as the measure of capital input and the total value of materials consumed as the measure of material input. The measure of material input is clearly not satisfactory since large and small scale units may consume materials of different type, different quality, or in different proportion.[30] This affects the estimates of relative material productivity and relative efficiency.

Comparing material productivity between large and small scale units, it has been found that small scale units are less efficient in the use of materials in almost all (thirty-five out of thirty-seven) industries. This agrees with the findings of Hajra. Relative material productivity is less than 0.9 in twenty-five industries, but less than 0.8 in only four industries.

Table 2 shows the distribution of industries by levels of efficiency. Columns 1 and 2 are based on the value added version (corresponding to Series A and B in Table 1) and column 3 on the gross

[29] Ho arrives at a similar conclusion, analysing variations in productivity and capital intensity across size classes, for Korean small scale Industry.

[30] The data sources for this study do not provide data on materials consumed in sufficient detail. It is, therefore, not possible to correct the measure of material input for these differences between large and small scale units.

output version of the production function. It is seen from the table that relative efficiency estimates based on the gross output version are less than unity in thirty-four out of thirty-seven industries, implying thereby that in most industries small scale units are relatively inefficient. In this regard, these efficiency estimates are not different from those presented in Table 1. It is, however, seen that the extent of inefficiency is much smaller in the third set of estimates. In thirty-one industries, the relative efficiency indices are above 0.85, and in twenty-two above 0.9. It would appear, therefore, that relative efficiency estimates based on the value added version tend to exaggerate inefficiency in small scale industry. It may be mentioned here that the rank of industries in terms of relative efficiency do not change much by the inclusion of the material input in the relative efficiency index. Also, the relationship between relative efficiency and employment potential holds good. Ranking industries according to relative efficiency estimates based on the gross output version, it has been found that for the top seven industries, capital intensity in large scale units is, on average, 1.6 times that in small scale units. The relevant ratio is 3.9 for the bottom seven industries and 3.7 for the bottom ten.

Table 2
Distribution of Industries by Levels of Relative Efficiency

Relative Efficiency Index	Number of Industries		
	(1)	(2)	(3)
Above 1.0	3	2	3
0.95 – 1.00	1	1	8
0.90 – 0.95	3	3	11
0.85 – 0.90	3	3	9
0.80 – 0.85	2	3	3
0.75 – 0.80	5	3	2
0.60 – 0.75	10	11	1
0.40 – 0.60	10	12	0
Below 0.4	1	1	0
Total	37	37	37

Note: Relative efficiency index for Cols. 1 and 2 are based on the value added version and for col. 3 on the gross output version of the production function.

Causes of Inefficiency in Small Scale Industries

Estimates of relative efficiency presented in Table 1 show considerable variation across industries. An analysis of this variation would be useful for understanding the causes of inefficiency in small scale industry. The explanatory variables chosen for this purpose are discussed below.

Dhar and Lydall, and Sandesara have attributed their finding of relatively higher efficiency in large scale units to (i) economies of scale, and (ii) better management. To capture the effect of scale economies on relative efficiency, relative size (measured by value added per unit in small scale industry divided by that in large scale industry) has been taken as an explanatory variable. If there are substantial scale economies, the average factory size in large scale industry will be high compared to that in small scale industry, so that the relative size variable will take a low value. This will be associated with a low value of the relative efficiency index, since scale economies will give large scale units an advantage over small scale units. Thus, a positive relationship is expected between relative size and relative efficiency.

To measure the quality of management in small scale industries, the ratio of closing stock of raw materials to consumption of raw materials has been taken. This ratio indicates how efficiently small scale units manage their inventories[31] (a lower ratio indicating better management), but it is also affected by uncertainties in the supply of raw materials. While the education and experience of the entrepreneurs could be taken as alternative measures of managerial ability, such information has not been provided in the RBI survey.

Whether small scale units use manual or mechanised methods of production should have an important bearing on their levels of efficiency. In a study of small scale units in Delhi, Dhar[32] compares labour and capital productivities between power-using and non-power-using small scale units. The findings of this analysis are broadly consistent with the hypothesis that power-using small scale units are more efficient. Accordingly, the proportion of small scale units using power has been taken as an explanatory variable.

[31] It is assumed implicitly that a small scale unit, efficiently managing its inventories, would also manage efficiently other activities relating to production.

[32] P.N. Dhar, *op. cit.*

Since inadequate credit supply is often a major constraint on the smooth functioning of small scale enterprises, one would expect greater availability of institutional credit (especially short-term credit) to be associated with higher levels of efficiency. To measure the availability of institutional credit to small scale industries the following three ratios have been taken: (*a*) ratio of short-term bank borrowings to inventories; (*b*) ratio of short-term bank borrowings to total short-term borrowings; (*c*) share of banks and financial institutions to total long-term borrowings.

The commercial orientation of entrepreneurs in small scale industrial enterprises may be an important source of production inefficiency. Analysing this aspect for unregistered small scale units in Gujarat, Van der Veen[33] finds commercial orientation to be widespread and notes that the industrialists tend to expend considerable effort on purchasing and marketing aspects of their enterprises and tend to expend negligible effort on the production aspect. Rather than applying their energies to reducing the costs of production, they apply their energies to reducing trade margins on purchased inputs and to gaining control of the marketing channels for their products. In the words of Van der Veen, 'The proprietors of these urban unregistered industrial units possess a strong commercial orientation. They operate small units for which flexibility is a highly prized asset. They operate in imperfect markets. As a result, they profitably expend considerable energy on purchasing raw materials and on marketing their products.' To capture this aspect of small scale industries, the ratio of value of goods sold in the same condition as purchased to total output has been taken. This ratio varies considerably across industries, from 0.5 per cent to 62.1 per cent.

Correlation coefficients between relative efficiency (Series A and B) and the explanatory variables are shown in Table 3. Correlation coefficients for relative size are positive and highly significant. Correlation coefficients for the ratio of closing stock to consumption of raw materials are negative, as expected, and statistically significant for Series A. Correlation coefficients for the proportion of small scale units using power are positive, again as expected, and statistically significant for Series B. Correlation coefficients for the variable representing commercial orientation do not have the expected negative sign. Rather, they are positive, though not statistically significant.

[33] J.H. Van der Veen, *op. cit.*

This is perhaps due to the fact that profits made in trading are included in value added. A significant negative relationship is observed between relative efficiency and the ratio of short-term bank borrowings to inventories. Also, correlation coefficients between relative efficiency and the ratio of short-term bank borrowings to total short-term borrowings are negative, though not statistically significant. On the other hand, long term borrowings from banks and financial institutions as a proportion of total long-term borrowings do not show any significant negative relationship with relative efficiency.

Table 3
Correlation Coefficients between Relative Efficiency and Explanatory Variables

Explanatory Variable	Correlation Coefficient	
	A	B
Relative size (value added per unit)	0.645†	0.594†
Ratio of closing stock to consumption of raw materials	− 0.326*	− 0.274
Proportion of small scale units using power	0.296	0.323*
Ratio of short-term bank borrowings to inventories	− 0.424†	− 0.381*
Ratio of short-term bank borrowings to total short-term borrowings	− 0.272	− 0.222
Share of banks and financial institutions in total long-term borrowings	− 0.036	− 0.047
Value of goods sold in the same condition as purchased as a proportion of total output	0.196	0.215

Note: *Significant at 0.05 level
†Significant at 0.01 level

The finding of a negative relationship between short-term bank borrowings and efficiency is somewhat surprising since one would expect credit facilities to help small scale units overcome the problem of insufficient working capital, and thereby contribute to the smooth running of the production process. This perhaps shows that providing credit to small scale units at concessional terms may lead to a waste of resources. This danger of subsidised credit schemes for small scale enterprises has been noted earlier. On this issue, Ho states:

Ideally, one would like to see the credit market less regulated and that small scale enterprises be given a chance to compete on equal terms with large scale enterprises for credit. But, when interest is regulated, providing subsidised credit to small scale enterprises may lead to a serious waste of resources. Small scale enterprises are extremely difficult to assess so that a general subsidised credit scheme aimed at supporting the small enterprise sector may end up financing many establishments that are wasteful users of capital.

The correlation coefficient between the ratio of short-term bank borrowings to total short-term borrowings and the ratio of raw materials stock to consumption of raw materials is 0.412, which is statistically significant at 5 per cent level. It suggests that greater availability of short-term bank credit induces the entrepreneur to maintain a larger stock of raw materials, which leads to lower capital productivity. On the other hand, if bank credit is not easily available, the entrepreneur has to borrow from other sources in which the interest rate is very high so that he is forced not only to cut down the size of inventories, but also to economise in the use of labour, materials, and other factors of production.

Considering the correlation coefficients, the following four variables have been selected for multiple-regression analysis: relative size (S), raw materials stock to consumption ratio (R), proportion of small scale units using power (P) and ratio of short-term bank borrowings to inventories (B). Regressing relative efficiency (E) on these variables, the following equations are obtained (t-values in parentheses):

For Series A

$$E = 0.76 + 1.74\,S - 0.46\,R + 0.19\,P - 0.30\,B$$
$$\quad\quad (4.27) \quad (2.54) \quad (-1.05) \quad (1.93) \quad (-1.53)$$

$$n = 37 \quad\quad R^2 = 0.50 \quad\quad F = 7.9$$

For Series B

$$E = 0.66 + 1.49\,S - 0.31\,R + 0.19\,P - 0.25\,B$$
$$\quad\quad (5.18) \quad (2.24) \quad (-0.73) \quad (2.03) \quad (-1.30)$$

$$n = 37 \quad\quad\quad\quad R^2 = 0.44 \quad\quad F = 6.2$$

The signs of regression coefficients match with the signs of the correlation coefficients presented in Table 3. The coefficients of S (relative size) and P (proportion of small scale units using power) are positive and statistically significant at 5 and 10 per cent level, respectively. The coefficients of R (raw materials stock to consumption ratio) and B (ratio of short-term bank borrowings to inventories) are negative, but not significant statistically. The elasticity of relative efficiency with respect to relative size (at the mean of the variables) is 0.13 using estimates for Series A and 0.12 using estimates for Series B. The regression models leave a large part of the inter-industry variation in relative efficiency unexplained. In part, this may be attributed to errors in the measurement of relative efficiency. Also, the measures used for the explanatory variables are not completely satisfactory.

Conclusion

Estimates of relative efficiency presented in this paper indicate that in a fairly large number of industries, small scale units are relatively inefficient compared to large scale units. The index of relative efficiency is found to be positively correlated with relative capital intensity, which implies that small scale units are efficient in those industries in which the difference in the capital-labour ratio between small and large scale units is relatively small. Thus, small scale industries cannot be relied upon to generate a large amount of employment efficiently. The relative efficiency index is found to be positively related to relative size, and the proportion of small scale units using power, and negatively related to the ratio of closing stock to consumption of raw materials and the ratio of short-term bank credit to inventories. The finding of a negative relationship between short-term bank borrowings and efficiency in small scale industries is somewhat surprising. It perhaps indicates that providing small scale units with subsidised credit involves some cost in terms of efficiency. It should be noted, finally, that the efficiency index used here measures only technical efficiency. Even if small scale units are inferior in terms of technical efficiency, they may be far superior in allocative efficiency so that the economic efficiency of small scale units may be as high as that of large scale units.

6 I.M.D. Little

Resource Use Efficiency and the Small Scale Enterprise

Introduction

This paper is a summary of Chapters 7 through 12 of the World Bank Study by Little, Mazumdar and Page.[1] It investigates the question whether there is any relation between the size of an establishment, and the social efficiency with which it transforms factors of production into useful output.

We all know that factor productivities and factor intensities are in themselves no indication of social merit. Nevertheless, a good first step is to see whether the usually hypothesised relations between these variables and establishment size (measured by the number of workers) are valid; these are that the larger the size, the greater the capital intensity, the lower the capital productivity, and the higher the labour productivity. Do they hold good? The short answer is that they hold good for manufacturing in the aggregate, with some exceptions for the smallest size class. This is true of India and many other countries.

But this by itself seems to me to be of little interest. It may arise, on the one hand, because some industries typically use little capital

---

[1] I.M.D. Little, D. Mazumdar and J. Page (forthcoming).

in small establishments and have high capital productivity and low labour productivity, and vice versa, but with little variation between units of different sizes within narrowly defined industries. If this is so, then the best way to increase labour demand in the economy is to increase demand for the products of industries that are typically labour intensive and have high capital productivity. The size of the establishment, and supply side intervention in favour of the small, become irrelevant. If, on the other hand, within an industry, small units are more labour-intensive than large units, and have higher capital productivity, while their products are closely competitive with those of large units, then supply side intervention in favour of the small could be appropriate. The moral is that, it is essential to disaggregate, and this idea lay behind the inclusion of new surveys in the World Bank research.

A Review of Evidence from Industrial Censuses and Samples

Let us briefly look at some census material, first for manufacturing in the aggregate. We find, as already indicated, that the factor proportions and productivities behave much as expected. Take Japan: there are no anomalies in the aggregate except that capital productivity rises from the smallest size, 1–9 workers, and peaks in the range 20–50. But as soon as one disaggregates, even to four groups of industries, anomalies start appearing and they are anomalies that are unfavourable to small scale industry, especially to the smallest size class. But here is an interesting point. We had the census reclassified on the basis of capital size. At this still high level of aggregation to four groups of industries, the anomalies vanished when size was measured by capital employed. This is something that will come up again.

Turning to LDCs, the work of Ohkawa and Tajima[2] and Tajima[3] based on census material for a number of countries was available. There were no figures for the smaller size groups (< 20 workers). For the rest, labour productivity and capital intensity rose with size with few anomalies. But capital productivity was highly erratic.

The latest available Colombian, Korean and Taiwan censuses

[2] K. Ohkawa and M. Tajima (1978).
[3] M. Tajima (1978).

were examined for the World Bank project. In the case of Colombia, capital productivity again behaves erratically but there is a tendency to peak in the range of 20–100 workers. Otherwise, if one excludes the smallest group (5–9 workers), the figures are reliable, behaving according to hypothesis. But the smallest size class shows both high capital intensity and capital productivity.

The Korean census (1968) is the most interesting, since results are published at the four-digit and, occasionally, five-digit levels.[4] The following account is based on the work of Samuel Ho.[5]

Taking the aggregated figures first, an interesting point emerges. Capital intensity is virtually constant in the range 10–100 workers. Capital productivity is almost constant in the range 5–50 workers, but then rises dramatically before falling again in the largest group. So we have further evidence of an inverted 'U' for capital productivity.

We looked particularly at the size class of 100–200, comparing it with 10–20, on the assumption that the figures for the smallest size class are the most unreliable and that the sample gets fairly small for the larger size classes. Comparing the two, we find that both capital and labour productivity are more than double in the larger size class, (that is, 100–200), while there was virtually no difference in the capital to labour ratio. This suggests increasing returns up to around 200 workers followed by decreasing returns, apparently quite a common phenomenon.

Turning to the more interesting results of disaggregation, it was found that the regularities prevailing in aggregated statistics very rarely carried over to industries defined at the four-digit level. For instance, monotonicity of rising capital intensity with size is found in only two of 160 industries, where there are entries in at least four different size categories. More than that would occur by chance. It is almost as if there was something causing irregularity. The figures do not support the belief that small enterprises, as measured by numbers employed, are typically labour-intensive. The incidence of lowest capital intensity is almost even over the various size classes from 5 to 500 workers. Highest capital intensity occurs as often in the range 5 to 50 as in the range from 50 upwards. Capital productivity peaks in the range 50 to 500 in about two-thirds of the 160 industries in which there were entries in at least four size categories.

[4] The Taiwan census that was also analysed by Ho was less detailed than the Korean census, while contradicting none of the broad impressions derivable from the latter.
[5] S. Ho (1980).

Both statistical weaknesses and reality doubtless contribute to the turbulence of the disaggregated figures. Capital measures are notoriously unreliable. In this census, capital comprises the book value of owned tangible fixed assets but excludes rented assets. So far as this goes, capital used is more likely to be understated for small enterprises than for large ones. The value added is also likely to be very unreliable, most especially for the smaller sized classes, many of which do not keep records. And where records are kept, value added may be falsified to deceive the tax-man. Turbulence is also present in reality. One enterprise or even a size class of enterprises may have a good or bad year for reasons quite unconnected with production functions or normal market conditions.

We made comparisons between 20 to 50 workers and 100 to 200 workers, that being the range in which the aggregate figures suggested strong increasing returns. Out of 213 industries in all, 139 had entries in both these two size classes. In 67 cases, capital intensity was lower and capital productivity higher in the larger class. In 40 out of the 67 cases labour productivity was also higher. So, to this extent, the feature of the aggregate figures-non-increasing capital intensity and higher productivities-carried through to disaggregation. In view of the declining productivity in still greater sizes, economies of scale seem a more likely explanation than increasing monopoly.

It should also be noticed that inter-industry variations in capital intensity are far greater than these average intra-industry variations by size group. The latter seldom vary by a figure of more than three, while the range of the former is over a hundred.

Ho also made a crude cost-benefit analysis using actual wages as shadow wages, and a 20 per cent rate of return as the shadow price of capital. Out of 138 industries,[6] the peak of the benefit/cost ratio was in the range 50–499 workers in eighty-eight cases, and was spread fairly evenly over this range. Thirty-two industries performed best in the range below 50 workers, of which seven cases were in the class 5–9 workers. Eighteen performed best in the range 500 + workers.

Turning to India, we reviewed the early work by Sandesara[7] and

[6] The number was reduced to 138 by excluding industries whose output was *prima facie* heterogeneous, and those that did not have establishments in at least four size classes.

[7] J.C. Sandesara (1966).

Mehta[8] which seemed to produce relatively inconclusive results. We also compared the factor ratios and productivities for the SSI and the ASI—results not particularly favourable to small scale, that is to the SSI firms. We next looked at the 1978–79 ASI, where one finds that the size class 200–500 very nearly dominates all other size classes in having both higher labour and higher capital productivity.

We finally examined the Reserve Bank of India Survey[9] of small establishments that had been assisted by the commercial banks. This tended to show that the larger small (16–20 workers) were better than the smaller small. It is also evident from the RBI Survey that if one ranges establishments by capital employed, the figures are much more regular, especially when using the original value of plant and machinery as the size discriminator. This speaks well for the Indian formulae for defining the small, but does not speak well for the fact that size distributions are not published on this basis. The survey also shows, as one might expect, that not using power certainly selects enterprises with very low labour productivity and very low capital intensity. An obvious conclusion is that if one is foolish enough to want to select by labour intensity alone, then one should look at techniques, not employment size.

Let me summarise the results so far. First, the greater the disaggregation, the more the expected ratios fail; and only disaggregated figures are interesting so far as supply side intervention goes. Secondly, the smallest size class, as measured by the number of workers, very often shows quite high capital-labour ratios and low productivites. However, this may be partly explained by the fact that censuses and surveys are snapshots of a seething mass and the smallest size class includes new born infants where capital has been laid down but there is little employment or production as yet, and it may also include some dying adults. Third, there is considerable evidence that in a great many industries, the medium class, (50–500) is the most beautiful.

Further Evidence from the IBRD Surveys

The industries covered in India were printing, machine tools, soap, shoes, metal castings, powerlooms and handlooms. The detail of

[8] B.V. Mehta (1969).
[9] Reserve Bank of India (1979).

the surveys can be found in the World Bank study. The results permitted sophisticated econometric analysis for the first five industries, but not for powerlooms and handlooms. This was because in these latter two industries there was insufficient variation in capital-labour ratios, that is, the firms were all using essentially the same techniques. But the first question is whether, before turning to the econometric analysis, our figures support the results obtained from the Korean census. The answer is that they do. In none of the industries, was there a monotonic relationship between employment size and capital intensity; and when the distribution is divided into size groups in the normal manner, the intra-group variance of factor proportion and productivities was so great that inter-group differences were rarely of statistical significance. It is worth adding that we believe our surveys were less susceptible to the probable bias of the census figures that was referred to earlier. No firm was included that did not have at least a full year's operation. There were cases of excess capacity, but they were not significantly more prevalent in the smaller size classes.

A few highlights concerning the factor proportions and productivities in the five industries follow. In *shoe-manufacturing*, the capital-labour ratio was almost flat up to 50 workers. There was no firm in the class size 50–99. Over 100 workers, there was a large jump in capital intensity, and this corresponded with a significant rise in labour productivity and a fall in capital productivity. These differences corresponded to a marked difference in techniques. In *soap-manufacturing*, there was no systematic or significant variation of factor proportions with size: in this case, it should be noted that although there were seven firms with over 100 workers in the sample, these did not include (unlike the shoe sample) firms using modern techniques. In *printing*, there was an erratic tendency for capital intensity to rise with size. Capital productivity falls sharply and significantly for firms with 50 workers or more. There was no accompanying large rise in labour productivity, so that the larger firms show up badly. In *machine tools*, capital intensity rises erratically with size. This is the only sample industry in which there is a statistically significant difference between the factor productivies of the very small (<10 workers) and those of larger sized firms. Both labour and capital productivity are low for the small. In *iron castings*, there are no large or significant variations of capital intensity with size. The size groups with over 50 workers have both higher capital and labour productivity than all smaller sizes, but the intra-group variation is large.

When establishments are ranked by capital, the factor proportions and productivities vary with size in a manner that is closer to expectations than when employment is used as the size discriminator. This confirms what has been found to be true in some other surveys or censuses, as already mentioned. Nevertheless, substantial ir-regularities occur, and the diffferences between size groups are frequently insignificant, intra-group variation remaining high. *Shoe-manufacturing* is the only industry in which there is a regular rise of capital intensity and labour productivity with capital size, and a regular fall in capital productivity. In *soap-making*, capital intensity peaks and capital productivity reaches its nadir in the middle group with Rs. 50–100,000 investment. Labour productivity does not vary significantly throughout the range. In *printing*, capital intensity also has a peak (in the range Rs. 200–500,000), while capital productivity falls above Rs. 10–20,000. Labour productivity rises up to Rs. 50–100,000 and then behaves erratically. In *machine tools*, capital intensity rises monotonically, and labour productivity almost so. Capital productivity is, however, erratic. But, over Rs. 1 million, there is a sharp break. Capital intensity trebles compared with the range from Rs 200,000 up, while labour productivity rises more than 50 per cent. Capital productivity does not decline significantly, so that the largest firms (seven in number) show up well. For *iron castings*, capital intensity and labour productivity are significantly low in size groups below Rs. 20,000, but capital productivity is not relatively high. Variations among larger size groups are not significant. They are all essentially using the same techniques.

Econometric Analysis of the Samples

The econometric analysis carried out by John Page consisted of fitting three factor translog production functions both of the average and the frontier kind. The three factors were capital (K), skilled labour (L_s) and unskilled labour (L_{us}). The log of output is expressed as a linear function of the logs of the factor inputs, the squares of those logs, and the interaction terms such as log K. log Ls.[10] This

[10] The method of fitting the functions is described in Chapter 10 of the book. It was criticised as inconsistent in the discussions. I do not think that this criticism is well

function has the advantage of permitting variable output elasticities, and variable elasticities of substitution. Using the frontier production function permits an examination of total factor productivity (TFP). It should be noted that differences in TFP may arise either because of differences in the technology used, or because of an inefficient use of factors within a given technology. The frontier was estimated without distinguishing different levels of technology. The strategy adopted was then to explain differences in productivity, by various regressors including a proxy for the 'vintage' of capital or level of technology.[11] This analysis could be satisfactorily carried out only in four industries, since the data for iron castings had too many gaps.

The size of the enterprise is positively related to its age. One might expect age to have two opposite effects. On the one hand, the employees of the older firm are likely to have more firm-specific experience. On the other hand, the older firm is likely to be using older equipment. In fact, the age of the enterprise (like size) was not significantly related to TFP, except in the case of soap.

For the same reason, two age-related variables were used— the firm-specific experience of the labour force (for short, 'workers' experience'), and the age of the equipment. Workers' experience was the most uniformly successful variable. It was positive in all four cases, and significant in three. The elasticity was such that a 10 per cent increase in the average period of employment in a firm reduced costs by about 2 per cent. The age of the equipment could be measured only for printing and machine tools: in both cases, the coefficient was negative and significant (and in soap, where the age of equipment was not measurable, the age of the firm was significant, after allowing for workers' experience).

We deal briefly with other explanatory variables that were tried. As might be expected, capacity use was positively related to TFP.[12]

founded. Differences of opinion as to the best method can exist, but I believe that the method adopted by Page is well defended in Chapter 10.

[11] The proxy was the average age of the items of fixed capital equipment weighted by their original cost. This was described as the 'vintage of the capital'. This, however, implies that an older item of equipment is of an earlier vintage, even if indistinguishable from a later item. It was pointed out in the discussion that equipment may be less productive merely because it is more used, and not because it 'embodies' less advanced technology (as perhaps the word 'vintage' and, certainly, a 'lower level of technology' may be taken to imply).

[12] It was pointed out in the discussion that low capacity use may or may not be due to bad management. In the former case, it does not explain technical inefficiency but is a part of it.

Oddly enough, industry-specific managerial experience was insignificant except in soap. A possible explanation is that old managers, while more experienced, also get out of date: the explanation for soap as the odd-man-out may be that the soap entrepreneur was very often also a worker, and he probably should, as it were, partly fall under the label of firm-specific workers' experience. The education of the entrepreneur is interesting in that only literacy turned out to be significant: but we got rather contrary results when relating some other educational variables to the profitability and growth of firms.

Apart from technical efficiency, two other subjects were investigated by estimating the production function parameters—economies of scale and factor substitutability. The hypothesis of constant returns to scale could not be rejected in three out of five industries. In one of these—machine tools—there was some evidence of increasing returns, but it was not statistically significant. In the other two industries—printing and shoes—returns were variable. There was evidence of both increasing and decreasing returns, although the differences were not significant. In soap, for instance, as size increased there were first economies and then diseconomies of scale.

Turning to factor substitutability, there was a high partial elasticity of substitution (about 3) between skilled and unskilled labour in the four industries for which estimates could be made (printing, machine tools, shoes, and castings). Substitutability was still high, but lower between capital and skilled labour (about 2.0). Between capital and unskilled labour the elasticity was considerably lower—about 1.0 in machine tools and castings, and about 0.5 in printing and shoes. This was consistent with the fact that the relative employment of unskilled labour was shown to be much higher in large establishments in all the above-mentioned industries, except printing, where the evidence was equivocal.

Finally, an attempt was made to explain the growth (value of sales), and the profitability of the sample firms. In considering growth (and indeed profitability and productivity), it must be emphasised that only survivors could be surveyed. Many enquiries bear witness to high death rates among new small firms. But young survivors grow much faster than older larger firms. However, shoes and soap (where primitive methods are used in the smaller units) are to some degree exceptional. In these industries, a large minority of new small units remain small. Controlling for age, we investigated the influence on growth of many variables, including a number of entrepreneurial characteristics. There was little of significance. But either college or graduate education, though not strongly influential, was positively significant for printing, soap, and shoes; but no educational variable was significant for machine tools or castings. 'Profitability' (or the rate of eonomic surplus) was defined as value added less the wage bill, divided by the original value of fixed capital in constant prices *plus* working capital. The relation of size to profitability was erratic, and differences were rarely significant. However, in shoes, machine tools and castings, the smallest size group (1–5 workers) did have significantly low profitability, while in printing the opposite was the case. College or high school education was a positive factor in soap, shoes and printing, but not for machine tools or castings.

Policy-Related Conclusions

Size, as measured by the number of workers, is a very poor indicator of anything of economic or social significance. But insofar as the evidence suggests anything, it is that the small (<50 workers) and, especially, the very small (<10 workers) are very often both technically and socially inefficient as compared with larger enterprises, especially those of medium size (50–499 workers).

Employment (and the greater equality that a higher demand for labour may be expected to promote) has been the major argument for promoting small enterprises. But employment size is a poor indicator even of labour intensity, which itself is a poor indicator of social advantage. Labour intensity is far better spotted by observing the technique used. This recalls the important distinction, made long ago by Dhar and Lydall, between traditional manufacturing and the small modern factory or workshop.[13]

Size (measured by capital employed) is a better, but still unreliable, indicator of factor proportions and productivities. Obviously, a viable enterprise that uses almost no capital is labour-intensive, and will have high capital productivity. Obviously, again, it is using traditional methods.

[13] P.N. Dhar and H.F. Lydall (1961).

Leaving aside traditional manufacturing, the differences in labour intensity between normally operating firms within any narrowly defined industry are very small compared with the differences to be found between the average labour intensity of different industries. Changes in the composition of output would do much more to increase the demand for labour than supply side intervention designed to change the establishment size structure of particular industries.

III Industry Studies

7 J. George
Waardenburg

Small Scale
Leather Shoe-
Manufacturing
in Agra: A Case
Study in Small
Scale Industry
in India's
Development

Introduction

Reasons for Interest in the Subject and Problem Formulation

The subject of this study is a part of a group of studies on 'Small
Scale Industries in India's Development' undertaken by a number
of Indian and Dutch researchers within the framework of the Indo-
Dutch Programme of collaboration in the social sciences on Alternatives in Development (IDPAD). Our interest in this subject was
awakened for several reasons.

Development processes cannot, or can no longer, be considered
as an unambiguous blessing for everybody involved in them. Therefore, not all development strategies or policies are good in a politico-

ethical .sense, differing only in degree of efficiency in reaching certain development goals (in other words, in degree of correctness). Personal income distribution effects, and especially the impact on groups around or below the poverty line, have become important yardsticks for the performance of development processes and policies, and employment effects also loom large in the discussion on development either for their own sake or because of their influence on the income distribution and poverty situation.

Moreover, the role of the state as the main actor or regulator for development processes has been recognised to be more limited and relative than some, especially economists, have thought it to be in the fifties and sixties. In this connection, more attention has been given to 'grass roots action' and 'participation' and their influence, while the real effectiveness of the state in all its branches and in its complex interaction with other actors in the development processes has become a subject of consideration and study.

Already, these two groups of insights have necessitated a considerable differentiation and disaggregation in studying development processes and policies, and their impact on the people and on society. In this context, we became interested in the scope of this impact by looking closely at one (or some) particular aspect of the industrialisation process in India, in order to gain some insight into it beyond what could be learned by studying its aggregate or roughly sectorally-disaggregated performance figures.

Though in general in the Third World, and so in India, modern industrialisation has been a pivotal element in the process and policy of economic development, it 'has not been able to change the structure of employment and income generation in any substantial way, nor has it made much of a dent in the problems of employment and poverty'.[1] Moreover, it has contributed to a process of hyperurbanisation as it appears to favour the rise of large industrial centres.

In the recent 'serious thinking on alternatives in the development process,'

the small scale industry sector has come to be regarded as an alternative to the process of development through the modern

---

[1] From the introduction of the project's description in 'proposal for Indo-Dutch Cooperation Programme on Alternatives in Development 1980–1981'. IDPAD, ICSSR, New Delhi, IMWOO, The Hague, 1980.

large scale sector. This recent shift of emphasis to the small scale sector, however, is based on a number of assumptions about the nature and characteristics of this sector, most of which have not been systematically examined.[2]

Therefore, we decided to look into these small scale industries, as one particular, admittedly rather small, segment in India's industrialisation and development process. From the inception of India's industrialisation policy around Independence in 1947 (with its emphasis on modern large scale industry) onwards, also, attention and some selective support has been given to the more Gandhian small scale industrial units[3]—including those of cottage type—as a means to provide employment and redress poverty.

However, there is quite a difference between a modern small scale industrial unit of production, which differs more in size than in technology—more precisely capital-labour ratio—and modern large scale units, and a traditional small scale industrial unit—including household and cottage units—which has not only a technology, but also a style of management which differs considerably from any modern, large or small scale unit. While the traditional type of units may be sitting in the draught of modern industrialisation, they appear to employ relatively more and poorer people.

It seemed appropriate to restrict the study considerably, limiting it to one sector and one area, in order to enable us to bring the study as close as possible to real life. In the first place, the study is confined to the small scale leather footwear sector in Agra. In this sector, a large number of traditional units of various sizes and with varying marketing practices exists. Also, a considerable variety of units according to size and according to marketing channels exist, including the ancillaries of large national companies like Bata and Carona and exporting units. Moreover, leather-working is the traditional occupation of the largest Scheduled Caste group, the Chamars, which is one of the poorest and most down-trodden. Finally, the government has been active in its support to this sector:

[2] *Ibid.*
[3] A small scale production unit was, in general, defined as having at most a gross fixed capital of Rs. 0.5 million and less than 50 workers if power is used, or less than 100 workers if no power is used (Planning Commission, 1955). Later on also definitions with Rs. 0.75 million or Rs. 1 million—and ancillaries with Rs. 1.5 million—as a maximum for gross fixed investment in plant and machinery were used.

this has been reserved for small scale production.[4] An All-India Bharat Leather Corporation was established in the seventies to support this sector, and the state of Uttar Pradesh also provided support to this sector by establishing, in 1975, the Uttar Pradesh Leather Development and Marketing Corporation (UPLDMC), which is located in Agra but has a state-wide responsibility.

Another reason for interest in the small scale sector (namely, the leather shoe sector in Agra) is that in the realm of planning it is the responsibility of the state government and, as such, it is an example of lower level planning. A more differentiated and disaggregated view of the functioning of a government tends to look beyond what happens at the national or central level and obviously becomes interested in activities at lower levels of government and their impact.

This study deals with the problems of the small scale shoe-manufacturing sector in Agra, taking account of the differentiation of the production units according to marketing channels and size of production. Our special interest is in the survival prospects or 'efficiency' of these different units, their employment effects, their functioning in relation to poverty situations, the impact of government measures on them and, finally, their social and human dimension. While our first intention is to understand and analyse along these lines the position of these production units, and some aspects of their marketing, possible suggestions for action which may emerge from the analysis as possibly suitable for improving the situation will be looked into and mentioned at the end of this report.

Approach

The basis of approaching the subject of this report is a stratified sample survey of eighty-eight production units in Agra, with additional smaller questionnaires answered by 43 workers, 7 traders, 6 raw material dealers and 8 shops in Agra. In addition, some 12 extensive free interviews with 'resource persons' occupying pivotal positions in the Agra leather footwear scene were held and extensively recorded. To the insight gained by these interviews were added several observations by other people, especially the work of H.A. Romijin (1982).

[4] Only units exporting more than half their production may surpass the small scale limits.

Useful material was also available from two other earlier survey reports. In 1975 the UPLDMC conducted a survey which covered, by a small questionnaire, some 2,700 of a total of about 4,000 leather footwear production units. A brief report of the results of this survey was available (UPLDMC, 1976). In 1981 the Uttar Pradesh Industrial Consultants (UPICO) conducted an all-U.P. sample survey of the U.P. leather footwear industry, the report of which was also available (UPICO, 1981). Finally, a few studies on the leather goods sector in India or developing countries in general are available and were used for background information.[5]

Though quantitative, statistical data were collected and used, it cannot be called a rigorous statistical study. For Agra, only a reasonable impression of the total population of production units is available, with a subdivision into marketing categories, on the basis of the UPLDMC (1976) survey. But even in this survey, covering 2,701 units, it is estimated that about 1,000 units of the traditional, smaller type were missing. Though the sample of production units drawn in Agra took account of the subdivision of the UPLDMC survey and in that sense was stratified, it is not claimed that, on the basis of this sample, rigorous statistical conclusions about the whole population of production units can be drawn. We consider the quantative part of this study rather a statistical analysis only of the properties of the sample itself. Without offering statistical proof for that, it is our impression that the results have a more general validity for the whole population.

In fact, we consider the non-quantitative, qualitative information collected and the impressions and conclusions gained from it as important as the quantitative data and conclusions. Therefore, we are also not too worried that the unreliability of some statistics and some answers to the questionnaires would radically distort the picture of the situation we get. In fact, some wrong data can easily be detected and rejected, an example of which will be given in the next section, while in other cases they are counterbalanced by more correct, qualitative information.

We distinguish the following seven '*marketing categories*' of production units in Agra:

[5] See G.K. Boon (1980), P.A. Cornelisse *et al.* (1980), Gokhale Institute (1969), Van Heemst (1977, 1982, undated), McBain (1977), Nayudamma (1980) and Nayudamma *et al.* (1980).

	Number in Sample	Number in UPLDMC Survey
Exporters (1)	13	300
Government suppliers (2)	3	9
Ancillaries (3)	17	50
Outside suppliers (4)	9	245
UPLDMC suppliers (5)	12	—
Local suppliers large (6)	17	833 (8)
Local suppliers small (7)	17	1,264
Total	88	2,701

1. Either via the State Trading Corporation or directly to foreign demand.
2. Supplying the government, mostly with army material, often via the Directorate General of Supplies and Disposals.
3. To Bata, Corona, Swastik or Flex.
4. Supplying directly on order to retail shops mostly outside Agra.
5. Rather regularly marketing their produce via UPLDMC.
6. Selling to wholesale agents more than 25 pairs a day, on order or not.
7. Selling to wholesale agents up to 25 pairs a day, normally not on order.
8. Not counted the about 1,000 units left out of the survey.

In addition, we distinguish the following '*size categories*,' according to production in pairs:

A: 6–10
B: 11–25
C: 26–50
D: 51–100
E: 101–200
F: > 200

The situation of the production units as well as the total system of production units in Agra are investigated with respect to these two sets of marketing and size categories.

In the next section, we present and discuss briefly quantitative material collected in this study on Agra. The third section briefly mentions some qualitative results and some conclusions which may be useful for policy-making.

Some Background Information on Agra

Historical records on Agra go back to at least the end of the eleventh century, but mythical tradition suggests a much earlier existence. When Sultan Sikander Lodhi of Delhi made it the capital of his Indian Mughal Empire, in 1504, it was brought into prominence, which it retained for a long time, even after Aurangzeb had again selected Delhi for his court in 1658. The British forces conquered it in 1803, making first Allahabad, and later Lucknow, the most important city of what is now Uttar Pradesh. Also Indian Independence did not give again to Agra its earlier prominence, though it has had considerable military forces on its ground.[6] Long before the advent of the British, the city of Agra was known for the production of a great variety of indigenously styled leather footwear, a necessary adjunct of the police uniform. Already, then, the footwear trade was in the hands of rich factors. Soon the British had introduced their own shoemakers in Agra. The local workers mastered not only the repair but also the production of shoes of cheap ordinary English style, which replaced the indigenous shoes. At the end of the nineteenth century, factories, technical footwear instruction and the first machines were introduced in Agra. However, its cottage industry could produce shoes at half the unit cost of factories with machines. In the beginning of the twentieth century, an association of shoe factors was formed and one central market for them in Hingki Mandi—still very much alive[7]—was established. However, the Agra Shoe Manufactures' Association was formed not before 1941.[8]

More important than these historical data for understanding the social climate of footwear production in Agra is the fact that making leather goods is one of the traditional occupations of one large sub-caste in India, the Chamars. They are the first-ranking Scheduled Caste in India, as well as in several states, notably in Uttar Pradesh where they constitute 56.5 per cent of the total Scheduled Caste population. Moreover, Uttar Pradesh is the state with the largest

[6] Srivastava (1979).

[7] H.A. Romijin (1982) has described the working of this market in her Masters' thesis 'Hingki Mandi', Agra University.

[8] S.P. Dhir, *A Brief History of the Footwear Industry of Agra*, Agra, The Shoe Manufacturer's Association, 1968.

number of Chamars. Though they are well known as workers in leather, hide and skin, their main occupation in Uttar Pradesh is in agriculture, 54 per cent being tenant cultivators, 20 per cent agricultural labourers, while only 1.5 per cent are in manufacturing industry—presumably not leather—and 4 per cent in (presumably mainly leather goods) household industry.[9] UPICO (1981) mentions for Uttar Pradesh of all artisans working in the leather goods sector, mainly of cottage type,[10] 20 per cent belonging to Muslim weaker sections[11] and the remaining 5 per cent belonging to other communities, among which Christians are said to be the largest group. While the real work is thus mainly done by Chamars, or Yadavs, they are not proportionally represented among the managing staff. Until Independence and Partition, a larger role was played by Muslims, but since they left in 1947 for Pakistan, one finds a considerable number of Sikhs or other people from the Punjab, who moved in 1947 in the opposite direction, in these functions. Certainly, also, some Chamars did move gradually into higher managing positions, even before 1947. These so-called 'big men' had already undertaken in the 1930s some political action for the improvement of the position of the Chamars as a whole, but the success of the Chamars was very limited, due to the difficulty of organising a unified front, as Lynch (1974) describes quite well.

Some Personal Observations

For a non-Indian researcher like me, even when personally professionally interested in development problems and seriously involved in Indian society, it is quite an experience to step into the work place of a tiny, traditional *dahliawalla* or shoe-manufacturing unit—offering its daily produce of pairs of shoes wrapped in a basket (*dahlia*) for sale to the local traders (commission agents) each day again. Five to eight people, sitting on the floor of one small, scantily lit room, working in a clear division of labour, produce the complicated and artistic product which a shoe is. Often they come mainly from one larger family, some of them helped by young boys (mostly a son) who get tea for them, shift their material around, and

[9] A.B. Mukerji, *The Chamars of Uttar Pradesh, A Study in Social Geography*, Delhi, Inter-India Publications, 1980.

[10] 75 per cent belonging to Scheduled Castes—presumably practically all Chamars.

[11] Notice that working on skin meets no ritual objection in the Islam.

so on. They stare friendly, humanly, slightly suspiciously, and with a mixture of hope and despair at the visitor, who is helpfully received by the owner, indistinguishable visibly from his company. Illiterate, poor, without expectations for improvement, they appear quite used to accepting the strange, ununderstandable but irresistible things which happen to cross their path. We cross not only the front of a production unit, but also the front of that undescribable and often misused 'informal sector.' We enter into a world not only of facts and figures, but also of human and social misery and hope. We wonder a while whether we can bear the responsibility of making our fellowmen, who live in many respects at such a distance, the object of our research. And so we continue.

But it is not only the *dhaliawallas*, mostly clinging together in their *mohallas*, who catch our eye. In considerable contrast we meet also the well established, clever local traders at Hingki Mandi or another local marketing place who receive us, this time without interpreter, in English, with suppressed suspicion and dignified respect. We meet the well-trained and instructed manager/owners of the ancillaries of Bata or Corona, and the very able and eager exporters, all well aware of the opportunities, requirements and vicissitudes of the national and international shoe market. And we meet also the busy but friendly people of the UPLDMC, in their lively office with that improbable, hardly visible entrance at the Sadar Bhatti crossing, where elephants instead of taxis pass by. Finally, we also meet the devoted and dignified people of the Khadi and Village Industries Commission, where the echo of Mahatma Gandhi still sounds.

Quantitative Material

Employment and Efficiency as Between the Marketing Categories

While studying the characteristics of this sector, we use as much as possible the seven-fold distinction mentioned earlier in order to gain insight into the possible differentially advantageous or disadvantageous features of these categories.

In order to find out whether there was any significant difference in employment generation between the seven categories of production units mentioned, the following procedure was followed.

For all production units in the sample, the people mentioned and the total investment per some unit of production (as a proxy for sales, which turned out to be a less reliable figure) was calculated and the results were plotted in a two-dimensioned scatter diagram with employment and investment per unit at the respective axes, not presented here. A distinction was made between figures for total production of the whole year ('long term') and for only one day ('short term'), the former having a special source of undesirable deviations inasfar as differences in long-term production between units may also reflect differences in sales opportunities between units which for some purposes one may like to include in the discussion, in other cases not.

As a next step for each point in the scatter diagram, the category to which it belonged was identified. For all points in one category the average as well as the standard deviation of the capital-output and employment-output ratios was calculated for the 'short term' and 'long term' data respectively (see Tables 1 and 2). While doing so a skipping procedure, known from the statistical literature, was used in order to delete extreme cases which could be expected to distort the results in an unjustified way, e.g., because of being obviously incorrect.

Before applying a rigorous statistical analysis for discovering significant differences between the categories, a first impression of such differences can be gained as follows. For each average, we check whether it differs from the average of any other category more than two times or one time the standard deviation corresponding to the latter average respectively, and display the result by ≫ or > respectively in the case of a positive difference, and ≪ or < in the case of a negative difference, in four 7 × 7 matrices (see Tables 1a and 2a).

We will call these relationships 'very significant' or 'significant' differences respectively, according to whether they refer to two times or one time the standard deviation. Notice that these relations are not necessarily reciprocal, as the standard deviations corresponding to two averages involved in a relation may be quite different. Notice also that, though we do not deal with a rigorous statistical test here, it is by no means without meaning that an *average* of a category differs from the average of another category by more than the latter's standard deviation.

From these tables we draw some results. For the short term data (Table 1a) we see:

Table 1

Average and Standard Deviation of Capital and Number of Workers Per Unit* of Production Per Day for the Marketing Categories

Category	Capital		Employment		Number of Observations			Employment/Capital Ratio
	Average	St. Dev.	Average	St. Dev.	Valid	Missing÷	Total	
(a) Export	4.14	2.56	37.7	25.1	8	5	13	9.1
(b) Government Supplies	1.37	0.40	41.5	34.9	2**	1	3	30.3
(c) Ancillary	3.18	3.62	39.5	17.5	15	2	17	12.4
(d) Outside	1.83	1.50	67.0	25.4	7	2	9	30.6
(e) UPLDMC	0.94	0.21	66.2	41.6	12	0	12	70.4
(f) Local (large)	1.44	1.24	57.0	22.9	14	3	17	39.6
(g) Local (small)	1.26	1.09	109.9	57.9	14	3	17	87.2
Total	2.02	2.28	63.4	42.4	72	16	88	

* 'Unit' is average production value per day. Rs.5,184.79.

÷ Out of the total sample of 88 units some did not provide the answers to the relevant questions or were removed by the 'skipping' procedure mentioned in the text.

** This amount is so small that the data for this category should be handled with care.

Table 1a

'Significant' and 'Very Significant' Differences Between Averages of the Categories for the 'Short Term' Data*

	a	b	c	d	e	f	g			a	b	c	d	e	f	g
a	×		⊘<			⊘<		a	×	⊗>		>	≫	≫	≫
b		×	<			⊗		b	⊘<	×		⊗			
c			×	<		⊗		c	≫	×		≫	>	>	
d	>	⊘>	×					d	>	×	⊗≫				
e	>	>		×				e	⊘<		×				
f		>			×			f			≫	×			
g	⊗≫	⊘>	⊗≫		>	>	⊘>	×	g						>	×

Employment/output figures   Capital/output figures

*See text for explanation. Circle denotes reciprocity.

1. Category *g* (small local suppliers) produces 'very significantly' more labour-intensively than category *a* (exporters), *c* (ancillaries), *f* (larger local suppliers), and 'significantly' so vis-a-vis the other categories. However, the reciprocal relationship holds only for the categories *a*, *b* (government suppliers) and *c*, and only 'significantly' so.
2. Category *d* (outside suppliers) and *e* (UPLDMC suppliers) produce 'significantly' more labour-intensively than categories *a* and *c*, but reciprocally so only *d*.
3. Category *a* produces 'very significantly' more capital-intensively than categories *b*, *e*, *f* and *g*, and 'significantly' so vis-a-vis category *d*, but reciprocally so only with respect to category *b* and only 'significantly' so.
4. Category *c* produces 'very significantly' more capital-intensively than categories *b* and *e*, and 'significantly' so vis-a-vis categories *f* and *g*.
5. All categories produce 'significantly' more capital-intensively than category *e*, and apart from category *g* even 'very significantly' so, but the reciprocal relationship holds only for category *b*, and only 'significantly' so.

The interpretation of these results is often rather straightforward, but falls outside the scope of this brief paper.

In moving to results of the 'long term' data, it should be noted that this introduces a general element of inefficiency into the data, due to seasonal (monsoon!) marketing and production (festivals!)

Table 2

Average and Standard Deviation of Capital and Number of Workers Per Unit*
of Production Per Year for the Marketing Categories

Category	Capital		Employment		Number of Observations			Employment/ Capital Ratio
	Average	St. Dev.	Average	St. Dev.	Valid	Missing†	Total	
(a) Export	2.97	1.30	26.46	14.62	8	5	13	8.9
(b) Government supplies	1.46	0.84	47.56	48.68	2*	1	3	32.7
(c) Ancillary	1.97	1.38	28.09	17.18	15	2	17	14.3
(d) Outside	3.11	4.00	93.88	59.83	7	2	9	30.02
(e) UPLDMC	1.01	0.81	78.23	63.18	12	0	12	77.5
(f) Local (large)	2.18	2.27	83.00	34.76	14	3	17	38.1
(g) Local (small)	1.27	1.03	129.37	70.16	14	3	17	101.9
Total	1.94	1.90	73.58	59.48	72	16	88	

* 'Unit' is average production value per day: Rs. 966,814

† See Table 1.

** See Table 1.

Table 2a

'Significant' and 'Very Significant' Differences Between Averages of the Categories for the 'Long Term' Data*

	a	b	c	d	e	f	g			a	b	c	d	e	f	g
a	×			⊘<		⊘<	⊘<		a	×	⊘>			⊗>		⊘>
b	>	×	>			<	⊘<		b	⊘<	×					
c			×	⊘<		⊘<	⊘<		c			×				
d	⊗>		⊗>	×					d		≫		×	≫		>
e	≫		≫		×				e	⊘<				×		
f	⊗>		⊗>			×			f					>	×	
g	⊗>	⊘>	⊗>		>		×		g	<						×

Employment/output figures	Capital/output figures

*See Table 1a.

problems, but possibly differentially so for the different categories. In particular, one would expect the categories *a* and *c* to be less affected by such problems. In general it should be noted, in addition, that the data used here reflect not only particular technologies in terms of labour and capital intensities, but also degrees of efficiency, related to size—due to economies of scale—or not. This complicates their analysis. We note in particular the following 'results', some of them formulated in comparison with those of the short term data (for easy reference, they are numbered similarly):

1a. Category *g* is no longer 'significantly' more labour-intensive than the categories *d* and *e*, and no longer 'very significantly' so vis-a-vis category *f*, which suggests that these three categories are more affected by seasonal marketing problems than category *g*.

2a. The latter interpretation is supported by categories *d* and *e*, but also *f*, now being 'very significantly' more labour-intensive than the categories *a* and *c*.

3a. Category *a* is no longer '(very) significantly' more capital-intensive than categories *d* and *f*, and no longer 'very significantly' so vis-a-vis categories *b* and *g*, which all indicates their relative 'change' in efficiency.

4a. The latter interpretation holds also for category *e*, which is no longer '(very) significantly' more capital-intensive than the categories *b*, *f* and *g*.

5a. No longer are the categories *b*, *c*, *f* and *g* '(very) significantly' more capital-intensive than category *e*, the latter apparently being considerably affected by seasonal marketing problems.

6a. Comparing the figures of Table 1 and Table 2 respectively, we see that the standard deviations of the categories *a* and *c* are smaller for the 'long term' data, but those of the categories *b*, *d*, *e* and *f* larger, both for capital and employment figures. This indicates that the seasonal marketing problems affect units within categories also differentially.

The general impression from these figures with respect to employment generation is as follows:

The small local suppliers (*g*) constitute an exceptionally labour-intensive category, the exporters (*a*) and ancillaries (*c*) exceptionally capital-intensive ones, and the UPLDMC-suppliers (*e*) are exceptionally capital-extensive.

The categories *g* and *e* have high employment/capital ratios, the categories *a* and *c* relatively low ones.

These impressions remain qualitatively the same for the 'short term' and the 'long term' data, but those of the first paragraph become quantitatively less pronounced, as categories *a* and *c* have less seasonal marketing problems than particularly categories *d* and *f*.

Gaining impressions about the relative efficiency in production of the categories is somewhat more difficult.

Clearly category *g* is, in an absolute sense, less efficient than category *e*. This holds less clearly—given the margins of error—for category *d* vis-a-vis category *b*—and for category *f* vis-a-vis category *e* for the 'long term' data.

If prices are used, cost comparisons could be made, but we refrain from it because of the separated labour and capital markets and, consequently, different prices with which the different categories are confronted.

The following procedure was applied to examine the efficiency problem, without using prices. For the whole sample a Cobb-Douglas production function is estimated[12] and drawn in the above-mentioned imaginary diagram. As a next step, the parameters of this function are changed by one time their standard deviation, first

[12] In the form $\ln\left(\frac{Y}{L}\right) = A + (1-\alpha)\ln\left(\frac{K}{L}\right)$ in which A and $(1-\alpha)$ are estimated, Y, L and K respectively being production, employment and capital respectively, and $(1-\alpha) = \beta$ assumedly.

the individual parameters separately, next both together, and all functions with these changed parameter values are drawn in the diagram, thus providing a ribbon. The unconventional idea is now that any average of a category which falls outside the ribbon should be recognised as indicating a quite exceptional category, and possibly an inefficient—above the ribbon—or very efficient—below the ribbon—one.

If we apply this procedure to the 'short term' data, it turns out that category *g* falls above the ribbon. We would not immediately take this as an indication of severe inefficiency—though the average of category *e* uses both less capital and less labour—but rather as a signal that a Cobb-Douglas function may not be appropriate (too rigid) for describing the technologies of such diverse categories of production units.

Applying this procedure to the 'long term' data, we see category *d* being clearly above the ribbon and categories *a* and *c* touching the ribbon from below. The result, with regard to category *d*, is due to a shift of the average, mainly to the right. This may be due to some arbitrary effect of the skipping procedure, whilst categories *a* and *c* may have less seasonally-determined marketing difficulties than the other categories.

Employment and Efficiency as Between the Size Categories

In the calculations made in the former section, the effect of the size of the production unit was not taken into account. In order to investigate this effect, and thus the possible presence of economies of scale, we put the units into the size categories A–F described in the first section. For these size categories we apply the same procedure as described in the preceding section (deleting the extra tables).

The following results can be seen from the tables. For the 'short term' data we see (Table 3):

7. Category F is 'significantly' less labour-intensive than any other category, all the reciprocal relationships holding 'very significantly'.
8. Categories E and D are 'significantly' less labour-intensive than the categories B and A, the reciprocal relationship holding also 'significantly'.

9. Categories C and B are 'significantly' less labour-intensive than category A, the reciprocal relationship holding also 'significantly'.
10. Category D is 'significantly' more capital-intensive than any other category, the reciprocal relationships not holding.
11. Category E is 'significantly' more capital-intensive than category A.

For the 'long term' data we see (Table 4):

7a. Category F is 'significantly' less labour-intensive only than categories B and A, the reciprocal relationship holding for the categories D, C, B and A.
8a. Categories E and D are again 'significantly' less labour-intensive than categories B and A.
9a. Categories C and B are no longer 'significantly' less labour-intensive than category A.
10a. Category D has lost its special position (probably due to an anomaly in the skipping procedure).
11a. Also, category E has lost the special position (probably also due to the skipping procedure) but now category C is significantly more capital-intensive than categories F, B, E and A.

Table 3

Average and Standard Deviation of Capital and Number of Workers Per Unit* of Production Per Day for Size Categories

Size Category Production	Capital		Employment		Number of Observations		
	Average	St. Dev.	Average	St. Dev.	Valid	Missing†	Total
F > 200	1.55	1.44	9.76	2.46	3	2	5
E 101–200	2.13	1.47	39.34	17.05	13	2	15
D 51–100	4.41	4.27	42.10	19.42	12	4	16
C 26–50	1.50	1.25	56.76	30.54	11	3	14
B 11–25	1.38	1.09	73.24	27.24	26	3	29
A 6–10	1.09	0.84	141.16	64.97	7	2	9
Total	2.02	2.28	63.37	42.42	72	16	88

*'Unit' is average production value per day: Rs. 5,184.79.
†See Table 1.

Table 4
Average and Standard Deviation of Capital and Number of Workers Per Unit*
of Production Per Year for Size Categories

Size Category Production	Capital		Employment		Number of Observations		
	Average	St. Dev.	Average	St. Dev.	Valid	Missing†	Total
F > 200	1.38	1.30	15.81	14.64	3	2	5
E 101–200	1.62	1.31	30.40	16.02	13	2	15
D 51–100	1.62	3.00	42.90	40.97	12	4	16
C 26–50	3.45	2.54	83.57	72.89	11	3	14
B 11–25	1.61	1.13	87.56	31.53	26	3	29
A 6–10	1.14	0.77	103.49	84.57	7	2	9
Total	1.94	1.99	73.58	59.48	72	16	88

*'Unit' is average yearly production: Rs. 966,814.
†See Table 1.

Comparing Tables 3 and 4, a less clear conclusion than for the marketing categories can be drawn—looking at the capital figures, the larger firms appear to have less seasonal marketing problems, but the employment figures do not confirm this; there, only category E appears to have relatively few such problems. category C, however, has many.

As far as 'absolute inefficiency' is concerned, both in the short and the long term data, category B appears very inefficient, being dominated strongly by category F and clearly less strongly by category E, which also dominates clearly category C in the long term case. Incidentally, category D appears to be plagued by a few exceptionally capital-intensive members.

There is, in the figures, a strong suggestion of economies of scale, with a very remarkable feature that with increasing size labour-intensity decreases without capital-intensity increasing. In other words, the machines in the larger unit are hardly more costly per unit of output, but they do strongly replace labour. In such a situation, smaller—labour-intensive—units would immediately be wiped out by the larger units without adequate protection (like reservation of the sector).

The calculations were repeated with employment figures including not only the workers involved but, also, the administrative and managerial personnel. The results are not essentially different. But, in the short term, category-wise results employment figures for categories a, b, c and d go up by 7–12 per cent, against those in categories e, f and g which go up by 0.5–3 per cent. In the short term size-wise results, employment figures go up by 10–12 per cent in the categories F and D, but by 0–2 per cent in the categories B and A. All this confirms the obvious hypothesis that in more organised and larger production units, the administrative and managerial personnel occupies a relatively important place. The same hypothesis was confirmed by a direct investigation of the available data.

Some Social Issues

In this section, we will take up some of the many issues which have been dealt with in the questionnaire. These link up very well with the more qualitative impressions.

(a) The Size and Composition of the Labour Force According to Function and Skill

Total employment per production unit is hardly correlated with the marketing categories ($R^2 = 0.127$) and not really significantly so ($F = 1.9$). Categories a and c have higher than average values, categories d, e, f and g lower than average values.

The *percentage of workers* in the total of employees in the production units is rather strongly correlated ($R^2 = 0.61$) with the marketing categories and highly significantly so ($F = 20.5$). Categories a and c have a clearly lower than average percentage, while the categories f, e and g have in increasing degree a considerable higher than average percentage, categories b and c having percentages only slightly above average. This whole difference is a nearly literal translation of the notion of organised (a, c) and unorganised (f, e, g), with b and d as intermediate cases.

The *percentage of formally skilled workers* has only a low correlation with the marketing categories, and not significantly so ($F = 0.7$). For whatever it is worth under these circumstances, we may mention that category c has a considerably higher than average percentage, category a hardly so and all other categories at the same level are somewhat below average.

The same investigations for the size categories show that the *total employment* is somewhat correlated with size ($R^2 = 0.19$) but significantly so ($F = 3.7$). Remarkably, category E far above average,[13] category F less so, category D hardly so and categories C, B and A increasingly clearly below average.

The *percentage of workers* among the employees is rather strongly correlated with size ($R^2 = 0.48$) and very significantly so ($F = 14.5$), category D being most below average, categories F and E also considerably so, but categories C, B and A increasingly clearly below average.

The *percentage of formally skilled workers* is hardly correlated with size ($R^2 = 0.06$), not significantly so ($F = 1.0$), category D being again exceptionally above average.

(b) The Relation between Workers and Production units

There is a widespread system of contract workers attracting helpers, often family members, to assist them in their work. The *ratio* of such helpers and total employment is hardly correlated and not significantly so with the marketing categories ($R^2 = 0.12$, $F = 1.1$), categories *b* and *c* being above average, categories *e* and *f* being below average.

Also, the *percentage* of family members among the helpers is not clearly correlated to the marketing categories, nor significantly so ($R^2 = 0.18$, $F = 1.3$), categories *b* and *e* being clearly below average, categories *f* and *g* being clearly above average. But this ratio and this percentage are correlated, and significantly so to the size categories ($R^2 = 0.24$ and 0.29, respectively, $F = 3.0$ and 3.1, respectively), the ratio being above average for category D and less so for category A, the percentage being above average for the categories B and A, and less so for category E.

The *workers remained attached to the same unit*, even after a period of work interruption, throughout the last years, especially in the categories *f*, *a*, *g*, *d* and *e* in this decreasing order, category *a* displaying remarkably more attraction than categories *b* and *c*, probably because of its payment and work conditions, but the significance is low (sign. level = 0.88), the largest units being relatively more, the one but largest relatively least 'attractive'. When asked specifically whether the same workers could be hired again when the production unit was restarted after a seasonal interruption, the answers indicated in decreasing order, categories *a* and *g* 81 per

---

[13] This suggests that category E still belongs to the continuous spectrum of technolgies in terms of labour intensity, but that category F has become a separate case.

cent, *f* and *c* above 50 per cent, *e*, *d* and *b* down to 33 per cent, category *c* displaying a remarkable difference with the result of the former question. Again, the significance is low (sign. level = 0.14), while for the size categories it is even lower (sign. level = 0.70).

(c) Views and Attitudes vis-a-vis the Future of Footwear Production
With respect to the future, we started with a factual question whether sales and/or investment had gone up or down over the last years. There turned out to be a significant difference in the *change in sales* between the marketing categories (sign. level = 0.02), categories *a*, *b*, *c* and *d* having experienced clear increases, categories *f* and *g* having experienced clear decreases. Also, between the size categories, there existed significant differences (sign. level = 0.02), categories F to C displaying in majority (decreasing from 100 per cent to 66 per cent) increases, categories B and A displaying in majority decreases.

There was no clearly significant difference between the marketing or the size categories (sign. level 0.1 and 0.2 respectively) with respect to *changes of investment*, though categories *g* and A, D and B mentioned at least 25 per cent of the units with no increase in investment. Apparently, the local marketing units (with these units trading with UPLDMC as possible exception) as well as the smallest units have experienced in general bad times.

Asked (subjectively) what *prospects* one sees *for one's own firm* or *for the sector as a whole*, categories *a*, *b* and *e* say good for more than 20 per cent, *f* and *g* say so for more than 10 per cent, but category *b* scores 50 per cent on bad, with category *c* 30 per cent, categories *e* and *g* around 20 per cent, and categories *a*, *d* and *f* around 10 per cent. Here the subjective/objective discrepancy for category *c* (auxillaries) is especially interesting. The significance level is 0.03. For the size categories, the latter is 0.08 (not really significant) and the pattern less clear. There are more than 50 per cent with 'no answer' and in the motivation for those prospects the pattern is diffused.

Under this heading we asked also two indirect subjective questions with respect to the attitude vis-a-vis the opportunities of children in the footwear sector, first what the respondent (normally the manager/director/owner) thought about the attitude of Scheduled Caste workers, and then about his own attitude. To appreciate the differences between these two questions it may be useful to know that Scheduled Caste workers (normally Chamars) are to be found significantly (F = 2.2 but R^2 = 0.15) more in categories *g, f, e* and *c* (!) (in decreasing order) than in categories E, D, C and F (in increasing order). So one may say that in the locally-oriented and small units, Scheduled Castes are dominantly present, but much less so in the organised and larger units.

However, there was a highly significant (sign. level = 0.001) difference between the marketing units with regard to 'their' opinion of Scheduled Caste people's attitude to their children's future in this trade, but it is very difficult to interpret it.

. The following marketing categories attributed with the following decreasing percentages of units a positive attitude to the Scheduled Caste people on this point: categories *f* 93 per cent, *a* 85 per cent, *e* 73 per cent, *g* 71 per cent, *c* 68 per cent, *d* 66 per cent, *b* 33 per cent, with practically no 'can't say' answers.

For the size categories there was no significant association (sign. level = 0.44). But when asked about their own children's future in this trade[14] the picture changes. A positive future for their children is seen by the following categories with the following percentages (the second percentage mentioned gives the negative future answers, which we mention as there were also many 'can't say' answers): category *a* (66, 17), *b* (50, 50), *f* (39, 66), *g* (23, 53), *e* (14, 60), *d* (12, 62), *c* (12, 70). The significance level of this result is not known, nor has any clear pattern been discovered as yet in the motivations given.

(d) Labour Problems

The occurrence of complaints of owners of the units about three kinds of labour problems was investigated: (*i*) absenteeism, (*ii*) 'mentality' of labourers, (*iii*) power position of labourers. The results were briefly as follows:

Of the thirty-four respondents in categories *f* and *g*—local channels—no complaints (the one exception complaining about absenteeism). Of the seventeen respondents in category *c*—ancillaries—four complained about absenteeism and four about the power position of workers. Of the sixteen respondents in categories *a* and *b*, one complained about absenteeism, one about 'mentality' and two about the power position of the workers. Of the UPLDMC

---

[14] Notice that in the categories *a–d* the respondents are by no means always themselves Scheduled Caste people.

suppliers (*e*) only two out of twelve complained about absenteeism, and of the outside suppliers (*d*) four out of nine complained, all about absenteeism.

What interpretation can be given to these results?

Some Qualitative Observations and Conclusions

Shoe-making as a Traditional Occupation

As noticed in the first section, in India, shoe-making is traditionally the domain of the Chamars or Jadavs. A former sub-caste, they now belong to the Scheduled Castes, which occupies a low position on the ladder of social prestige, and usually live in groups together in so-called *mohallas* (a group of houses with some common ground). The personalised significance of this traditional occupation may be elucidated by the following experience during the investigation. A Muslim owner of a tiny shoe-manufacturing unit complained during the conversation that he and his family could hardly survive on his earnings from the unit. But to the question why, during slack periods in shoe production, he did not take up another job (like, for instance, rickshaw-cycling as some of his colleagues had done), after having reacted so far with a certain indifferent sorrow, he answered, with an air of pride and helplessness (in Hindi): 'Sir, if ever I take up any occupation other than shoe-making, I will never return to the latter.' This answer suggests that the traditional oc-cupation, shoe-making, lends to the owner a sense of identity, without which he would become an anonymous 'unit of labour'. This suggestion may have a wider application than only this indi-vidual case, and may also indicate a social significance, which has a cohesive function in society.

In view of this situation and possible interpretation, it is relevant to note that, increasingly, Jadavs tend to send their children for some education, at the same time dissociating them from the tradi-tional occupation of shoe-making. This tendency occurs, however, less within the units of marketing categories *e*, *f* and *g*, the smallest, weakest and most traditional ones. On the other hand, people from other social groups move into the shoe-making occupation and, recently, not only in the managing and trading jobs but also in actual manufacturing. While the first tendency may also be influenced by government reservation of a part of the educational facilities for Scheduled Caste people, the second phenomenon reflects the great pressure of unemployment on the labour market, also pushing people into socially unattractive occupations.

Technological Choice in Agra Shoe-Making

The figures presented in the second section suggest a considerable range in technological choice possible as well as occurring at the generally modest levels of production of individual production units in the small scale shoe-making sector in Agra.

Broadly speaking it appears that three groups of marketing categories could be distinguished according to technology utilised in terms of labour and capital used per unit of production. The exporting and 'ancillary' categories appear to constitute a relatively capital-intensive and labour-extensive Group I; the UPLDMC, government, outside and local large suppliers appear to constitute a second, less capital-intensive but hardly more labour-intensive Group II; while the local small suppliers on their own constitute a third Group III, distinctly more labour-intensive, but alas not less capital-intensive than Group II. These same three groups appear also to make different products. Group I has to deliver a relatively high standard quality, with considerable risks to brand names or export opportunities in case of failure. Group II should supply a solid medium quality, with limited damage in case of failure. For Group III, a sturdy low quality, low price shoe suffices.

Roughly half the shoe-makers (with considerable skill by experience) and helpers are employed in Group III. This group constitutes not only a different method of production, but also of management, social and cultural life. In short, it constitutes a world in itself. A massive 'escape' from this world cannot be expected, while 'upgrading' Group III units by technical and management education is likely to cause mainly a shift in technology away from labour, throwing out a considerable part of the earners in this group with little hope for employment elsewhere. Even if the government abstains from such active 'upgrading,' a gradual shift in technology appears unavoidable. A major change could be made if their marketing problems could be attacked and the earnings of the middlemen could accrue largely to the producers. The attempts in this direction by the UPLDMC, of providing marketing services and encouraging cooperations, are laudable but they have not made a rapid or major difference in the situation. Further research on the situation would be useful.

On the other end of the spectrum, there is an occasional change from Group II to Group I, mainly from 'outside supplier' to 'ancillary,' obviously at the cost of sacrificing identity and independence but gaining the certainty of a continuous market. Here, the national firms like Bata and Corona, providing the marketing services, are comparable to the middlemen for Group III, who also occupy a comparable position of strength. These ancillaries, however, are still quite different from the 'exporters,' either those delivering uppers mainly via the State Trading Corporation to Eastern Europe, or those having direct contacts with foreign traders and markets. The difference is mainly in size, but also in product sophistication, management styles, the un-. traditional lineage of the owners and the composition of the personnel. Though all units in Group I belong to the formal, organised sector, the exporting units still somewhat constitute a world of their own.

Group II allows for little generalisation.

The Workers' Relationship to Production

The answers to the question about the occurrence of labour problems displayed a striking difference between the marketing categories as mentioned earlier. The virtual absence of labour problems in the categories f and g—the local suppliers—is quite interesting, as the situation of the employees is worst there. One explanation is that whatever problems between people arise here, they are not recognised as labour problems, as many employees are relatives or neighbourhood dwellers. Another, related, explanation could be that the employees here do not conceive of themselves as labour, thus not creating 'labour' problems. Most problems with labour are to be found with the categories 'ancillaries' and 'outside suppliers,' in which the employees have become more independent in a situation similar to emerging capitalism. Finally, the workers in the 'exporting' category, hardly creating problems, are an envied labour elite with stable work and relatively high wages.

Some Recommendations

One result is the clear difference between the various marketing categories of production units, which suggests that any policy or action for small scale shoe-manufacturing units not making this distinction is bound to have a varied effect on the different categories' units, thus probably failing to achieve any general end. Specific policies and actions are required, based on specific, detailed, further investigations, and carefully watched as to their consequences in reality.

A second result is that employment in this sector, especially in Group III, is seriously threatened. As a permanent protection of this employment may not be financially feasible, one should consider designing policies for two different phases. Phase I, covering two generations or a few decades, would be both one of preparation for the future development of the sector in Phase II and one of 'inefficient' protection of employment in this sector, in view of the social significance of this employment and of the production units as focal points of (social) living.

A third result is that any policy designed to further the cause of the really poor in this sector appears necessarily to start from or to be combined with the mobilisation of these poor themselves, which constitute a separate and contained world to which government policies have hardly any access.

Finally, government policies and institutions aimed at helping his sector require a continuous scrutiny of their progress.

8 **H.H. de Haan**

Sugar Processing in India: The Scope for Intermediate Technology

Introduction

Sugar processing in India is characterised by a large variety of products, technologies and scales. Traditionally, cane is processed into jaggery or *gur*, a substance which contains both sugar crystals and molasses. Though its importance has gradually declined, it still accounts for more than 30 per cent of total cane use. A minor part is produced on a tiny scale by bullock crushers for household consumption. The larger part is manufactured in commercial units using power-driven crushers; their scales of production vary from 10 to 50 tonnes of cane crushed per day (tcd).

Sugar is mainly produced by large modern sugar mills with capacities ranging from 1,000 to 8,000 tcd. The modern large-scale process is often called the vacuum pan sulphitation (VPS) method. The share of the mills in total cane has only increased slowly and has fluctuated in the recent past between 30 and 40 per cent.

Sugar is also produced by more traditional methods in so-called *khandsari* factories (*khandsari* is the Hindi word for sugar entrepreneur). The traditional *khandsari* process is carried out in units with scales from 50 to 100 tcd. These units are highly flexible as they can produce both sugar and *gur* in any desired proportion, depending on the price ratio of *gur* and sugar. During the fifties, the traditional method was improved, mainly by the application of sulphitation to juice clarification. The improved process is usually denoted by an open pan sulphitation process (OPS) or, in popular language, sulphur *khandsari*. In the sixties and seventies, the OPS process showed a spectacular growth, reaching its height during 1977–78 with an estimated number of about 1,800 units according to the 'sulphur crusher holder list' of the western U.P. Gur and Khandsari Manufacturers' Association. At the time their estimated share of total cane use was about 10 per cent but, in recent years, its role seems to have declined considerably. The large majority of OPS (i.e., 75 per cent) units is located in U.P., while western U.P. alone has 50 per cent of the total number in the country. The only other state with a sizeable number of units was Andhra Pradesh (360 units). In northern India, the scales vary from 50 to about 200 tcd, but in Andhra Pradesh the capacities may attain 300 tcd. It is this process that has also attracted so much attention from outside India.

Particularly in western U.P., all these sugar-processing units often co-exist close to each other. They compete heavily for cane, especially when it is in short supply. The rules of the game are different, however. The *gur* sector is largely exempt from regulation; tiny units which are not allowed to purchase cane are left completely free, but commercial units have to pay cane tax. The *khandsari* sector, both traditional and improved, also needs a license and pays both cane tax and excise duty, but the duty is a fraction of the rate paid by the mills.

The sugar mills are subject to various rules. They have to deliver 65 per cent of their output at fixed prices to the government and are obliged to pay the farmer at least a minimum price for the cane. This implies that they often run into trouble in times of cane scarcity, when the free market price of sugar is high. The *gur* and *khandsari* units can sell their output on the free market at high prices, and thus pay high cane prices, while the mills have to deliver 65 per cent of the output at a relatively low price, which is based on the minimum cane price. Further, the release of sugar to the free market is regulated by the government and the molasses cannot be sold freely.

As the factor proportions of the different cane-processing methods vary considerably, changes in the composition of cane use have important consequences for the use of factors of production. Obviously, the more traditional methods use more labour and less capital per unit of output. Their main deficiencies, however, are the relatively low crushing and boiling efficiency. The first drawback implies much higher cane costs, while the second leads to lower sugar recovery and a lower quality of output. Another shortcoming is the fuel inefficiency of the furnaces. Without technological improvements, the OPS process is unable to survive if it has to compete with the sugar mills under equal conditions.

Since the sixties, experimental research has been carried out by the Planning Research and Action Division and the Appropriate Technology Development Association. The experiments are aimed at increasing the efficiency of juice extraction by replacing the crusher by a screw expeller and at increasing the boiling and fuel efficiency by improved furnace designs. The test reports available in the early eighties have shown positive results.

In the paper presented at the IEG/World Bank Conference, which was based on De Haan (1983), the conclusion was reached that the improvements would be insufficient to make the OPS a viable alternative to the VPS. A contrary result was obtained by Kaplinsky[1] which I did not know at the time of the Conference. I have, therefore, fully revised my paper, which also considered the traditional *khandsari* and *gur* industry, and focused my analysis exclusively on the OPS and the VPS in order to compare our result with Kaplinsky's.

The earlier study was carried out under the purview of the Indo-Dutch Programme on Alternatives in Development (IDPAD) sponsored by the Indian Council of Social Sciences Research (ICSSR) and the Dutch Institute of Social Science Research in Developing Countries (IMWOO). The research started at the beginning of 1981 with a sample survey of *khandsari* plants using the open pan sulphitation process in district Bijnor (western U.P.). During the season 1981–82, a sample survey was applied to *gur* and non-sulphur *khandsari* units in districts Ghaziabad, Meerut and Muzaffarnagar. A large amount of secondary data and qualitative information was also collected from various associations, institutions and government departments.

R. Kaplinsky, *Sugar Processing: The Development of a Third World Technology*, London, 1984.

A short visit to Meerut/Ghaziabad district in 1984 to make a video report on small scale *gur* and sugar plants, showed that the production process of the OPS units in that area had not undergone significant changes.

The first section of this paper provides a review of the debate on appropriate sugar technology. The second section exposes briefly the methodology of the evaluation procedures. The third section gives the basic results of the evaluation. The next section deals with the prospects for survival of the OPS process. To keep this paper within reasonable limits, the estimation of the data and parameters used in the evaluation is not explained.[2]

The State of the Debate

The co-existence of various cane-processing technologies has been subject to continuous debate in India since the beginning of this century. In 1920 the Indian Sugar Committee, set up to study the desirability of sugar import protection measures, discussed the merits and demerits of the *khandsari* industry vis-a-vis the sugar mills. Since then, all official documents on the sugar industry have filled many pages with the analysis of and recommendations on the interaction of the three competitors for sugar cane—the sugar mills, the *khandsari* industry and the *gur* sector. However, in the late seventies the debate intensified, and received increasing attention from abroad. The ILO was the first organisation to show an interest, followed by the UNIDO and some foreign research institutes, in particular the Livingstone Institute of the University of Glasgow. The debate focused on the improved *khandsari* process, also denoted by the open pan sulphitation process (OPS).

Within India, basically two points of view prevail with respect to the OPS method. The first stream of thought[3] holds that the vacuum pan sulphitation process (VPS) is superior, both technically and economically, to the other technologies. However, since a shortage of investment funds prevents crushing all the cane by this method,

---

[2] For details, see H.H. de Haan, *The Sugar Cane Processing Industry in Western Uttar Pradesh,* Main Report to IDPAD, Rotterdam, 1983.

[3] See K.K. Gupta, N.C. Jain and N.A. Ramiah, 'Appropriate Technology for the Production of Sugar and Other Sweetening Agents,' in *Appropriate Industrial Technology for Sugar,* New York, UNIDO, 1980, pp. 75–76.

even in the medium long run, less efficient techniques have to be accepted in order to ensure that the demand for sweetening agents is satisfied.

The other viewpoint, while recognising the technical superiority of the VPS process, suggests that the lower recovery and thus higher cane costs of the OPS would be compensated by the lower capital costs and the high degree of employment generation.[4] Further, it refers to other advantages, such as, better dispersal of economic activity and linkages at the local level. Even if these benefits could not fully outweigh the lower recovery, it is believed that the OPS method can be improved by technical innovations, which might even make the OPS superior to the VPS.

The protagonists of the OPS process received support from an ILO study, which concluded (on the basis of a cost comparison between the OPS and VPS) that the present value of the costs of both processes would be equal for a crushing season of a hundred and fifty days, while the costs of the OPS would be lower for seasons of shorter duration.[5] The study was biased in favour of the OPS by assuming an unduly high recovery rate of 8 per cent and by not allowing for differences in the quality of the output between the VPS and OPS. It also contained a methodological error by applying a shadow price to capital at the cost side but not to the reinvestments of savings at the benefit side. As shown by the UNIDO, the correct procedure does not affect the ratio of net present values of the two projects and leaves the signs of the NPVs unchanged, if the savings behaviour does not change in the future.[6] Since the net benefits of the VPS exceed those of the OPS, the application of a shadow price of capital would lead to an increase in the absolute difference between the NPVs of both processes. Surprisingly, this methodological error has remained unnoticed by the various authors who contributed to the debate.

The latter-mentioned view was reinforced when the Planning

[4] See M.K. Garg, 'Mini Sugar,' *Project Proposal and Feasibility Report*. Appropriate Technology Development Association, Lucknow, 1979; M.K. Garg, 'Mini Sugar in India,' in *Appropriate Industrial Technology for Sugar*, New York, UNIDO, 1980; and PRAI, Report of the Fourth Technical Seminar on Open Pan Sugar Manufacture (24–26 September 1966), Lucknow, Planning and Research Action Institute, 1968.

[5] C.G. Baron, 'Sugar Processing Techniques in India,' in *Technology and Employment Industry*, Geneva, ILO, 1975.

[6] UNIDO, *Guidelines for Project Analysis*, New Delhi, 1972.

Commission proposed to impose a ban on the licensing of new sugar mills in the Draft Five Year Plan, 1978–83. This decision was expressed in the following words:

> The alternative technologies available for the production of white sugar, consistent with desirable capital-employment parameters show that future demand for sweetening agents, after allowing for fuller utilisation of the existing and licensed sugar mills, can be met by necessary expansion through OPS Khandsari plants. It is proposed to work out the policy framework for the further expansion of the sugar industry in the light of these studies. For the time being, therefore, no new sugar mills will be licensed, although expansions of existing units may not be ruled out where this is necessary for maintaining their viability.

The proposal of the Planning Commission was partly based on a linear programming exercise, formulated by Raj Krishna,[7] in which the distribution of the increase in sugar production during the plan period over the OPS and the VPS was determined by minimising a cost function subject to a minimum constraint for output and employment and a maximum constraint for capital. While various values for the right-hand variables were used, in the main variant 68 per cent of the increase of sugar production was to be allocated to the VPS, whereas the OPS would get the balance of 32 per cent. As demonstrated in De Haan, the validity of this result is dubious because of the unduly high shadow price implied by the employment constraint.[8]

A new government came to power in 1980 and a new plan was prepared for the period 1980–85, in which the earlier proposal was deleted. This was hardly surprising since India was undergoing one of its worst post-Independence sugar crises at the time of preparation of the plan. Sugar-cane was in short supply and sugar prices rose to record levels. In the circumstances, the policy makers were disenchanted with the 'cane wasting' *khandsari* industry.

The most recent attempt to provide support for the OPS is

[7] C.R. Reddy and R. Krishna, Choice of Technology in the Sugar Industry, Planning Commission, Project Appraisal Division (mimeo). See also C. Rangarajan and A.H. Karlo, Choice of Technology in the Sugar Industry, Planning Commission, Project Appraisal Division (mimeo), 1980.

[8] See de Haan, *op. cit.*

Kaplinsky, who admits that the OPS is not viable on the basis of its present mode of operation.[9] He believes, however, that technological improvements will render the OPS sufficiently cost efficient to withstand competition from the VPS under equal conditions.

Remarkable in the debate on sugar technology is the minimal attention paid to the *gur* sector. Obviously, *gur* is not a direct substitute for sugar, but it cannot be taken for granted that the production of OPS sugar is superior to *gur* manufacturing. The higher profitability of the OPS can be largely attributed to the fact that the OPS sector can sell all its produce at an artificially high price in the free market. Further, the public distribution of cheap sugar is likely to diminish the demand for *gur* and thus its price.

The debate on sugar technology assumed international dimensions when international organisations, (such as, the ILO and the UNIDO) and foreign research institutes got involved. One of the main issues in the discussion was the appropriateness of the OPS process for African countries. One of the first studies examined the relationship between scale and technology and obtained the result that the OPS was only desirable at the smallest scales.[10] This implied that OPS should be applied only when cane supply is so deficient or dispersed that a sugar mill of larger capacity would not be viable. This situation is of limited relevance for India, where sugar-cane is cultivated intensively in a large number of regions. It would seem unlikely that in African countries, where there is less pressure on land compared to Asia, no land could be made available to supply sugar-cane to a sugar mill of a capacity of about 1,500 tonnes of cane per day. And if this is really impossible, importing sugar might be a better proposition.

The uncompromising view of Forsyth evoked reactions from others more congenial to small scale enterprise. Hagelberg[11] questioned some data and assumptions but was, in our opinion, unconvincing in his rebuttal.[12] More substantial contributions were made by Bhat and Duguid[13] and, in particular, by Alpine and

[9] See Kaplinsky, *op. cit.*

[10] See D.J.C. Forsyth, 'Appropriate Technology in Sugar Manufacturing,' *World Development*, Vol. 5, 1977, pp. 189–202.

[11] G.B. Hagelberg, 'Appropriate Technology in Sugar Manufacturing—A Rebuttal,' *World Development*, Vol. 7, 1979, pp. 893–99.

[12] D.J.C. Forsyth, 'Appropriate Technology in Sugar Manufacturing: A Reply,' *World Development*, Vol. 8, 1980, pp. 165–66.

[13] B.A. Bhat and F. Duguid, 'Appropriate Technology in Cane-Sugar Production,' in *Appropriate Industrial Technology for Sugar*, New York, UNIDO, 1980.

Pickett.[14] The latter compared technologies under the assumption that these would be used in a plantation system. They also considered, therefore, different cane cultivation techniques in combination with processing techniques. Their basic assumption was that on account of less inputs (like fertilizers), the OPS would be supplied with cane of lower yield that was cultivated and harvested in a labour-intensive way. This would not be possible for the VPS as the lower yield would increase the area of sugar-cane to such an extent that transportation costs would become prohibitive, given the bad road conditions. It was further assumed that the cane delivered to the mill had to be harvested mechanically. In this way, it was found that in rain-fed areas, where land is cheap relative to capital, growing cane with less capital inputs over a wider area might reduce the cost of cane so much that the OPS would have a higher net present value than the VPS if the season was long. Even in irrigated areas with a long season, the net present value of the VPS did not exceed that of the OPS so much that the latter had to be discarded at once. It was not examined, however, whether the return on growing cane with low capital input was higher than that of alternative crops. However, their results are unlikely to apply to a land-scarce country like India.

The UNIDO/UNDP organised a seminar at Nairobi in 1977 on the implications of technological choice in the African sugar industry.[15] The suitability of the OPS to African conditions played an important role in the papers presented in the discussions. While there was some scepticism towards the OPS, it was nevertheless recommended that a study of the OPS process under Indian conditions be carried out with a view to establishing its appropriateness for Africa. It was further proposed to start a number of pilot OPS units in certain African countries in order to evaluate the operation of these plants.

The sequel to this seminar was held in India in 1978, where the central theme of the discussion was the comparison of the OPS and VPS. The seminar concluded that OPS would be 'appropriate to situations characterised by conditions such as mixed agricultural cropping patterns, small domestic markets, inadequate

[14] R. Alpine and J. Pickett, 'More on Appropriate Technology in Sugar Manufacturing' *World Development.* Vol. 8, 1980, pp. 167–74.

[15] UNIDO, Final Report of the Joint UNEP/UNIDO Seminar on the implication of Technology Choice in the African Sugar Industry, 18–22 April 1977, Nairobi.

infrastructure, capital scarcity and wide-spread unemployment or underemployment'.[16]

The proposal of the Nairobi seminar to install a few pilot OPS plants was implemented and an Indian manufacturer exported equipment to East Africa. Kaplinsky[17] has assessed the functioning of OPS units in Kenya. In Indonesia four OPS units were built, but during a field trip to that country in 1984 we learned that none of them functioned properly.

Another study worth mentioning was conducted by Delasanta and Morgan on Pakistan.[18] They compared four technologies—VPS, OPS, modernised *gur*-making, and two bullock-driven crushing units, one making traditional *khandsari* and the other *gur*. The comparison was made on the basis of the Little-Mirrlees method of evaluation and applied shadow prices to all inputs and outputs in a detailed way. Only the VPS and the improved *gur* plant showed a positive net present value (NPV). The value of the *gur* unit exceeded that of the VPS by such a large margin that the former was considered the most appropriate technology.

Whereas there is some similarity between India and Pakistan in the area of sugar-cane processing, the parameters for VPS do not tally with those prevailing in western Uttar Pradesh or even in the country at large. In particular, the recovery rate of 8.5 per cent is considerably lower than the Indian figure. Further, not all scales of production considered are representative of the Indian situation, where bullock-driven crusher units account for a minor proportion of the total cane crushed. The modernised *gur* unit refers to a hypothetical unit which uses a hydraulic crusher of the size applied in the OPS process. In India, hydraulic crushing in *gur* manufacturing is an exception, since the entrepreneurs who can afford to set up hydraulic crushing plants prefer to produce *khandsari* which yields much higher profits. On closer examination, it appears that the favourable conclusion with respect to *gur* has to be attributed to the assumpion of a recovery of 14 per cent. If this rate were 12 per cent, which is a more realistic estimate, the NPV of VPS and *gur* would hardly differ. Since we did not have the more extensive report on

[16] UNIDO, Appropriate Industrial Technology for Sugar (Monograph on Appropriate Industrial Technology No. 8), New York, 1980, p. 9.

[17] Kaplinsky, *op. cit.*

[18] D.W. Delasanta and R.P. Morgan, 'The Choice of Sugar Cane Processing Techniques for Pakistan,' *World Development*, Vol 8, 1980. pp. 725–39.

which Delasanta and Morgan[19] is based, we were unable to compare all their data and assumptions with the Indian figures.

The evidence available at the start of this study did not permit unambiguous conclusions to be drawn. At present, on the basis of De Haan and Kaplinsky,[20] it has become clear that at least in India the OPS process in its present mode of operation is inferior to the VPS. Whereas its higher cane costs are compensated by its lower capital costs, particularly at higher discount rates, the quality of its output falls too much behind that of the VPS to make it sufficiently competitive. The much higher employment generation of the OPS does not outweigh the large difference in NPVs. The main issue now is whether the technical efficiency of the OPS can be significantly improved in the near future. As will be shown in the fourth section, we do not share the optimistic view of Kaplinsky.[21] And even if we did, the OPS is unlikely to become a viable alternative to the VPS in India.

The Evaluation Methodology

In this section, we shall briefly discuss the basic parameters of the comparison and the method of appraisal. The prices of output and production costs are considered in the next section.

Basic Parameters

We shall compare only two sugar-producing technologies—the vacuum pan sulphitation process (VPS) and the open pan sulphitation process (OPS). The area of reference is western Uttar Pradesh, one of the main sugar areas of India. Though both processes are carried out on various scales, only one scale was selected for both. We shall briefly discuss the implications for the results.

In western U.P., the scales of the VPS vary from 1,100 to 4,200 tcd, but we shall consider only a 1,250 tcd plant as this is the size for which new lincenses are issued. This factory, however, is so designed that an expansion to 2,000 tcd can be easily realised. Economies of scale are important in the large-scale sugar industry, and a 1,250 tcd

[19] *Ibid.*

[20] See de Haan, *op. cit.*, and Kaplinsky, *op. cit.*

[21] Kaplinsky, *op. cit.*

factory is well below the estimated minimum efficient size (about 5,000 tcd) given a sufficient supply of cane. The Government of India considers sugar factories as instruments of rural development and allows, therefore, for the sub-optimal size of 1,250 tcd.

The capacities of the OPS plants vary from 50 to more than 200 tcd. Though the most frequently used crusher is a 50 tcd non-hydraulic three-roller crusher of size 11" × 14", we selected a unit with a hydraulic 13" < 18" six-roller crusher with a capacity of 100 tcd. This was the largest crusher used in western U.P. in the period 1980–82; there was only one unit with a nine-roller 13" × 18" crusher. In the western districts of western U.P.—like Meerut and Muzaffarnagar—this crusher sometimes attains capacities of 180 tcd, but at the cost of lower recovery. The hydraulic 16" × 24" six-roller crusher of 200 tcd capacity is only used in Andhra Pradesh. In western U.P. larger capacities are attained by increasing the number of crushers and not by shifting to a 16" × 24" crusher.

Also, in the case of OPS, unit production costs tend to be lower as the scale of production increases. According to the NSI[22] the unit cost of production of a 200 tcd factory with two hydraulic 13" × 18" crushers will be 14 per cent lower, as a consequence of a relative decrease in capital and labour costs. The estimates of labour costs were rather hypothetical and far removed from actual practice, which is based on the contract system and which does not employ permanent labour as suggested by several authors.[23] In fact, the increase in the scale of production may require the replacement of (part-time) family workers by permanently paid workers for administrative and supervisory tasks. Further, most of the equipment has standard sizes and much work is done manually, which implies that economies in labour costs are probably limited.

By choosing for the OPS and VPS scales of 100 tcd and 1,250 tcd, respectively, we consider for both processes sub-optimal sizes. As economies of scale are likely to be more important for the VPS, our results will be somewhat biased against the VPS.

As a basis for comparison we consider the annual amount of sugar produced by a VPS mill that crushes 120 days at full capacity (i.e., 14,250 tonnes during a fixed period of twenty years). The same amount can also be produced by seventeen OPS units in the same

[22] NSI, Project Report for Setting up Modern Khandsari Sugar Manufacturing Units, National Sugar Institute, Kanpur, 1979.
[23] See Garg, 1979, op. cit. and Kaplinsky, op. cit.

period at full capacity. The actual number of crushing days of existing VPS mills may vary from 70 to 220 days per year, with an average between 140 and 150 days. The rates of capacity utilisation are close to 90 per cent but as I want to carry out the comparison to the extent possible on the basis of equal parameters, we assumed a full capacity equivalent of 120 days, derived from a season of 140 days with a rate of capacity utilisation of 86 per cent. The assumption of 120 full capacity equivalents for OPS (135 days at 89 per cent capacity utilisation) is rather on the high side.

The basic parameters are presented in Table 1. For the more important ones, ratios between the OPS and VPS are given to facilitate the comparison. The OPS uses 36 per cent more cane per unit of sugar due to its lower recovery rate. Its capital-output and capital-labour ratios are much lower. Its 54 per cent higher employment-generating capacity per unit of output is quite striking. This figure would have increased to 131 per cent, if we had used standard person-days of 8 hours, since working days of 12 hours are normal in OPS units. Another major difference, not presented in Table 1, is the lower average quality of OPS sugar, resulting in a price margin of about 20 per cent with respect to VPS sugar.

Table 1
Basic Parameters of the Processing Technologies

	VPS	OPS	OPS:VPS
Number of units	1	17	
Sugar produced (tonnes)	14,250	14,250	
Annual days of crushing at full capacity	120	120	
Recovery rate (% on cane)	9.5	7.0	0.74
Total cane crushed (tonnes)	150,000	204,000	1.36
Fixed capital (1,000 Rs.)	68,000	25,000	
— per tonne of cane (Rs.)	453	123	0.27
— per quintal of sugar (Rs.)	477	175	0.37
Total employment (persons)	850	140	
— permanent	340		
— seasonal	510	140	
Annual number of person-days	185,300	285,600	
— per tonne of cane	1.2	1.4	1.17
— per quintal of sugar	1.3	2.0	1.54
Fixed capital per annual number of man-days (Rs.)	367	88	0.32

Source: Compiled from De Haan (1983), Chapter 5.3.

Method of Appraisal

The method of evaluation is based on the principles proposed in Hansen,[24] which differ only slightly in substance from Little and Mirrlees[25] or Squire and Van der Tak.[26] The numeraire in which the cash flows are expressed is consumption at the base level, which is defined as

> the level of per capita private consumption at which an additional rupee of income has the same social value as an additional rupee of government income, as indicated by the fact that the government neither taxes nor subsidises people at this income level, assuming, of course, that the government's tax/subsidy structure is socially optimal.[27]

The rate of discount refers to the numeraire and is, therefore, not necessarily equal to the opportunity cost of capital.

Hansen makes the useful distinction between the following five stages in the evaluation procedure:

1. Calculation of financial profitability at market price;
2. Shadow pricing of resources to obtain the net benefit at economic prices;
3. Adjustment for the project's impact on savings and investment;
4. Adjustments for the project's impact on income distribution;
5. Adjustment for merit or demerit goods.

To restrict the size of this paper, we present only an evaluation at economic prices.[28] Economic prices reflect the real scarcities of the outputs and inputs of the production process or, in terms of development policy, they are geared to the growth objective. A proper evaluation at social prices, which refer to the objective of income distribution, is extremely difficult because of the little knowledge of

[24] J.R. Hansen, *Guide to Practical Project Appraisal*, New York, UNIDO, 1978.
[25] I.M.D. Little and J.A. Mirrlees, *Project Appraisal and Planning for Developing Countries*, London, 1974.
[26] See L. Squire and H. van der Tak, *Economic Analysis of Projects*, Baltimore and London, 1975.
[27] Hansen, *op. cit.*, p. 100.
[28] For financial and social prices, see De Haan, *op. cit.*
[29] Kaplinsky, *op. cit.*

marginal saving rates of the economic factors and the subjectivity in assigning weights to different income groups. We do not believe, however, that social pricing will affect the results at economic prices substantially.

To facilitate the calculations, a number of simplifying assumptions were made with respect to the operation of the project. First, an equal lifetime for both technologies, namely twenty years, was taken. It is doubtful whether the equipment for the smaller units have the same quality as that of the VPS, but in the absence of any firm evidence I decided to take an equal figure. On the other hand, a difference of five years would not affect the results significantly. Second, once the plants have started effective operation we assumed that the flows of annual costs and benefits are constant over the project cycle. As noted by Kaplinsky,[29] this may be a rather heroic assumption for the VPS because of capacity underutilisation in the beginning of the production period. In the fourth section, the validity of this assumption is tested. The value of Rs. 68 million for investment in fixed capital, given in Table 2, contains a correction for the increase in capital costs caused by a construction period of two years. Third, no scrap value is assumed at the end of the project period. This is unlikely to apply to the VPS which will still have a considerable resale value. It certainly does not apply to the land occupied, but since investment in land is a very minor proportion of total capital investment, we did not deduct the value of land.

As recommended by the standard literature on cost-benefit analysis, the net present value (NPV) of costs and benefits was taken as the selection criterion. This implies that in our case of mutually exclusive projects, the one with the highest NPV is considered superior as it gives the highest return after deduction of all costs. A discount rate of 10 per cent was used as the basis for the evaluation. In some cases, results at a rate of 20 per cent and the internal rate of return (IRR) are also given, to show the consequences of this assumption.

Contrary to the usual practice, we shall not present the results in terms of the total NPVs but rather of its annual equivalent. In the case of constant annual costs and benefits, both procedures are fully equivalent; the NPVs only differ by a constant multiplication factor. This way of presenting the results facilitates the comparison between the various technologies, because prices and costs, except capital

[29] Kaplinsky, *op. cit.*

costs, are simply the first year figure. Our procedure can be represented by the following formula:

$$NPV = B - C - K/a$$

Where B and C are constant annual benefits and costs, respectively, K is investment in fixed capital and a is the annuity, determined by the discount rate and the lifetime of the project.

The Evaluation Results

This section contains a brief discussion of the choice of the reference season, the costs of production and the sugar price. The results of the evaluation are then presented. As we are comparing different technologies rather than trying to assess whether a project has to be accepted or rejected, we have focused attention on the crucial parameters. In fact, three differences are of overriding importance— the lower quality of OPS sugar, the higher cane costs of the OPS and the higher capital costs of the VPS. Labour and energy costs play a relatively less important role.

The Season of Reference

Since sugar-cane production shows large annual fluctuations, the parameters to be used in the evaluation are far from stable. The length of the crushing season, sugar prices, cane prices and production costs vary so much that some caution is required in the choice of the year of reference. At the time of field-work, the last year for which reliable data were available was 1978–79. Fortunately, in that season the number of crushing days was close to the average, which allows a reasonable estimation of the costs of production and the levy price of sugar. Ironically, in that season, partial decontrol was replaced by full decontrol because the release of large sugar stocks carried over from the preceding season had depressed the free sugar price to the level of the levy price. We determined the free sugar price, therefore, by applying a multiplication factor to the levy price, based on the average ratio of the free and levy sugar prices during the period 1973–74 to 1978–79, derived from the price data of six sugar mills. In this way, we obtained a representative picture in spite of the abnormal situation during 1978–79.

Cost of Production

The market price was adjusted for only two inputs, namely sugar-cane and unskilled labour. The most important is the correction of the cane price, as cane costs are usually more than 60 per cent of total production costs in financial or market prices, while the difference in recovery rates between the OPS and the VPS is 36 per cent. As most land is under cultivation and yields are unlikely to increase rapidly in the future, an increase in production can only be attained at the cost of other crops. The economic price of sugar-cane is, therefore, the value of the crops replaced by cane, which in northern India is on the average lower than the financial or market price of sugar-cane. To allow for this, I took as the economic price of cane the minimum price fixed by the government (i.e., Rs. 100 per tonne of cane). This price has to be paid by a mill with a recovery rate of 8.5 per cent, whereas for every 0.1 per cent increase in recovery the price increases by Re. 1. In the two years prior to the exceptional seasons of 1977–78 and 1978–79, the actual price paid was about Rs. 130. Since the mills procure the cane from larger distances, their actual cane costs have to be increased by transport costs and costs of cane collection centres, which amounted to Rs. 7 per quintal (i.e., 100 kg) of sugar.

The wages of unskilled labour were corrected by considering the wage paid by the tiny *gur* sector as the economic price of unskilled labour. This assumption diminishes the wage costs of the VPS and the OPS by Rs. 6 and Re. 1, respectively. Compared to the cane price adjustment, this one affects the evaluation marginally.

The costs are given in Table 2. In the last column, the differences in cane and capital costs indicate that the higher cane costs of the OPS are more than compensated by its lower capital costs on the basis of a discount rate of 10 per cent. This clearly demonstrates that the OPS is not inferior in terms of costs of production on the basis of an economic price of cane.

Sugar Price

Obviously, a comparison of the OPS and the VPS on the basis of the regime of partial decontrol is not fair, since the OPS sells all its produce at the higher free market price, while the VPS sells 65 per cent of its output at the lower levy price to the government. We, therefore, used two prices: the average price obtained by the VPS under partial decontrol (also called the dual price system) and the free market price. The former is a weighted average of the levy price and the free price with weights of 0.65 and 0.35, respectively. In 1978–79 the average levy price of sugar for western U.P. and central U.P. was Rs. 220 per quintal. By applying an excise duty rate of 13 per cent we obtain a market rate of Rs. 249. The free price was determined by multiplying the levy price of Rs. 220 by 1.67, that is, the average ratio between both prices, as obtained from the data of six sugar mills. By further applying an excise duty rate of 20 per cent, we obtain a free market price of Rs. 440. The average price under partial decontrol is then Rs. 316. Since this price is not sufficient for new mills to operate profitably, the government uses an incentive scheme which permits new mills to sell all the output on the free market during the first five years and 65 per cent in the sixth year. At a discount rate of 10 per cent, the annual equivalent of the benefits is Rs. 59, which has to be added to the price of Rs. 316. In short, we take an average dual price of Rs. 375 and a free price of Rs. 440.

The price of the OPS is assumed to be 80 per cent of the free price. On the basis of the accounts presented by some OPS units to the tax authorities, a figure of 75 per cent was obtained. As the OPS owners tend to underestimate their receipts to evade taxation, we increased it to 80 per cent. This increase is reasonable since the price of the lower quality traditional *khandsari* sugar, for which regular market prices are published, shows a margin of about 25 per cent. The price of the OPS thus determined is Rs. 352 per quintal, that is, lower than the average dual price, if the incentive scheme is allowed for.

Finally, a market price under full decontrol was simulated by assuming that the willingness to pay off the ration-card holder is 20 per cent higher than the levy price. By using again the weight of 0.65 and 0.35 for the adjusted levy and the observed free price, and by applying an excise duty rate of 20 per cent to both, we obtain a price of Rs. 360—that is, Rs. 15 lower than the average dual price. Changes in the multiplication factor applied to the levy price hardly affect the relative values and the absolute difference of the NPVs of the OPS and the VPS. Obviously, the OPS price falls drastically (namely, from Rs. 352 to Rs. 288). Since these prices are more realistic, they will constitute the basis for the sensitivity analysis.

The Results

The results presented in Table 2 leave no doubt about the superiority of the VPS. Even if the VPS is subject to partial decontrol, the difference in NPVs is significant. Particularly, under the assumption of a free market price the margin between the OPS and the VPS assumes gigantic proportions. In this case, it was further assumed that the release of VPS sugar to the free market is not regulated, which reduces the requirement for working capital to finance the sugar stocks and thus also the costs of production. Under decontrol, the internal rate of return (IRR) of the OPS (51 per cent) is higher than that of the VPS (40 per cent) but, as mentioned before, the IRR is no correct selection criterion. As the last column of Table 2 shows, it is especially the large difference in output prices that is responsible for the negative result for the OPS, and not its higher cane costs, which are more than compensated for by its lower capital costs.

Table 2
Costs and Benefits of Producing Annually 14,250 Tonnes of Sugar.
(Rs. per Quintal of Sugar)

	Partial Decontrol			Full Decontrol		
	VPS (Dual)	VPS (Free)	OPS	VPS (1)	OPS (2)	(2–1)
1. *Total income*	375	440	352	360	288	−72
— normal sales	316					
— extra sales (at 10%)	59					
2. *Total costs*	226	220	220	226	220	
— cane	113	113	143	113	143	−30
— processing	57	51	56	57	56	
— capital (at 10%)	56	56	21	56	21	+35
3. *NPV (at 10%) (1−2)*	149	220	132	134	68	
4. *IRR*	43	58	87	40	51	

Source: Compiled from De Hann (1983), Chapter 5.4.2.

The relative values of the NPVs are rather insensitive to changes in the length of the crushing season, the cane price and the output price of the VPS. The parameters have a significant bearing on the results—namely, the output price ratio and the recovery rate of the OPS—the former being the most important. We, therefore, analysed the sensitivity of the results with respect to the assumptions of a sugar-price ratio of 80 per cent and a recovery rate of 7 per cent for the OPS. Table 3 gives the results of various combinations of higher price ratios and recovery rates. In the case of a ratio of 85 per cent and 8 per cent recovery and a ratio of 90 per cent and 7.5 per cent recovery, the NPV of the OPS would exceed that of the VPS at a discount rate of 20 per cent. At a rate of 10 per cent, however, the VPS remains superior by Rs. 9 at a price ratio of 90 per cent and 8 per cent recovery. This means that if the OPS would attain the performance displayed in the last column of Table 3, the probability of survival would be enlarged considerably, particularly if we allow some economies of scale for larger OPS units and the possible difficulties in feeding a sugar mill sufficiently in the initial period of production.

Table 3

Sensitivity Analysis for OPS Under Simulated Free Market Conditions
(Rs. per Quintal of Sugar)

	Actual		Hypothetical OPS			
	VPS	OPS	I	II	III	IV
Price ratio (%)	100	80	85	90	85	90
Recovery rate (%)	9.5	7	7.5	7.5	8	8
Capital investment	477	175	163	163	153	153
Income	360	288	306	324	306	324
Total costs	170	199	189	189	181	181
— Cane	113	143	133	133	125	125
— Processing	57	56	56	56	56	56
Surplus	190	89	117	135	125	143
Capital charges (20%)	98	36	34	34	31	31
NPV (at 20%)	92	53	83	101	94	112
Capital charges (10%)	56	21	19	19	18	18
NPV (at 10%)	134	68	97	115	107	125
IRR	40	51	71	82	82	93

Source: Compiled from De Haan (1983), Chapter 5.4.2.

These results deviate considerably from those obtained in De Haan[30] where we wrongly deducted a 5 per cent trade and transport margin from the output price of the OPS. This reduction decreases the price ratio by 5 per cent, which has a great effect on the comparison. Further, in our revised analysis, we assumed a shorter crushing season of the VPS, which increased its capital costs by 17 per cent.

We shall now proceed to an assessment of the chances of survival of the OPS in India.

The Future of the OPS

In this section the scope for survival of OPS will be examined. This depends essentially on the possibility of increasing both the rate of recovery and the quality of output. Table 3 showed that the gap in NPV between the OPS and the VPS had narrowed considerably at a recovery rate of 8 per cent and a price ratio of 90 per cent. We shall, therefore, examine to what extent these figures can be attained by technological improvement.

First, we discuss the possible overestimation of the NPV of the VPS by not allowing for initial underutilisation of capacity. If this is important, the relative profitability of the OPS would also increase.

Capacity Utilisation

A new sugar factory sometimes encounters difficulties in procuring sufficient cane in the initial years of production, particularly if cane is grown by small holders rather than at an estate. Kaplinsky[31] assumes that the VPS reaches its normal capacity of 83 per cent four years after the start of production as follows—first year 58 per cent, second 66 per cent, third 75 per cent and fourth 83 per cent, which he considers to be a good average without presenting much empirical evidence. To test his argument we examined the initial performance of nine 1,250 tcd factories recently built in western and central U.P. Table 4 gives the average daily rates of capacity utilisation during the period 1977–78 to 1981–82.

The low starting rates of Nadehi, Nanauta and Ramala (74 per

---

[30] de Haan, *op. cit.*
[31] Kaplinsky, *op. cit.*

Table 4

Average Rate of Daily Capacity Utilisation of Recently Built 1,250 tcd VPS Factories in Western and Central U.P. (Percentage of 1,250 tcd)

Sugar Mill	Season						Average
	1976–77	1977–78	1978–79	1979–80	1980–81	1981–82	
Anupshahr		73	89	85	73	98	85
Bilaspur		58	76	89	93	89	85
Bilaspur		73	86	89	99	83	85
Budaun		71	88	80	78	79	79
Chandpur		75	84	95	104	99	91
Chattha		68	89	86	94	95	88
Nadehi		80	83	90	81	82	82
Average	74	71	85	88	89	89	82
Nanauta				53	83	97.	90
Ramala			50	75	80	87	82

Source: Compiled from National Federation of Cooperative Sugar Factories, New Delhi (1981 and 1984).

cent, 53 per cent and 50 per cent) refer to extremely short seasons of 6, 19 and 11 days, because these factories were completed in March or April when the crushing season has usually reached its final stage. Obviously, Kaplinsky's average does not apply to the mills constructed in the recent past.

Nevertheless, his argument may be correct in another sense. It is quite possible that the under-utilisation of capacity is not caused by low daily crushing rates but, rather, by a shorter crushing season. Table 5 gives the length of the crushing period for the seven mills which started in 1977–78.

To provide a yardstick for comparison, we present the average for the older factories in the districts of Meerut/Ghaziabad, Muzaffarnagar and Bijnor. Only in the first season did the new factories have a significantly lower number of crushing days, partly since most of them started late in the season. If we exclude the first year, the average of the new factories increases slightly from 128 to 129, whereas the three district averages decrease from 146, 146 and 154 to 130, 129 and 137, respectively. If the latter three figures are weighted by the number of factories in the district (8, 4 and 3, respectively) we obtain an average of 131, if the first year is excluded. This means that the length of the crushing season of the new factories after the first year is on the average similar to that of the older factories.

These figures suggest that only a correction for the first year would be required. We do not know the length of the construction period of the new factories, but it is unlikely that those which started later in the season were built in less than two years. Given our assumption of a two-year construction period, the low production in the first year may reduce the NPV of the VPS significantly, as discounting implies assigning larger weights to the first year. It also means a shift in the investment pattern implying lower capital costs. However, the net effect is negative, particularly if the season is short (as in the case of Bilaspur and Chattha). Table 5 indicates that the average season of the new mills was only 59 per cent of the three districts' average. If we take this figure as the first year rate of utilisation, the NPV of the VPS would still exceed that of the OPS, but with a rather small margin. In the case of Chattha and Budaun, adjustments would be required for all the five years. Compared to those mills the performance of the OPS is better. It is a moot question, however, whether the alternative of seventeen OPS units

Table 5

Length of Crushing Season of Recently-Built 1,250 tcd VPS Factories in Western and Central U.P. (in Days)

Sugar Mill	Season					Average	
	1977–78 (1)	1978–79 (2)	1979–80 (3)	1980–81 (4)	1981–82 (5)	1–5	2–5
Anupshahr	183	127	78	98	220	141	131
Bilaspur	51	136	118	121	198	125	143
Bisalpur	123	130	63	102	219	127	129
Budaun	124	122	56	96	200	120	119
Chandpur	165	137	73	132	203	142	136
Chattha	66	144	68	70	158	103	110
Nadehi	168	143	68	126	211	143	137
Average (1)	125	134	75	106	201	128	129
District:							
Meerut/Ghaziabad	213	132	80	105	201	146	130
Muzaffarnagar	210	140	81	101	192	146	129
Bijnor	223	160	94	134	160	154	137
Average (2)	214	140	83	110	190	147	131
Ratio (1):(2)	.59	.96	.90	.96	1.02	.87	.98

Source: Compiled from NFCSF (1981) and NFCSF (1984).

would have had a longer season. On the other hand the performance of Chandpur and Anupshahr was much better than that of the OPS.

Finally, we would like to point out an interesting aspect of the difference in the construction period between the two alternatives. In our discounting procedure at a rate of 10 per cent, we started discounting with weight of 0.91 in the first year of production of both the VPS and OPS. The longer construction period of the VPS was accounted for by 'discounting' back to year-1. This procedure implies that the OPS does not produce during the construction period of the VPS. This derives from the way of defining the project, namely, the production of 14,250 tonnes of sugar per year during a given period of twenty years, which implies that production should start in a fixed year. Obviously, the OPS would become superior to the VPS if the comparison would be made with the OPS starting production in year-1, since its NPV will be multiplied by a factor 1.21.

We may conclude that though the OPS is not a better alternative in economic prices, the gap in NPV has narrowed enough to be compensated by its larger employment generating capacity. It is, therefore, worthwhile to examine whether the realisation of 8 per cent recovery and a 90 per cent price ratio is possible.

The Scope for Improvement

There are essentially two conditions for the viability of the OPS— improving the quality of sugar to get a higher price and increasing the rate of recovery to reduce cane costs. We shall briefly examine the possibilities.

It is somewhat misleading to talk in terms of recovery, because this depends not only on the efficiency of the production process, but also on the sucrose content of the cane. The hydraulic six-roller $13'' \times 18''$ crusher is able to extract 80 per cent of the sucrose in cane. During boiling and centrifuging a further 30 per cent is lost, which implies that the total extraction of sucrose is 56 per cent. This gives a recovery of 7 per cent on cane with a sucrose content of 12.5 per cent. A sugar mill extracts about 76 per cent, which gives a recovery rate of 9.5 per cent on cane of the same sucrose content. It is on the basis of these figures that we choose the recovery rate of 7 and 9.5 per cent.

Already in 1965 it was found that a screw expeller could increase the rate of sucrose extraction from the 80 per cent obtained by a crusher to almost 90 per cent, which would lead to 0.8 per cent higher recovery.[32] The application of some expellers in a few commercial units, however, was a complete disaster. Attempts have been made to improve the design in order to prevent the problem of jamming, which was responsible for the failure. New trials in the early seventies did not show much improvement, but recent experiments were more hopeful. Nevertheless, we do not know of any expeller that has worked satisfactorily throughout a full season. So far the evidence presented is based on trials of only two hours.[33] We consider it, therefore, highly premature to conclude that the recovery rate of the OPS has increased by 0.8 per cent, as suggested by Kaplinsky.[34] In my opinion, a definite judgement is not possible before reliable data are available on the performance of an expeller that has functioned continuously for longer periods.

Even if the expeller could function satisfactorily under commercial conditions, it is uncertain whether it will be attractive to the owners of the OPS units. The capacity of the commonly used crushers has increased over time because of technical improvements and the application of motors of larger power. It seems that the capacity of a properly constructed hydraulic six-roller 13″ × 18″ crusher can easily attain a daily capacity of 150 tcd without much loss in extraction, if any. The existing expellers have a capacity of only 50 tonnes. Three expellers are considerably more costly than one crusher as the former consume more power. Further, it is a common practice in the western districts of western U.P. to crush in excess of the optimal rate, which is impossible with the expeller. The first results of a partial resurvey of units in Bijnor in the first three months of 1986 do not indicate that expellers are used. The successful test of two hours, on which Kaplinsky's optimistic view is based, was carried out in February 1982. If the expeller is really such a successful improvement, as he suggests, it is difficult to understand why, after four years, no expeller is found in the district with the largest number of OPS units in the country.

Another possible improvement is the use of a new furnace design.[35]

[32] See Garg, 1979, *op. cit.*

[33] See F. Almond, 'Operating Performance of the Screw Expeller and the Shell Furnace,' Appendix to Kaplinsky, *op. cit.*

[34] Kaplinsky, *op. cit.*

[35] See Almond, *op. cit.*, or M.K. Garg, and I. McChesney, The Development of Wet Bagasse for Open Pan Sugar Boiling, ATDA/IITS, Lucknow/Rugby (mimeo), 1980.

The existing furnaces, which are fed with bagasse (i.e., the residual of cane after crushing), require more fuel than the bagasse produced. Since the cost of additional fuel is considerable, many OPS units overfeed the crushers at the cost of lower extraction. In this way, the amount of bagasse per unit of juice increases, and also the caloric value of the bagasse due to its higher sucrose content. It is, therefore, desirable to attain self-sufficiency in fuel by improving the furnace designs. Fuel efficient furnaces will reduce the need for overcrushing and thus enhance the prospects for the expeller.

Another advantage is that these furnaces can function on wet bagasse. At present, the bagasse has first to be dried before it can be used as fuel. The use of wet bagasse will diminish the costs of production because bagasse dryers, who account for about 15 per cent of the labour employed, become redundant. It also reduces the loss of crushing days because of rainy weather, when the bagasse cannot be dried.

In the letter enclosed to the test report of February 1982 it is mentioned that, at that time, three units were operating exclusively on the new furnaces. The first results of the resurvey in Bijnor district in the beginning of 1986 do not, however, indicate that they are used there. On the basis of the information presently available, one wonders whether the new furnaces have really passed the experimental phase.

Table 3 clearly shows that the difference in profitability between the OPS and the VPS is largely due to the lower price of OPS sugar. Surprisingly, this aspect is hardly dealt with in the debate on OPS. Baron[36] did not even include the output price in his calculations and Kaplinsky[37] mentions only in a footnote that his assumption of a price ratio of 90 per cent has a key bearing on the analysis. In this respect we do not know of any research programme which aims at the improvement of the quality of OPS sugar. Garg and McChesney mention that the new furnace decreases the caramellisation of the juice during boiling, but we do not believe that this alone will lead to a significant improvement in the quality of sugar.[38]

On the basis of the prices given by OPS units, we consider a price ratio of 90 per cent too high. The output prices of first, second and third sugar given by Garg would render a ratio of 80 per cent, if we

[36] Baron, *op. cit.*
[37] Kaplinsky, *op. cit.*
[38] Garg and McChesney, *op. cit.*

assume that the price of first OPS sugar is on the average of 10 per cent lower than the price of VPS sugar.[39] As Table 3 shows, the more realistic assumption of 85 per cent gives a difference in NPVs of Rs. 24, even if the recovery is increased to 8 per cent.

Finally, it should be mentioned that the labour costs of the OPS are low because of the long working days and the use of migrants, sometimes from distant places (like Bihar or eastern U.P.). If the OPS units obeyed the labour regulations, its wage bill would increase considerably. Therefore, we did not allow for the lower costs of production caused by the use of the new furnace.

It is our, admittedly partly subjective, expectation that, even if all the improvements mentioned are realised, the best one might expect is an average recovery rate of 7.5 per cent, a price ratio of 85 per cent and a small average need for additional furnace fuel. Table 3 leaves no doubt that the OPS is not viable under such conditions.

[39] Garg, 1979, *op. cit.*

9 Nirmala Banerjee

Small and Large Units: Symbiosis or Matsyanyaya?

Introduction

This paper examines the relative efficiency of large and small units which are engaged in producing closely competing items. It is noted that large and small units are not always rivals; there is often a complementary relationship between the two. However, this relationship is dominated not so much by motives of mutual profitability but of blatant exploitation of the small by the large to an extent which makes it difficult to understand the behaviour of the small in terms of standard concepts (such as, profitability or cost minimisation). Furthermore, there are indications that while individual small units are often inefficient and therefore non-viable, they serve the purpose of making production more profitable for large units and, therefore, though there is a high mortality rate amongst such units, the species survives and plays an important role in the market. The problem as illustrated here relates to the units in the electric fan industry of the Calcutta region. However, the conclusions probably apply to units of various other similar industries because of the basic character of small units which is discussed later in the paper.

The Electrical Fan Industry

The Indian fan industry has had a rather chequered history over the last thirty years. Though fans have been domestically manufactured since the beginning of the First World War, production expanded fast only after Independence. In the twenty odd years since 1950, the number of fans produced increased ten-fold. In 1950 the number was 193,000. In 1972 it had gone up to 2.5 million. Since then, in the next ten years, production has doubled[1] though the progress from one year to another was not quite smooth. Previously, the industry was concentrated in and around the Calcutta industrial belt. It has now spread over most parts of India and has been successful in Maharashtra, Gujarat, Haryana, Punjab, Tamil Nadu, and so on.

The production of a domestic fan, especially a ceiling fan, is a simple process which can be done by fairly simple tools and standardised skills. The blades are cut from readily available aluminium sheets. The tie rod and the top and bottom parts of the case to house the electrical wiring (or the armature as, it is called) are made of cast iron. These can be manufactured either by a pressure die-casting method or by a simple gravity die-casting method. The former initially requires more capital but is much more productive than the latter. The parts are then smoothed and painted. The electrical fittings of a fan consist of a stamping or electrical core on which copper wires are wound either by experienced hands or by a coil-setting machine. Other parts (like ball-bearings and regulators) are standard bulk-produce items.

Because of this availability of low capital techniques of production, it has long been possible for small or cottage units to assemble fans from readily available bulk items and intermediate parts produced by other small units who sell them independently in the market. Traditionally, products of smaller units without well-known brand names were sold somewhat cheaper than those of bigger units whose quality was considered superior. The two types of units shared the market as competitors and, till the early 1970s, the share of the small units was not insignificant. In 1972, small units or at least units which were not members of the Fan Makers' Association

[1] India Central Statistical Organisation, *Annual Statistical Abstract*, New Delhi, 1970, 1974 and 1980.

had produced about one-third of the total production of 2.5 million fans.[2]

The majority of small units in the fan industry, however, are not engaged in assembling final products of the industry but in performing any one or two of the earlier stages of production (such as, die-casting parts, sanding, painting and finishing blades, rods, tops and bottoms, winding armatures, and so on). It is interesting to note that large units, which formerly used to undertake all stages of fan production within their integrated production process, have, since the 1960s, started to farm out work on several intermediate stages of production to various small units. Thus firm X (which is one of the two largest fan producers of Calcutta) farms out orders for die-cast parts, sends out parts for sanding and painting and also gives out work of winding armatures for table fans. A very large number of small units are now engaged exclusively in only one or two of these tasks for big units. What is more interesting is that, generally, large units do not rely on these ancillaries for fulfilling their entire requirement of any of the operations. They continue to produce the bulk of their requirements in their own factories but supplement their own production from time to time with the products of small units. This is true of all the operations that are being put out.

There are no direct estimates of the extent of the work being put out by large units but one can make some indirect guesses about its dimension. For example, the large unit X claimed that the number of fans it produced in 1982–83 was 1.573 million. It had two large workshops for finishing and painting fan parts: a conventional one where standard spray painting machines were used and the other where a Ransberg Electrostatic paint machine was in use. The capacity of the first at two shifts a day was for finishing and painting all parts of 600,000 fans per annum. The capacity of the other at two shifts a day was 780,000 fans per year. The supervisors of the two paint shops confirmed that this was about the extent of their annual output. Therefore, finishing and painting of parts—at least for the additional 193,000 fans—had presumably been put out to small units.

An indirect indicator of the proliferation of small units meant mainly to serve as ancillaries of large units is provided by the fact that we found no small units working on the final assembly of fans

[2] Subir Das, 'Economies of Scale and Implications for Policy: A Study of the Electrical Ceiling Fan Industry,' in A.R. Bagchi and N. Banerjee (eds.) (1980).

even though we surveyed those areas of Calcutta where small fan units are concentrated on two occasions—once in May 1983 and again in the winter of 1984–85. (The methodology of the surveys is given in the Appendix.)

This increasing reliance on small units for certain operations by big units leads one to expect that for those operations, the small units are more efficient. However, against this presumption is the fact that the rate of mortality amongst small units doing this work is fantastically high. Workers in this area reported that most of them had shifted from a moribund unit to a new one several times and that the average life of most such units was five to six years. In the period between our two surveys, not less than 30 per cent of the units we had seen on the earlier occasion had turned moribund and/or changed hands.

One way to compare the efficiency of small and large units is to compare their total unit cost for a given operation. The operations selected were finishing and painting of fan blades and parts because it was possible to do this work either by a completely mechanised process or by hand with very simple tools. The stages are:

1. Application of a coat of red oxide to the shaped parts and drying them by heat.
2. Application of a paint-primer to the parts and drying them by heat.
3. Application of a putty made of a mixture of red oxide, paint primer and french chalk to any holes or depressions in the parts and once again drying them.
4. Another inspection and use of a special putty to smooth the parts and also heat drying them.
5. Sanding the parts by water and sand-paper to smooth them.
6. Painting them by spray process and drying the paint by heat.

In the small units, red oxide and paint primer are applied by a compressor machine: the rest of applications are done by hand with a rag by a worker. Only the final paint is sprayed on by a hand-held spray-gun. The sanding is done by women who dip each part in plain water and rub it with sand-paper. Drying is usually managed in a mud chamber heated with a kerosene stove, or sometimes in the sun if time and weather permit it.

In the large units, the entire operation is done by putting the parts on conveyer belts where they move from one stage to the next. The heating is done in closed metal chambers heated by domestic gas. For the sanding a worker puts the part on a fast moving disc operated by electricity. A strong jet of water hits the part from above. The worker presses a piece of sand-paper on the surface and depresses the pedal to operate the disc. After that, these pieces are again dried, then paint is applied to parts moving on a conveyor belt through a closed chamber where a paint spray is operating. The parts are then sent to dry in an electrically heated chamber. In the Ransberg process of painting, the operation is further improved by electrically charging the paint and the parts by opposite charges so that the paint is pulled to the parts and very little is wasted by spillage or random spraying.

Besides these common operations, the large unit also uses a process for initially degreasing the parts by passing them through a hot solution of caustic soda and then dipping the aluminium blades in an allochrome solution. This ensures that paint sprays on evenly and lasts much longer.

Cost Comparisons

Table A gives a comparison by items of costs for the large and small units for the operation of finishing and painting tops, bottoms or blades of a fan. It can be seen that the per piece total cost (item No. 7) is somewhat lower for the large unit than the small unit. Also, the per piece cost to the small scale unit of operation exceeds the rate given to it by the large units (item No. 8). This is so even when the average wage rate of the large unit at Rs. 32 is about 3.55 times the average wage rate of about Rs. 9 prevailing in the small unit.

As against their low cost of labour, the major problem for small units is their high cost of material. This is because the paint machines of the large unit are designed mainly to avoid wasting costly paint. The standard closed chamber of the paint shop of a large unit uses about 25 per cent less paint than a hand-held spray-gun. The Ransberg process, where parts of the fan and the paint are both charged with an opposite electrical charge, saves up to 40–50 per cent of the paint used in the hand method.

The results shown in Table A are unfavourable to small units, despite the fact that the calculations assume (*a*) that large and small units pay the same price for inputs. This is obviously not the reality, since large units buy in bulk and get a discount of up to 30 per cent on their purchases, (*b*) small units are assumed to borrow capital at 16 per cent per annum. In fact, some of the units can get advances only on the unofficial money market and pay significantly more for these short-term loans for working capital. These two factors would substantially aggravate the cost disadvantage to small units, (*c*) that the output of the two kinds of units is strictly comparable. This, again, is not a fact. As mentioned before, large units incorporate additional stages of production (namely, degreasing and allochrome treatment). Skipping these operations means that the paint-work of small units is short-lived in comparison with that of large units.

These facts give rise to two questions—if the unit costs of large units are lower, why then do large units put out operation and, moreover, are doing so increasingly? And, secondly, how and why do small units go in for this kind of work when they are patently losing on it? The answers give us some idea about the objective functions and constraints of the different kinds of units in the fan industry.

Large Units

Initially, the management of large units claimed that work was put out only in emergencies when a machine broke down. Later, however, they admitted that the vast scale of putting out operations was meant mainly to supplement their normal supply in case of extra orders. In fact, electrical fan units have fast proliferated in all parts of the country, and old established units (like firm X of Calcutta) have felt the pressure of their competition. Due to this, orders fluctuate not only seasonally but from year to year and firms cannot plan for investment towards a steadily increasing production. They have to adjust their production in a wide range around a steady core, which is itself probably shrinking as new units come up to serve areas where older firms had a near monopoly till recently.

For firm X, records for 1981–83 are given in Table 1.

Not the least part of the uncertainty is introduced by export orders, which vary widely from year to year for India as a whole as Table 2 shows.

Table 1

	Number
1981–82 sales	1,653,448
1982–83 sales	1,574,261
Installed capacity	1,561,000
1982–83 production	1,573,000

Source: Figures from the *Annual Report 1982–83* for Firm X.

These variations in export demand are no doubt further compounded for individual firms. Customs records show that in the year 1984 for the months when Calcutta customs recorded large exports of fans, the distribution is shown in Table 3.

These orders were divided between several countries—Singapore, Malaysia, Nigeria, Saudi Arabia, Iran, United Arab Emirates, and so on. Neither of the two large firms X or Y had a firm hold on the market of any one country. Singapore, the largest market, received supplies from all four of these Calcutta firms—so also did Malaysia and Saudi Arabia.

The small firms were then being used by the large firms to avoid investing in additional capacity, which is likely to be underutilised both because additional demand fluctuates widely from time to time and also because it does not reach the level of the optimal scale of production for some of the processes used by large firms.

The small units by themselves are not efficient in various operations of fan production: but the combination of large firms producing the basic bulk load of supply and supplementing it as and when necessary by putting out orders to small units works efficiently for the large firms because (*i*) it saves locking up capital in capacity likely to be under-utilised, (*ii*) it utilises marketing and sales overheads of large firms more efficiently, (*iii*) it overcomes the large mechanised units' problems of matching the capacities of different machines meant for different stages of production of a given product, and (*iv*) it passes on the problems created by uncertainty of demand entirely to the small units. The latter provide the flexibility that the system needs for catering to a fluctuating demand. When orders expand, new small units come up or the existing units hire extra workers. When orders are scarce, they dismiss workers or seek orders from other industries for similar processes. Large firms,

Table 2
All India Exports of Electrical Fans

Year	Ceiling Fans		Table Fans		Pedestal Fans	
	No.	*Value (Rs. '000)*	*No.*	*Value (Rs. '000)*	*No.*	*Value (Rs. '000)*
1977–78	822,552	15,81,36	61,724	11,413	3,346	1,025
1978–79	625,096	12,16,58	33,756	6,784	3,784	1,600
1979–80	1,033,978	21,85,41	38,066	7,163	5,428	1,348
1980–81	1,158,864	26,40,78	49,582	10,094	4,198	1,483
1981–82	811,356	19,70,00	27,340	3,152	1,540	488

Source: *India Monthly Statistics of Foreign Trade,* March issues of relevant years.

Table 3
Monthly Exports in 1984 Under Calcutta Customs House

Month	Firm X	Firm Y	Other Firms
January	28,800	1,050	Nil
March	Nil	4,280	Nil
May	6,004	2,012	Nil
August	8,214	30,563	8,351 (one firm)
October	2,400	Nil	Nil
November	Nil	49,261	22,612 (two firms)

Source: Daily records of the Calcutta Customs House.

regulated by various laws and committed to one or another technology, cannot do this frequently. Mixing of low quality supply from small units with their own production should affect the market of the large units in the long run, but the risk is probably not high since supplies from small units are small as compared to the total output and sales of big firms. The latter probably pass those parts to customers who are generally less discerning. It is likely that public sector purchases fall in this category.

Small Units

The question how a small unit continues in business is easily answered—small units do not do the work properly. They save on inputs. For example, for sanding purposes, the water in which workers are to dip parts is supposed to be a weak acid solution. Even two years ago, this was being done. Now the workers are simply asked to use plain water. This makes the work slightly harder for the workers and leaves the parts somewhat unprepared to receive paint, but the difference in quality is not necessarily obvious at the time of delivery. Similarly, paint is not applied in the required thickness, number of coats, and so on. This cheating is not peculiar to fan units alone. Small shoe-makers who do put-out work for large shoe firms save on the glue given to them by large firms.[3] Handloom weavers, while weaving parts of saris which are not immediately detectable, save on yarn given to them by agents. In each case the

[3] Timir Basu, 'Calcutta's Sandal Makers,' *Economic and Political Weekly*, 6 August 1977.

rate quoted for the work is so unattractive that the work is un-remunerative to the small unit unless some materials are put aside.

Why do small units go into a business where cheating is the only way of survival and where the entrepreneur apparently gets no returns for risk taking? The answer to these questions lies in the nature of the small units. The standard small unit engaged in the fan industry is not a firm in the sense of an entrepreneur employing capital and labour in anticipation of demand. Rather, it is one version of the operation of an artisan who has developed some skills, has some conventional tools and is trying to make a living. He expects to get his payment mainly as a wage and also to collect whatever residual he can by keeping costs below the price set by the buyer in the contract. He produces goods only on order and has no means to gauge the potential demand for his products.

In the depressed industrial area of Calcutta, the main aim of most small unit owners is to find some employment for a living. Since wage employment is hard to come by, the next-best alternative is to set up a unit as a self-employed worker. In such a unit, he not only puts in labour but also undertakes some more functions. (a) From time to time he has to locate some customer who will give him orders. Since the competition amongst small units is keen, this is a demanding task. (b) He puts in working capital at least to the extent of paying his wage bill. Most such units do not have the resources to buy inputs for the work and then to await payment for them till the final bill. Often, some inputs are given by the large unit—for example, in the case of paint, the brand is specified and paint is often supplied by the buyer. The owner worker still has to find credit to pay rent, heating bills and wages, both to his hired workers and to himself and his family members in order to survive. (c) He takes the risk of the products being rejected by the buyer after the order is completed. He has already had to pay wages of the hired workers and also the cost of some of the inputs: he has ultimately to find money for the other inputs also, even if he fails to collect for the order. (d) He has to await final payment by the large unit. Usually, this needs a lot of running around and can take as long as three months. The owner of the small unit has to find credit for this period. (e) For him the system provides no mechanism against the risks of varying demand. Most small units work for one or the other of the large units because, over time, they have built contacts with them; but often they will also work for their rivals if they can make contact with them. Also, when fan orders are scarce, they try for orders from other firms using those processes. In case none are forthcoming, they dismiss the workers, and try to make a living by doing something else, even if it means leaving their few tools idle and taking to occupations like buying and selling scrap, running errands, and so on.

Owners of most small units collect no payment for these tasks or for bearing the risks involved. Indeed, their maximand is not profit or even their own wage-cum-payment. What they aim to maximise is the period in which they can earn at least a living wage.

In this aim, the main constraint on the owner/worker of a small unit is his lack of information and knowledge. Admittedly, limited access to an imperfect capital market acts as a big barrier to his undertaking business at a viable scale with adequate tools; but even if there are efforts made to make credit easily available, his major bottleneck would remain. He has little knowledge of techniques other than those he has learnt by rote from his friends and family. And, he has no access to markets other than the few contacts he has established. In our earlier survey, we had found that the owners of small units often had to resort to a middleman to get orders of fan parts. The middleman or agent got the orders, gave some advance and got the worker owner to do the work. He specialised in collecting information and contacts for orders, credit and cheap inputs. The worker owner took the risk of paying workers and producing the supply. In case of rejection of the supply, he lost the lot. The middleman often lost his advance and also his goodwill with the customers. In return for this part of the work the latter took a commission from the price agreed with the customer. In the two years since our first survey, the small units under study had established direct contacts with large fan units. Even then, for orders other than fans, they often had to go back to some middleman.

The small unit, therefore, is not a firm of the standard kind. The owner and his family are also part of the work force; if the wages for himself and his family were to be included, his costs would exceed the returns, allowing him only a negative return for the entrepreneurial function. The production is only for orders received and the price is fixed patently to take advantage of the worker/owner's need to survive by any means. The small unit owner often shares the risk of his business with some middleman; but in case his output is accepted, the latter takes his cut as the first call on the payment. The small unit owner has neither the knowledge, the information nor the contacts to break into the charmed circle, even when the market is buoyant.

Summing Up

For the owner of a small unit, the main aim is to make a living for as long as possible with the limited skills at his disposal. To this end, he tries hard to acquire orders under conditions of fierce competition from numerous others with similar qualifications. The only way for any one of them to succeed is to undercut the price quoted by rivals; competition on any other basis is not permitted since the high quality of workmanship is neither possible nor in demand. The only saving that he can achieve is by economising on his own remunerations as well as on those of his workers. Generally, even for small units, wage rates per job are fairly standardised between similar units and one owner cannot normally undercut others in this. He, therefore, tries to use the labour of his family members as far as possible. He also utilises women whenever possible in unskilled operations and pays them relatively low rates. Actually, the operations of sanding and checking are by and large overlapping; but if women do them, the work is called sanding and paid at the rate of Rs. 4.25 per day. If men do it, it is called checking and paid at Rs. 6.25 per day. All such devices are used to get out as much margin as possible from the operation.

In the short run, this kind of pragmatic solution appears to fit in with the general economic policy of the country. It keeps down the costs of the large firms; it creates some self-employment and it also earns some foreign exchange through exports for the country. However, it must be acknowledged that this has been made possible by the gross exploitation of a section of the country's workers to whom the country has failed to give not only a guarantee of a minimum living but even access to technical knowledge, and information about the market and about facilities offered by the public sector to industrial units.

Moreover, in the long run, the organisation can be nothing but a low level trap for all concerned. Given the comfortable cushion of flexibility provided by the readily available and highly vulnerable small units, the large firms have no incentive to invest in R and D or to improve their technology. They are themselves veering towards unethical practices of selling goods of uneven quality and this is likely to backfire on them in the long run by further shrinkage of their markets. Since this option of putting out work is open to all big firms, it is not in anyone's interest to mount an aggressive policy of sales promotion and expand its own market up to a more optimal scale of production. There is always the danger that other firms will undercut the former by pushing the small units harder. In the export market too, large firms are at present content with looking for an occasional 'kill'—a quick order here and there. They obviously have some margin in their sales organisation and management to look for such orders and one possible incentive for doing so could be the export incentive offered by the government. However, they are not trying to build any long-term steady market on the basis of quality products and low prices.

The small units are all locked in the traditional role of artisans, in spite of participating in a modern industry. They have no scope of learning skills (other than the imitation of family members or friends) and no hope of ever acquiring the status of an entrepreneur, with its possibilities of learning and adopting newer and more profitable techniques or expanding to a more economic scale. They are condemned to go on scrounging for a living on the margin of the industrial economy. The only method of survival open to them is to further exploit their own workers and family members, to look for still cheaper labour, to increase the work load and/or to dismiss workers arbitrarily as and when necessary.

For the country as a whole, there is a lot of wastage of labour and expensive materials due to the crude techniques employed by the small units. Also, when the demand prospects of the industry improve, this does not lead to the establishment of new efficient plants; rather, the additional demand is shared by existing firms supplying more than their installed capacity through work being put out. This leads to an overall fall in the quality of Indian fans.

In the export market especially, there is now no serious large-scale attempt to build up an efficient production capacity and country-wise marketing networks to sell Indian fans on the several markets that are open to them. India, however, does have an abundant supply of the materials, technical knowhow and expert work force required for the industry to expand in the international market. The only thing is, as the wise pundits of India had maintained since long ago, this kind of '*Matsyanyaya*'—with the big preying on the small and the small on yet smaller—can never be conducive to overall growth.

Conclusion

It is by no means the claim of this brief study that the portrayal of a particular group of ancillaries to one industry in one region is typical of the genre of ancillaries even within that industry for the country as a whole. It is merely to point out that the reality can be vastly different from the standard concept of an ancillary that is prevalent in academic literature or in policy documents. Theoretically, setting up of an ancillary or separating some stages of production under different management is said to be profitable when there is a mismatching between the technically efficient scales of different processes in the production of a given product. Or setting up an ancillary may be recommended if it reduces the burdens of management in a firm with a particularly elaborate production process. This consideration might become doubly important if one particular stage can profitably use a more labour-intensive technology; segregating that particular process under a different banner, preferably one where unit labour costs are low (either by removing it to a cheap labour location or by farming it out in the informal sector) can appear very attractive to the large parent unit. However, for such a relation between the ancillary and the integrated large unit to be mutually profitable, the two have to be of similar status—the entrepreneur of the ancillary could have a smaller capital base, but he has to have a comparable knowledge of and access to various markets and facilities. Otherwise, the relation between the two types of units cannot be essentially complementary. For example, in the industry discussed here, there is a case for setting up a sophisticated modern ancillary unit for finishing and painting fan parts which can relieve the various large units of keeping a large unutilised capacity for those processes in an uncertain market. Such an ancillary unit can, in principle, set up a Ransberg paint process machine and keep it fully operative throughout the year by fulfilling occasional orders of various large units as well as of other industries which use painted metal parts. The arrangement could be highly profitable for not only the ancillary (since the technique, when worked at full capacity, is very efficient), but also for the various integrated production process units in that they would get efficiently processed products with a better finish. Its production cost being lower, the ancillary would make a reasonable profit.

However, if this type of ancillary is set up, it will destroy the employment of most of the self-employed and hired workers now working in the numerous small paint shops around Calcutta. What is more, the entrepreneur of that mechanised ancillary will in all probability come from a totally different background than the present participants, since he will not only need access to a substantial capital stock (which the former, in the absence of any assets, cannot easily acquire) but also a thorough knowledge of the industrial scene and techniques.

On the other hand, the existing ancillary units with their present technology could also possibly have been viable if they could have bargained from a position of greater strength when negotiating with the large units on the latter's sudden orders. However, the objective reality of the situation is such that one cannot envisage how the small units can do this. Even a cooperative effort of all existing units may not succeed in this. In a stagnant economy with a huge backlog of the unemployed, it is difficult to ensure that a new group of workers does not undercut the cooperative.

If the aims of public policy are to ensure a continuation of employment for workers in the existing small units and at the same time expand the fan industry of the region, it is necessary to enquire why the earlier tradition of small units assembling complete electrical fans for a somewhat cheaper market is giving way to this new trend of more units serving as ancillaries to the big names. The former system had the advantage that the savings in labour charges or other inputs by small units could be utilised to put a cheaper product on the market and thus expand sales to a wider set of customers.

The usual difficulties of those small units which had been producing an alternative type of fan have been frequently discussed. Perhaps there is further scope for a more thorough investigation and analysis on the nature of small units competing with large units for different segments of the Indian market. Or, the policy measures suggested by earlier analysis have not been put into practice. The subject deserves to be reopened for investigation.

The present practices of large units also need to be fully examined. It is not within the scope of this paper to examine the possibilities of designing public policy measures for ensuring better quality control of industrial products, closer checks on the misuse of export incentives or more efficient marketing of Indian products abroad; but there is little doubt that the long-term interests of the country require such measures. And fairness demands that the enormous advantage to large units arising from imperfections in access to capital and information should not be allowed to turn into a double-edged sword in their hands; it should not enable them to exploit a very vulnerable section of the labour force and at the same time avoid fulfilling their due obligations to the customers.

APPENDIX

A Note on Methodology

For this study, large units were defined as those registered under the Factories Act. Small units were those outside this category. In none of the units were there more than 10 workers, although they did use electricity. Therefore, they did not come under the sample sector either.

There is no official or other reliable listing of small units in the fan industry. In 1983, we went through the daily returns of the Calcutta Customs House and located the Calcutta-based firm with maximum exports in 1982. We contacted this firm (which is a very large unit with a licensed capacity of 1,523,000 fans) and studied their production process. Then we located the two agents through which the firm farmed out its orders for certain operations. These agents, when contacted, were reluctant to give us any precise information but indicated the area where the small units of Calcutta's fan industry were concentrated. In this area of about one square mile, we found housed in tiny crude sheds and huts numerous units engaged in one or another of the operations of fan-making. Our research assistants randomly selected twenty units working on finishing and painting fan parts and made detailed reports about their working. In December 1984, we visited the same area; though we could not find eight of the original units, we found new ones working under a new owner, often with some of the original workers in the same place.

Table A

Costs of Finishing and Painting Tops, Bottoms and Blades of Electric Fans for Large and Small Units in Calcutta

	Small Unit		Large Unit	
1. Output Per Shift	200pcs.	1. Output		2500pcs.
2. Labour Cost	Rs. 82.00	2. Labour Cost*		Rs. 1,212.50
(a) 3 workers for sanding at Rs. 4.50 per day	Rs. 13.50	(a) 23 semi-skilled workers at Rs. 27.50 each		Rs. 632.50
(b) 2 workers for checking and applying putty at Rs. 6.25 per day	Rs. 12.50	(b) 13 skilled workers at Rs. 40.00 each		Rs. 520.00
(c) 1 worker to operate compressor to apply red oxide and primer at Rs. 14.00 per day	Rs. 14.00	(c) Supervisor at Rs. 1,500 p.m. for 25 working days		Rs. 60.00
(d) 3 workers to paint with the help of spray-gun at Rs. 14.00 per day	Rs. 42.00			
3. Energy Input†	Rs. 21.00	3. Energy Costs†		Rs. 250.00
(a) Kerosene for heating the hot chamber	Rs. 15.00	(a) Cooking gas for hot chamber		Rs. 150.00
(b) Electricity for working compressor machine and spray-guns	Rs. 6.00	(b) Electricity		Rs. 100.00

4.	Overheads†			4.	Overheads†	
(a)	Rent of shed	Rs. 33.00		(a)	Interest at 15%, maintenance at 5% on invested capital of Rs. 0.8 million used in two shifts per day; per shift liability	Rs. 1,100.00
		Rs. 4.00				Rs. 266.00
(b)	Rent for compressor machine	Rs. 10.00		(b)	Maintenance cost of Rs. 0.5 million per annum for Ransburg machine used in two shifts per shift liability	Rs. 833.00
(c)	Interest on working capital of Rs. 36,000 at 16%	Rs. 19.00				
5.	Other Inputs	Rs. 400–415		5.	Material Input	Rs. 3,500.00
	Material cost per unit	Rs. 2.00–2.07			Material cost per unit	Rs: 1.40
6.	Total Cost	Rs. 536–551		6.	Total Cost	Rs. 6,062.50
7.	Total Cost Per Piece	Rs. 2.68–2.75		7.	Total Cost Per Piece	Rs. 2.42
8.	Rate Paid by Large Unit	Rs. 2.50				

* The labour cost of a large unit is exclusive of other benefits (such as, bonus, holiday payment and retirement benefits). If, on this account, labour cost is increased by 30 per cent the total unit cost for the large firms would be about Rs. 2.57.

† Costs for energy as well as other overheads are averaged over a month assuming 25 working days per month.

Altogether, in the second visit, our impression was that there were, if anything, more units working on these tasks in that area.

The purpose of our first survey was to study the gender-wise specialisation in occupations in the industry. For this we had looked at details of job content, equipment and remunerations in each task. We had, incidentally, looked at the cost structures of small and large units which suggested some interesting possibilities regarding the logic of the organisation. Therefore, we went back to the problem in 1984.

10

K.B. Suri

Technology, Firm Size and Product Quality: A Study of Laundry Soap in India

Introduction

Laundry soap is manufactured in India both in the organised and the decentralised sectors. The former is distinguished from the latter by the use of electric power, modern technology and large scale operations. As the difference in technology and the scale of operations between the two sectors rests on the use or non-use of electric power, and since the government policy on soap industry has also been guided by this critical factor, the two sectors can as well be identified as power and non-power sectors. The organised sector has forty-five firms which in 1984 manufactured 147,000 tonnes of laundry soap, along with toilet soap and synthetic detergents. The decentralised or the non-power sector, for which information is patchy and hard to obtain, comprises 5,000–6,000 units, most of which are small in size, working with family labour or with a few hired workers. They manufactured 650,000 tonnes of laundry soap in 1984, thus accounting for about 82 per cent of the total annual production. Most of the units in the decentralised sector produce only laundry soap, though some of the relatively large units have recently taken up the manufacture of synthetic detergents. Toilet soap is produced exclusively in the organised or the power sector.

Reliable data about the manufacture of laundry soap as an exclusive item are not available at the three digit level of the National Industrial Classification. Moreover, hardly any information is collected from small scale decentralised units, most of these being outside the purview of the Factories Act of 1948. A few available estimates (see Table 1) give recent trends in the production of laundry soap in the two sectors.

Table 1

Production of Laundry Soap in Organised and Decentralised Sectors in India (1967–84) (thousand tonnes)

Year	Organised Sector	Decentralised Sector	Total
1	2	3	4
1967	151	307	458
1968	181	n.a.	n.a.
1969	201	n.a.	n.a.
1970	192	350	542
1977	n.a.	560	n.a.
1984	147	650	797

Sources: (a) Government of India, Bureau of Industrial Costs and Prices, 'Report on Fixation of Fair Selling Price of Soap,' New Delhi, 1972.

(b) 'Soaps and Cosmetics: Need for Cooperation between Organised and Small Manufacturers,' *Commerce* Bombay, 17 June 1978, pp. 1016–17.

(c) Indian Soap and Toiletries Association, *Soap, Detergents and Toiletries Review*, Vol. 15, No. 5, Bombay, May 1985.

During 1967–84, while the organised sector stagnated in the annual production level (ranging between 150,000–200,000 tonnes), the decentralised sector made rapid strides, more than doubling its output from 307,000 to 650,000 tonnes and raising its share from 67 per cent in 1967 to 82 per cent in 1984. The change in the relative strength of the two sectors is mainly the result of the government policy to protect and encourage the decentralised sector. The policy, put in operation in 1967 (*i*) froze the licensed capacity of the organised sector and reserved the production of laundry soap for the small scale and cottage sector to meet incremental demand, and (*ii*) levied excise duties on the power-using firms in the organised sector.

This study attempts to lay bare factors which have contributed to the co-existence of the organised (power) and the decentralised (non-power) sector in terms of the effect of production techniques on the quality of the product, intra- and inter-sectoral variations in the quality of the product and level and structure of costs, prices and product markets for the power and non-power sectors. It largely draws on the findings of two sample surveys organised by the World Bank in Delhi. The first survey, conducted in 1978, covered fifty non-power and three power using units. The second survey conducted in 1982 supplemented the first survey by focusing on the quality and marketing of laundry soap. It covered twenty-three non-power and four power using units. The 1982 survey also included a chemical analysis of forty samples of laundry soap, thirty-five of which were manufactured by non-power firms and the remainder by power using firms.[1] Reference is also made to the Government of India study of laundry soap units located in different parts of India, conducted in 1970.[2]

Methods of Production

Soap is formed by mixing fatty materials with caustic soda. The chemical reaction, known as 'saponification,' splits the fatty matter into sodium compounds of fatty acids (that is, soap) and a residue which contains glycerine.

Manual Method

The non-power firms use a 'semi-boiling' process, consisting of

[1] For sample design and a detailed analysis, see John M. Page, 'Firm, Size, the Choice of Technique and Technical Efficiency: Evidence from India's Soap Manufacturing Industry,' World Bank, Development Economics Department (mimeo), December 1979; Dipak Mazumdar, 'Product Quality and the Choice of Techniques,' Development Research Department, World Bank (mimeo), June 1982; K.B. Suri (1983); and I.M.D. Little, D. Mazumdar and J.M. Page (forthcoming).

[2] Government of India, Bureau of Industrial Costs and Prices, 'Enquiry into the Price of Soap,' New Delhi (mimeo), 1972.

completely manual operations and requiring simple, inexpensive and indigenously available equipment. The mixture of fatty materials, caustic soda, brine solution and water is boiled in a cauldron on open fire for 4–6 hours. The contents are continuously stirred manually. The mixture, as it boils, is periodically tested to gauge the degree of saponification achieved. The contents, with fresh additions of caustic soda, brine solution and water are boiled repeatedly if better quality of soap is desired. On the completion of the chemical reaction, the contents are allowed to cool and settle and impurities (known as 'lye') including glycerine—a by-product—are drained off as industrial waste. Builders and fillers are then mixed with the soapy matter and the resultant soap is left to cool and harden. The paste, as it thickens, is transferred to iron frames and allowed a whole night (or sometimes longer) to dry, set and solidify under atmospheric conditions. The blocks of soap are ejected out of the moulds and manually cut into bars and cakes which are stamped, wrapped and packed in board or wooden boxes. Sometimes, soap bars and cakes (particularly of low quality or manufactured by relatively small/cottage units) are not stamped or wrapped but packed in gunny bags or retailed as loose products. The entire process of soap-making takes 6–7 days and is carried on without mechanical power.

Mechanised Method

Firms in the organised sector make use of a fully mechanised 'boiling process' which involves steam boiling a mixture of fatty matter, caustic soda solution, brine solution and water for 50–60 hours. It requires the use of power-fed steam boilers and an elaborate and expensive plant which ensures complete saponification and also separates glycerine from neat soap. The neat soap is transferred to a tank or a container and mixed with builders and preservatives. The mixture is thoroughly milled and plodded and on thickening and hardening, is extruded into a continuous bar which is cut, stamped, wrapped and packed. Most of the large organised firms use mechanised means to cut, stamp, wrap and pack soap bars and cakes, though some use partly manual methods for these operations. Soap technology has made great progress during the last few decades. The boiling process is now fully automated with a built-in provision to test and control the quality of soap at various stages of the process.

Effect on Use of Materials and Quality of Product

The manual method of production of laundry soap employed by the non-power sector cannot ensure the complete neutralisation of fatty matter leaving behind unsaponified fats. In the absence of adequate quality control arrangements, non-power firms would have unsaponified fatty matter rather than leave free alkali which, beyond the specified limit of 0.2 per cent, is injurious to the skin. It has also been observed that many firms, in order to save on the cost of materials, use only 50–60 per cent of the caustic soda required for a complete chemical reaction. As a result, up to 40 per cent of the oils and fats remain either partially saponified or are suspended in soapy matter. The unsaponified matter does add to the weight of the product but it is neutral so far as the washing quality of the soap is concerned. Its presence shortens the shelf life of soap.[3]

Soap manufacturers in the non-power sector do not have the technical competence to separate glycerine from soapy matter, a valuable by-product which forms about 5 per cent of the cost of oils.[4] It remains partly in the soap without adding to its desired qualities and a larger part is wasted in 'lye' which is run off on the completion of chemical reaction.

The large scale units in the power sector have the technical capability to use non-edible oils (such as rice bran oil) and oils from forest seeds like sal, mahua, neem and karanja in place of edible oils (which have increasingly been in short supply and their domestic consumption supplemented through heavy imports). Mechanised units are also in a position to 'upgrade' or 'harden' soft oils (like rice bran oil) through the process of hydrogenation and thus save on some of the scarce hard fatty materials.[5]

Mechanised processes in the finishing stage, which includes milling, plodding and drying under vacuum in the Mazzoni plant (or a plodding machine) produce more homogeneous soap with a better appearance and finish. Silicates—builder for soap—are also uniformly mixed so that the saponfied matter is amenable to rapid cooling and drying and easier handling and cutting of the finished product. The finishing operations bring about a change in the structure of soap from a Beta phase to an Omega phase, so that the

[3] *Ibid.*
[4] *Ibid.*
[5] T. Thomas (1978) and B.N. Goldar (1982).

wearing and lathering properties of soap are optimised and its shelf life is increased.[6]

Differences in the Quality of Soap: Survey Results

The quality of soap depends not only on the method of production—manual or power-operated—but also on the composition of materials used, specifically (*a*) the proportion of total fatty matter (TFM), (*b*) the extent to which builders/fillers are used, and (*c*) the percentage of free (i.e., un-reacted) caustic soda. Other things being equal, the larger the quantity of TFM in unit weight of soap, the better is the quality of the product. Regarding substances mixed with the saponified matter, a distinction is made between builders and fillers—the former (sodium silicate) is added to improve the washing quality of soap while the latter (soap stone, earth, etc.) is mixed just to increase the weight of the product. In built soap, sodium silicate used up to 20 per cent of the weight of soap adds to the washing and cleansing quality of the product. With the exception of sodium silicate up to the limit of 20 per cent, the higher the proportion of 'matter insoluble in alcohol' found in soap, the lower is the quality of soap. The presence of free alkali (on account of the incomplete neutralisation of caustic soda exceeding 0.2 per cent) reacts with the skin and damages garments. The Indian Standards Institute has laid down standards for laundry soap (see Table 2).

Table 2
ISI Specifications for Quality of Laundry Soap (Percentage)

Indicator	Specification		
	Grade I	*Grade II*	
Total Fatty Matter (TFM)	62.0	45.0	Minimum
Matter Insoluble in Alcohol (MIA)	2.5	20.0	Maximum
Free Alkali (FA)	0.1	0.2	Maximum

Source: Indian Standards Institution, Government of India, *Specifications for Laundry Soap*, I.S. 284, New Delhi, 1974; Table 1, p.6.

[6] W.J. Corlett, *The Economic Development of Detergents*, London, Gerald Duckenworth, 1958, pp. 92–93; see also Government of India Survey, 1972, *op. cit.*

Detailed data on the quality of laundry soap were collected in 1982 from twenty-three non-power units and four power-operated units in and around Delhi. These firms, of varying employment size, produced 99 brands of soap. Of these, a sample of 40 brands was collected for chemical analysis with respect to the three indicators of quality mentioned in Table 2. The distribution of 40 samples by employment size of the firm and ex-factory price of soap is given in Table 3.

Table 3

Distribution of Laundry Soap Samples by Employment Size of Firm and Ex-Factory Price of Soap Produced

Employment Size of Firm	Price Per Kg (Rs)							Total
	2.50–3.50	3.50–4.50	4.50–5.50	5.50–6.50	6.50–7.50	7.50–8.50	8.50–9.50	
Non-power Sector								
0–5	—	—	5	1	1	—	—	7
6–10	3	2	1	4	—	—	—	10
11–20	—	1	1	2	—	—	—	4
21–50	—	3	1	1	—	—	—	5
51–100	—	—	—	1	3	—	—	4
101 and above	—	—	—	—	3	2	—	5
Total	3	6	8	9	7	2	—	35
Power Sector	—	—	—	—	1	—	4	5
Grand Total	3	6	8	9	8	2	4	40

Source: *World Bank Survey on Quality and Marketing of Laundry Soap, 1982.*

In the non-power sector, larger units with an employment size of 51 and above seem to produce brands of higher price levels compared to the smaller units. The brands manufactured by the power-operated firms are concentrated in the highest price categories. The results of the chemical analysis are summarised in Tables 4 and 5.

Nearly half the samples from the non-power sector and none from the power-operated firms were found to be sub-standard in TFM. Similarly, the use of builders/fillers was more common in the non-power sector than in the power sector. Within the non-power sector, larger firms employing over 51 people produced fewer brands of deficient quality with respect to TFM as well as the use of

Table 4

Distribution of Samples of Laundry Soap by Proportion of Total Fatty Matter (TFM) in Unit Weight and Employment Size of Firm

Employment Size of Firm	TFM (per cent)			Total
	Grade I (62.0 and above)	Grade II (45.0– 62.0)	Sub-standard (below 45.0)	
Non-Power Sector				
0 – 10	2	4	11	17
11 – 50	1	3	5	9
51 and above	4	4	1	9
Total	7	11	17	35
Power Sector	2	3	—	5
Grand Total	9	14	17	40

Source: *World Bank Survey on Quality and Marketing of Laundry Soap, 1982,* Chemical Analysis of Sample Brands.

Table 5

Distribution of Samples of Laundry Soap by Proportion of Matter Insoluble in Alcohol (MIA) in Unit Weight and Employment Size of Firm

Employment Size of Firm	MIA (per cent)			Total
	Below 20.0	20.0–30.0	30.0 and Above	
Non-Power Sector				
0 – 10	3	3	11	17
11 – 50	1	4	4	9
50 and above	8	—	1	9
Total	12	7	16	35
Power Sector	2	3	—	5
Grand Total	14	10	16	40

Source: *World Bank Survey on Quality and Marketing of Laundry Soap, 1982,* Chemical Analysis of Sample Brands.

builders/fillers. As the chemical test of the MIA does not distinguish between the use of silicate (which up to 20 per cent adds to the washing quality of soap) and inert fillers (like soap stone, earth, etc.), we examined all the brands produced by the sampled firms. The analysis showed that whereas 71 out of 90 brands from the non-power sector were of filled soap, all of the brands manufactured by the power operated firms were of built (silicated) soap (Table 6). The use of fillers was almost universal in the non-power sector while the power sector manufactured only silicated soap, though some of the varieties contained silicate in excess of the ISI limit.

Table 6
Distribution of Brands of Laundry Soap by Use of Builders and Fillers and Employment Size of Firm

Employment Size of Firm	Use of Builders/Fillers			Total
	None (Pure)	Builder Only	Builder and Fillers	
Non-Power Sector				
0 – 10	8	2	33	43
11 – 50	3	1	22	26
51 and above	5	—	16	21
Total	16	3	71	90
Power Sector	1	8	—	9
Grand Total	17	11	71	99

Source: *World Bank Survey on Quality and Marketing of Laundry Soap, 1982.*

Non-power units, regardless of size, were successful in controlling the amount of free alkali, in spite of their poor access to modern facilities to regulate and control the chemical reaction. Only 2 out of 35 brands were found with free alkali in excess of the ISI limit of 0.2 per cent. All the brands from the power sector were found to be within the specified limit.

In short, the survey results show that the non-power sector has, on the one hand, been deficient in the use of fatty materials and has extensively used fillers to cheapen the product, on the other. The differences in the composition of the product, compounded with the adverse effects of manual methods of production on the use of materials and the use-efficiency of the product, do lead to the conclusion that as compared with the power-operated firms, the non-power units produce laundry soap of inferior quality. It may be pointed out that though the varieties produced by the larger units (employment over 51) in the non-power sector compared favourably with those by the power-operated units in the content of fatty matter, the qualitative deficiencies in the former (on account of the use of traditional methods of production) cannot be easily ignored.

Costs and Prices

Factor Markets

The factor markets facing power and non-power units were reported to be highly differentiated. Regarding labour markets, the wage differentials between the two sectors were quite substantial—the average starting wages for unskilled labour were more than twice as much for power-using firms. This is evident from the Bank borehole surveys of 1978 and 1982 (see Table 7).

Table 7

Average Minimum Unskilled Monthly Wages in Power and Non-Power Firms Manufacturing Laundry Soap in Delhi (1978 and 1982)

	Year	Non-Power Sector—Employment Size				Power Sector
		0 – 5	*6 – 10*	*11 – 20*	*21+*	
Average Minimum Monthly Unskilled Wage (Rs.)	1978 :	197	199	196	193	492
	1982 :	294	330	309	386	686

Source: Computed from World Bank Sample Surveys of Laundry Soap, 1978 and 1982.

Non-power units paid starting wages to unskilled workers close to the minimum prescribed by the law (namely, Rs. 175 in 1978 and Rs. 300 in 1982). Within the non-power sector, there was very little variation in starting wage levels between the various size classes of firms in 1978. However, the 1982 survey reported slightly higher wages paid by larger non-power firms, but even these were almost half the wages paid by the power-using firms. Wide differentials in the starting wage levels for unskilled workers point to likely differences in the labour market characteristics, including personal and demographic characteristics of workers recruited by the two types of firms.[7] Field surveys in Delhi revealed that non-power units, specially of small and medium size, whose owners and partners were adept at soap-making, depended far less on skilled hired labour than large manual and power-using units. These units, in the absence of trade union pressure, never felt threatened by absenteeism or high turnover of workers, made labourers work strenuously for long hours in the heat, smoke and stench and paid them wages very close to the legal minimum.

Regarding capital markets, it is widely believed that small firms suffer from poor access to institutional finance. The Bank surveys supported this belief—nearly 80 per cent of the non-power units had depended totally on their personal savings/sources while almost all the power based firms had borrowed large sums from financial institutions. Non-power units, with few exceptions of relatively large firms, had complained about financial stringency to meet working capital requirements, but had not approached commercial banks or other institutions due to cumbersome and time-consuming procedures, involving a lot of paper-work and occasional kick-backs.

Structure of Costs

We examine the production and marketing costs of laundry soap produced by non-power and power using firms on the basis of the Government of India study (1970), for which data with requisite details are available (Table 8). There are marked differences in the level and the structure of costs of the two types of firms, which may partly be attributed to differences in the techniques of production and the quality and composition of raw materials used.

The cost differentials (expressed as cost of power using units divided by the cost of non-power units) work out to 1.16 for raw materials, 1.87 for conversion costs, 5.56 for other costs (overheads, packing materials, selling costs and excise taxes), 4.30 for non-material costs and 1.51 for total costs. It is clear that the non-power units manufacture inferior quality soap at about two-thirds the costs incurred by the power-using firms—important sources of lower

[7] For a detailed examination of wage differentials between small and large firms, and theoretical explanations of the same, see Dipak Mazumdar, 'Labour and Product Markets' in this volume.

Table 8

Costs per Tonne of Laundry Soap for Non-Power and Power Using Firms
(Rupees)

Item	Non-Power Firms	Power Using Firms
1. Raw Materials	1,630	1,890
2. Conversion Costs	76	163
(a) Wages, including labour cost of packing	54(26.1)	102(11.4)
(b) Fuel and power	15	41
(c) Depreciation	7(3.4)	20(2.2)
3. Other Costs	131	728
(a) Overheads, including repairs, maintenance, etc.	66	127
(b) Packing material	43	142
(c) Advertisement, distribution	18(8.7)	175(19.6)
(d) Selling commission	4(1.9)	92(10.3)
(e) Excise	—	192(21.6)
4. Total Costs	1,837	2,781
5. Total Costs − Raw Materials (4 − 1)	207	891

Source: Government of India study, 1970. Computations based on seven non-power and seven power using firms. Figures in brackets give percentages of non-material costs for each category of firms.

costs for the non-power sector are (*i*) selling costs, including publicity and distribution costs, selling commission, (*ii*) packing materials, (*iii*) excise taxes, and (*iv*) raw materials.

As expected, absolute wage costs for the non-power units are nearly half the costs of the power using firms. It may, however, be noted that expressed as a proportion to the non-material costs, wage costs form only 11.4 per cent for the power using firms, compared to 26.1 per cent for the non-power units. Wage costs do not, therefore, appear to have influenced the choice of capital-intensive techniques. There is also a very large differential with respect to selling costs being nearly 30 per cent for power using firms and just 10.6 per cent for non-power units. Large amounts spent by mechanised units on advertisement, distribution and sales commission indicate the need for them to establish organised sales networks over relatively extensive and dispersed markets as well as organise intensive publicity campaigns in the oligopolistic or monopolistically competitive markets in which the qualitative differences—real and artificial—in the product have to be impressed upon existing and potential clientele.

Prices and Product Markets

There is a sharp difference in the prices of laundry soap produced by power using and non-power firms on account of the large differential in the level of costs, as shown earlier. According to the government study (1970), the prices charged by the power using firms were 50–60 per cent higher than those by the non-power units (see Table 9):

Table 9

Selling Prices per KG of Laundry Soap (Rs.) Produced by Power Using and Non-Power Firms (1970)

Price	Non-Power Units	Power Using Units	Differential (%)
Minimum	1.77	2.67	+51
Maximum	2.49	3.96	+59
Median	2.02	3.07	+52

Source: Computed from Government of India study, 1970, based on five power using and seven non-power units.

The Bank surveys conducted in and around Delhi in 1978 and 1982 produced similar results. According to the 1978 survey, the average price charged by power sector firms was 35 per cent higher than that by manually operated units. The price differential according to the latter survey works out to be 53 per cent (See Table 10).

Within the non-power sector, firms of varying sizes using the same technology charged similar prices for their products in 1978. However, according to the 1982 survey, larger firms seemed to be charging higher prices for their products, which were also found to be of better quality.

The relative importance of the quality of laundry soap and the firm size in explaining the variation in the price of soap within the non-power sector and in both the sectors taken together has been assessed by a step-wise regression analysis of the data obtained from the chemical analysis of 40 samples of soap as a part of the Bank survey of 1982.

Table 10
Average Price per KG of Laundry Soap Produced by Power and Non-Power Sector Firms in Delhi (1978 and 1982)

	1978	1982
Non-Power Sector		
Size of Firm (Employment)		
Below 10	3.82	4.70
10 – 29	3.89	5.55
30 – 49	3.75	5.58
50 and above	3.39	6.53
Total	3.78	6.24
Power Sector Firms	5.12	9.55
Price Differential (%)	+35	+53

Source: World Bank surveys, 1978 and 1982.

$$P = f(T), P = F(T, E):$$
where P is Ex-factory price
T is Total Fatty Matter, indicator of quality of soap
E is employment size of the firm.

The results of the analysis are given in Table 11.

In the non-power sector, the quality of soap appears to exert a strong influence on its price and the addition of firm size further improves the explanatory power of the regression equation from 71 per cent to 78 per cent. The inclusion of five samples from the power sector firms dampens the importance of the quality variable and markedly increases the influence of firm size on the price of soap. Large firms (specially in the power sector) charged higher prices only partly on account of higher percentage of fatty matter. It is likely that TFM, the indicator of quality used in the analysis, does not fully capture all the qualitative dimensions of the soap produced by the mechanised firms. It is, however, possible that firms of varying sizes, viewed as belonging to the power and non-power sectors, operate in a structured product market which generates price differentials in excess of the corresponding differences in the quality of the product.

Product Markets

Variations in the quality of laundry soap over a wide range within

Table 11
Determination of Ex-Factory Price of Laundry Soap

A. *Non-Power Firms Only*

$P = 1.58 + 0.08T$ $\qquad$ $R^2 = 0.705, N = 35$
(78.7)

$P = 1.93 + 0.06T + 0.008E$ $\qquad$ $R^2 = 0.783$
$(55.0) \quad (11.6)$

B. *All Firms* (including power sector firms)

$P = 1.51 + 0.08T$ $\qquad$ $R^2 = 0.570, N = 40$
(50.3)

$P = 1.57 + 0.07 + 0.008E$ $\qquad$ $R^2 = 0.785$
$(71.7) \quad (36.9)$

(F – values are given in parentheses)

Note: Sample correlation coefficients between E and other variables:

	T	P
Sample A:	0.47	0.64
Sample B:	0.20	0.61

Source: IMD Little, D. Mazumdar and J.M. Page, 'Small Manufacturing Enterprises: A Comparative Study of India and other Countries,' The World Bank (Mimeo), January 1985.

the non-power sector and between the non-power and power sectors, and sizable price differentials point to a highly segmented product market. Interviews with sample firms during the 1982 survey revealed that the socio-economic status of the consumers of laundry soap varied directly with the quality and the price of the product. Low varieties of soap manufactured by the tiny and medium size manually operated firms were consumed mostly by poorer households (including industrial workers, coolies and other un-skilled workers), while medium varieties with a comparable pro-portion of TFM) produced by large non-power firms or power sector firms were sold to upper-middle and high income house-holds. The power sector firms, in particular, developed their markets among the affluent sections characterised by low price elasticity of demand.

In addition to the variations in quality, artificial differentiation in the product is introduced by using brand names and attractive packaging. All the firms, manually operated as well as highly mechanised, covered in the Bank survey of 1982, used the brand names of all the varieties of soap produced by them. The brand war is fuelled by intensive publicity campaigns, particularly by power sector firms and the larger non-power firms.

The product market is also spatially segregated. The tiny and small firms in the non-power sector sell in a limited, localised market and protect it by lowering price and the quality of their products. The large manually operated firms and the power sector firms with a strong resource base spread their marketing network widely in search of safe though distant markets where competition from local non-power firms is not so acute. Almost every such firm attempts to carve out for itself an exclusive market in prosperous, middle-income or hilly regions where it caters to the demand of special socio-economic and cultural groups.

Conclusion

The manually operated units using traditional technology, as well as the highly mechanised power based firms using modern plant and equipment, have been making laundry soap. The foregoing analysis points to explanations for their continued existence. In the first instance, the product is heterogeneous, varying over a wide range of quality. The qualitative differentials are on account of the production techniques employed as well as the quality and composition of the raw materials used by the power and the non-power sector firms. The non-power sector firms, particularly the tiny and the small scale units employing less than 50 persons, produced low quality sub-standard soap, while the power sector units and large manually operated units produced better quality or standard varieties.

The factor markets facing the two sectors are differentiated. There are substantial differences in the structure and level of costs of soap produced in the two sectors. The product markets are highly structured. The soap produced by the power sector firms commands higher prices among affluent sections, largely on account of its superior quality. Large firms in the power as well as the non-power sector also attempt to acquire a monopolistic hold over the market by introducing artificial differentiation in the product through intensive publicity and the spatial segregation of the markets. The discontinuities in the cost and demand functions of a heterogeneous commodity like laundry soap provide the economic rationale for the co-existence of the power and non-power sectors.

The fiscal and other regulatory policies of the government have also played an important role is protecting and promoting the non-power sector. The production of laundry soap has been reserved for the small scale manually operated sector since 1967. In many instances, the licensed capacity of large mechanised units has been kept well below their installed or rated capacity, so that the total licensed capacity of the organised (power) sector has been frozen at 215,000 tonnes. The power sector units are permitted to produce in excess of their licensed capacity only for the export market which, on account of sporadic external demand, is totally undependable for production/investment planning. The more important instrument to restrain and restrict the power sector is the imposition of a 5.25 per cent ad valorem excise duty. The manually operated units, have been totally exempted from this duty. The official policy has also discriminated against the power sector firms in many diverse ways, one of these being to supply imported tallow, an important fatty material, exclusively to the manually operated firms at relatively low prices.

The power sector has reacted by (*i*) maintaining the price of its products at a relatively high level and even up-grading the quality of soap and raising its prices, (*ii*) developing a high income clientele in traditional markets through massive publicity, (*iii*) searching for new markets in distant regions where the local non-power sector is weak, and (*iv*) diverting their existing capacities and capabilites to manufacture toilet soap and synthetic detergents which are high priced items. The data on the organised (power) sector available from the government study of 1970 and the annual reports of the Directorate General of Technical Development show that comparing the period 1967–70 with 1984, the production of laundry soap had declined from 75.2 per cent to 28.2 per cent, while that of toilet soap had gone up from 15.5 per cent to 41.7 per cent, and of synthetic detergents from 9.3 per cent to 30.1 per cent.

The unprecedented growth of the non-power sector implies (*i*) substitution of better quality soap by poor, sub-standard varieties with comparable weight but less detergency, shorter shelf-life and less ease of use along with a wasteful use of materials and waste of glycerine, a valuable by-product; (*ii*) low wages, close to the minimum prescribed by labour legislation, and (*iii*) loss of excise tax revenue to the government.

IV Factor and Product Markets and Linkages

11 Dipak Mazumdar

Labour and Product Markets

Labour Markets

The labour market issue in the context of the economics of small scale enterprises is the problem of the wage differential between small and large units. We need to assess insofar as we can how much of this differential is due to institutional factors which might cause distortions and how much of it is probably due to economic factors. First, the facts.

In spite of all the efforts of researchers and government agencies, the empirical estimate of wage differentials by size of firms is still extremely limited in India. The best body of data which exists is for Bombay city, due to a labour market research project in which the World Bank was fortunate in collaborating with Bombay University. Lalit Deshpande of Bombay University did an excellent job of carrying out a survey of wage earners in three sectors of the Bombay labour market—factories, small scale establishments and casual workers.[1] The analysis of wage differential from this survey is given in Table 1, where we attempt an analysis of wages by sectors controlling for other factors in a multivariate framework. We utilised the Multiple Classification Analysis Programme of the SPSS.

[1] Details of the survey, sample design and methodology are to be found in L.R. Deshpande, 'The Bombay Labour Market,' Bombay University unpublished report, 1979, and Dipak Mazumdar, 'Paradigms in the Study of Urban Labour Markets in LDCs: A Reassessment in the Light of an Empirical Survey in Bombay City,' *World Bank Staff Working Paper* No. 366, December 1979.

Table 1
Log of Monthly Earnings of Male Manual Workers in Bombay City (1978)

Grand Mean = 5.73

	1	Unadjusted		Adusted for Independents		Adjusted for Independents + Covariates	
		2	3	4	5	6	7
Variable + Category	N	Devn.	Beta	Devn.	Beta	Devn.	Beta
Size							
1 Factory 10–99	498	0.11		0.10		0.06	
2 100–499	452	0.43		0.40		0.35	
3 500–999	174	0.58		0.50		0.41	
4 1000+	1,339	0.54		0.53		0.41	
5 Small	1,580	−0.35		−0.34		−0.26	
6 Casual	900	−0.57	0.77	−0.54	0.73	−0.44	0.58
English							
0 No English	3,878	−0.07		−0.03		−0.02	
1 Some English	1,065	0.25	0.22	0.10	0.09	0.07	0.06
Training							
1 Trained	1,233	0.28		0.09		0.08	
2 Untrained	3,710	−0.09	0.27	−0.03	0.09	−0.03	0.08

	N						
Education							
0 Illiterate	1,022	-0.10		-0.04		-0.10	
1 Literate No Schooling	53	-0.34		0.08		-0.01	
2 GRDS 1–3	507	-0.03		-0.01		-0.05	
3 GRDS 4–6	1,319	-0.03		0.02		-0.00	
4 GRDS 7–10	1,029	-0.02		-0.02		0.02	
5 GRDS 11–12	943	0.17		0.02		0.10	
6 Diploma and Degree	70	0.33		0.18		0.23	
			0.17		0.05		0.12
Occupation							
2. Skilled Blue Collar	1,031	0.20		0.07		0.07	
3. Unskilled Blue Collar	3,912	-0.05		-0.02		-0.02	
			0.18		0.06		0.06
Multiple R Squared					0.619		0.688
Multiple R					0.787		0.830

The dependent variable is the average monthly earnings of male manual workers (including wages in kind). We give the analysis in terms of the log of earnings. The grand mean for the entire sample is 5.73, which appears at the top of the table. The earnings of each of the categories that are given in the first column are expressed as deviations from the grand mean. Column 2 gives the gross deviations with respect to that particular category. That is to say, for example, workers in the occupational category in factories of size 10 to 99 have monthly earnings, the log of which is 5.73 plus 0.11 in gross terms.

Column 4 of the table gives the net deviations from the gross mean in any particular category, after controlling for the influence of other variables which are included in this table in categoric terms (i.e., the variables entered in column 1).

Column 6 gives the net deviations after controlling for two additional variables which are entered continuously and which are called co-variates. These are age and $(age)^2$.

If we look again at the category of workers in factory size 10 to 99—these are, to repeat, all male manual workers—the workers have monthly earnings whose log value is 5.73 plus 0.06, after controlling for factors like knowledge of English, training, education, occupation and age and age square.

The other important point about the table is that the beta values in column 7 are of particular interest. These correspond to partial regression coefficients in the more familiar regression models. They give an idea of the degree of explanatory power of each of the categories that are presented in the table.

The major point that stands out from the results presented is the great importance of the occupational factor, which is related to the segment of the labour market compared to all the other variables. In a like analysis for a developed country, factors like education would probably top the list. But in the Bombay city context, the occupation category dominates the scene in terms of explanation of earnings either as measured by the beta values or by the range of the net earnings differential. For instance, the earnings difference between casual workers and workers in large factories with an employment size larger than 1,000 gives you a value in terms of log of 2.85, which is huge: workers in large factories, after controlling for other factors, earn two-and-a-half times the wage income of casual workers.

This is the major point that comes through in the empirical analysis—that the segment of the labour market influence, as related to employment size, is the major explanatory variable of earnings differentials in the Bombay labour market. Secondly, the results show that there is a ladder in earnings going all the way from casual workers to workers in small scale units to factories of different sizes.

The question arises immediately: how much of this differential is due to institutional factors? There are two points I will make in this connection.

The first—an important point which I certainly did not anticipate—is that the wage differential between the smaller factories within the factory sector and the larger units is considerable. I had expected that since the Factories Act defines the boundary of the sector which comes under the purview of labour legislation, and since institutional wage determination is enforced through a combination of trade unions and labour legislation, 'factories' will provide the cut-off point between the low and high wage sectors. I would have expected that there would be more uniformity in wages, at least within the factory sector. But here we see that though wages in smaller factories were higher than in small scale units outside the factory definition, wages in the larger factories were much higher. The cut-off point, in fact, seems to come around the factory size of 100 workers.

The second point to notice is that institutional influences in wage determination, as we know now, have become very important since Independence. There was a spate of labour legislation, and the support of labour unions from official tribunals took an upward jump after Independence. What do we find from historical figures about wage differentials in Bombay, where institutional influences were weaker? There isn't a great deal of material readily available. The best is from a study of Bombay, again by Bombay University, in the early fifties.[2] The earnings given are for unskilled workers only and for all factories taken together. Compared to the wages of small scale units, the unadjusted weighted average for 1978–79 shows that factory workers would be getting just about 118 per cent more. If you take the adjusted figures, then they are getting 80 per cent more. So there has certainly been a lift since the fifties. I will put the upper limit of this lift at something like 50–60 per cent. This

[2] D.T. Lakdawala and J.C. Sandesara (1960), p. 96, Table V-9, earnings of unskilled workers only.

might be the measure of institutional influence on wage determination in the early fifties. Probably the institutional factors were relatively weak.

The other sets of evidence, which are given in much more detail in an article I published in the *Economic History Review* some years ago, examine the historical material on wages in factories, particularly textile factories in Bombay.[3] Although this evidence is qualitative, from the Royal Commissions on Labour and similar enquiries, it is quite clear from the evidence that factory wages were higher than wages in other activities in the urban economy of Bombay even as early as 1892. This is the first reference on wage differential within the city. Of course, there is no question of any institutional influence in the early part of the century or in the inter-war period when more detailed wage data showed that wages seemed to be higher in the factories than in other segments of the urban economy, and higher than in agriculture.

From the foregoing one can conclude that there are some economic reasons why wages are established at higher levels in factories in large units irrespective of institutional factors, although the institutional factors seem to have pushed wages up somewhat in the decades of the fifties, sixties and seventies.

I have suggested a hypothesis for this phenomenon—i.e., why wages are high in factories—which is a combination of a 'turnover' theory of wage determination and the firm specific wage theories, which have been discussed recently in literature. The starting point of my explanation is that the supply price of stable family migrants from rural to urban areas is necessarily much higher than that of a lone migrant for three basic reasons: one, if the individual leaves the farm, other people can fill his role for a short time so that the loss of output is small; secondly, the earner-dependent ratio is much lower in towns than in the villages because women and children do not participate much in the work in towns whereas they do in the villages; third, the cost of living, of course, is much higher for families than for lone migrants (including housing costs, the cost of social security, old age and unemployment). For all these reasons the supply prices of family migrants are much higher than the supply prices of lone migrants.

---

[3] D. Mazumdar, 'Labour Supply in Early Industrialisation: The Case of the Bombay Textile Industry,' *Economic History Review*, Second Series, Vol. 26, August 1973, pp. 477–79.

I then add a second point to the argument: that at the margin, the supply of stable labour (i.e., stable for work in town and work in industry) would be the family migrants. This is not to deny that some temporary migrants have stability but if the marginal stable family migrants are there, their supply price determines wages. But the large mechanised units which value the productivity of stable labour will try to attract permanent stable migrants at the higher wage level corresponding to the higher supply prices of family migrants, whereas in the informal sector in casual work, or in small units (where the relationship between stability and productivity is not that important), the wages will be formed by the lower supply prices of temporary migrants.

This is only the first step. Labour, which is stable in terms of urban residence, is not necessarily stable with reference to its attachment to a firm. A firm, which values stability in terms of its technology or its size or whatever, will tend to have higher relative wages with respect to other firms. They will have a calculus that the higher the wage the lower the turnover rate and the higher the productivity. Different firms will arrive at different wage levels based on this calculus. The suggestion is that large firms would find it profitable to have a wage level that is relatively high because, in effect, when they are talking about the establishment of relative wage levels within the urban industry, each firm is more or less faced with an upward sloping supply curve of labour which will have long-term attachment to it; the higher the wage level, the lower the rate of turnover and the higher the potential productivity of the workers.

This is the second influence of relative wage differential on turnover rate. Once a firm specific labour force has been established, other influences which have been discussed in the literature enter and tend to push wages even higher. The two principal ones are the wage-efficiency relationship and internal labour markets. The wage-efficiency relationship can be regarded as a reformulation of the classical idea of the economy of high wages noted by economists as early as the nineteenth century. As long as the 'incentive effect' of the high wages increases the efficiency of an individual worker more than proportionately to the increase in wages, firms tend to benefit from a reduction of wage cost per efficiency unit of labour supplied. This type of high wage policy can and will be followed only by a firm which is convinced that it is dealing with an exclusive body of workers attached to it. Such a firm will also benefit from on-the-job training for its own workers for filling vacancies of higher skill categories. Incentive effects are strengthened and costs of search and information are minimised when firms with their own attached labour force develop systems of job ladder and internal promotion for the supply of labour of higher grades.

This is the kind of hypothesis I have for the formation of high wages in the large scale factories based on economic factors. The predictions from this hypothesis are that large factories will show evidence of a firm specific labour force as measured by the length of experience of workers in the particular firm and that a larger proportion of workers in these factories will be family migrants rather than individual migrants. Unfortunately, these predictions cannot prove the theory; they can only be consistent with the theory because we do not know which way the causation runs. It is possible for someone to argue that high wages are first established in the large scale sector and this creates the firm specific stable labour force and also induces the family migrants to come into these firms. And, if it is maintained that the causation runs contrary to what I have suggested (i.e., from wages to stability), then the supporters of this attractive view will have to tell us what are the other ways in which wages have been established at the relatively high levels in the factories.

The last point I will make is that this method of formulating the problem leaves the question of deciding how much of the wage differential is the distortion a bit in the air. I will go back to Table 1. If one starts off with, say, the low wages in the casual sector as measuring the pure supply price of temporary migrants, one can work out from there by taking into account the differential cost of living per family and temporary migrants, the lower earner dependent ratio and other factors—a supply price of family migrants which will give you an idea of the wage level that will attract family migrants. But this sets only the lower limit of the supply price. On top of that there will be premia due to firm specificity, the wage efficiency relationship and internal labour markets. Unfortunately, we do not have any means of quantifying the effect of these further considerations. So, if we want a shadow wage based on actual wages, we have to come to some sort of guesstimate or, alternatively, look at historical figures (say, in a period like the early fifties, which may have been relatively free of institutions). The difference between this historical wage level and the one observed in Table 1 for the large scale sector can be thought of as being due to institutional factors.

I have been referring to Bombay so far. Are these kinds of differentials to be seen in other parts of India, in the other urban labour markets? Our borehole surveys gave some information on wages, which is reproduced in Table 2. It shows that within the borehole units (that is, those units which are covered by the surveys in the small scale sector), there did not seem to be much increase in wages by firm size except in powerlooms. We compared these with wages in the factories. The reported wages of the lowest paid workers in textile mills in Kanpur served as comparators for power-loom wages in Mau, and those in Delhi for wages in all the other small scale units surveyed (which, in fact, were all in Delhi). The differences in wages between the factories and the small scale units were quite high—they were two to three times higher in the factories.

The last source I will refer to is Table 3, where we give some information at the aggregate level, average annual earnings for the ASI census sector, the sample sector and the unregistered sector of small scale units. We see that the differential between the sample sector and the census sector is huge. There is a relatively small differential between the unregistered urban small scale sector and the sample sector. This corresponds to the finding of the Bombay survey that the differential within the factory sector, between the small factories and the large factories, is very significant.

Product Markets

We turn now to another issue in the context of the co-existence of small and large firms in the same industry.

One reason for the co-existence is, of course, factor price differentials, of which the wage differential is a major element. We will now discuss the point that the co-existence of small and large firms can be also due to product market differentiation, even within the same industry.[4] We illustrate this point with reference to the laundry soap industry where it seems to be very clear.

The large mechanised firms produce qualitatively better products,

[4] A complete discussion will be found in Chapter 12 of I.M.D. Little, D. Mazumdar and J.M. Page (forthcoming).

Table 2
Average Earnings in Different Sectors of Employment (1974–75)

Period/Source	Sector	Annual Wages (Rs.)						
		Bihar	Gujarat	Maharashtra	Tamil Nadu	Uttar Pradesh	West Bengal	All India
(1)	(2)	(3)	(4)	(5)	(6)	(7)	(8)	(9)
		Registered Manufacturing						
ASI-74	Census	5,180 (100.00)	4,105 (100.00)	5,130 (100.00)	4,289 (100.00)	3,431 (100.00)	4,872 (100.00)	4,288 (100.00)
	Sample	1,763 (34.03)	1,732 (42.19)	2,669 (52.03)	1,666 (38.84)	1,636 (47.68)	2,402 (49.30)	1,913 (44.61)
		Unregistered Small-Scale Manufacturing						
NSS 29th round	Urban	1,489 (28.75)	2,033 (49.52)	1,778 (34.66)	1,230 (28.68)	1,528 (44.54)	1,560 (32.02)	1,551 (36.17)
(July 1974–June 75)	Rural	1,319 (25.46)	1,526 (37.17)	968 (18.89)	583 (13.59)	1,101 (32.09)	1,059 (21.74)	822 (19.17)

Note: The figures in brackets indicate percentages with wages in the census sector as 100.00.

Table 3
Average Annual Wage of Unskilled Workers in IBRD Surveys (Rs.)

Size	Machine Tools	Powerloom	Printing	Shoes	Soap
1 – 10	2,172	—	2,364	—	2,664
11 – 25	2,316	1,140	2,436	2,256	2,832
26 – 50	2,700	1,428	2,604	3,000	2,964
51 +	2,544	2,244	2,292	—	3,240

Source: World Bank surveys, 1979–80.

which cost more per unit of output measured in physical units. This is because the full-boiled process of soap-making requires a minimum amount of investment in machinery; also, it produces a quality of laundry soap which cannot be approached by non-mechanised processes which are found in the small scale sector. The cost per unit of output, if measured in tons or measured in physical units, is much higher in these mechanised units but because of the higher quality of the product it can be sold at a higher price. Typically, such a firm would spend more on advertising, would have more capital per unit of value added and much less labour per unit of value added compared to smaller firms. Because small and large compete in different parts of the market, they co-exist with different price levels.

The question arises: Why do the larger mechanised units not enter the mass market for the lower quality soap? The first point is that the preference system of the low income consumers is sufficiently different to exclude them from this market at a price which will cover their costs. A sequential question is: Why do they not attempt to reproduce the techniques of the less mechanised units; why do they stick to production in mechanised units? In our field-work we found a lot of non-mechanised units trying to break into the mechanised sector but we did not find any entrepreneur saying that they really would like to produce soap in the non-mechanised sector. The reason, I suppose, is that the management style for capital-intensive firms is so different from that in the non-mechanised firms that this is just not an option for them to consider. But there are other economic reasons which may be briefly mentioned.

It is likely that there are economies of scale in the highly mechanised firms—in production as well as in sales. In a monopolistically competitive market in which large firms would typically operate, it may not have exhausted the scale economies at its point of profit maximisation. (The equilibrium for the monopolistically competitive firm is reached at a point on the falling part of the average cost curve.) If market conditions change—with either the demand curve shifting outward or the cost curve shifting inward—marginal profitability will be higher in expanding the high income market compared to the alternative of producing lower quality products, even though the average return to capital might be the same in the two markets.

Another important point is that although non-mechanised techniques are much less capital-intensive, they are often intensive users of space. Expansion of the volume of production for a particular firm may be limited by the sharply rising marginal cost of land adjacent to its original location. Thus, production on a large scale by a firm using non-mechanised techniques may need wide dispersal of operations—making the cost of supervision and management prohibitive.

These, and similar costs of expansion of scale, explain the widely observed phenomenon in our field survey that a substantial proportion of the non-mechanised firms in our sample served only a localised market. We also noted that some firms which had taken the first step towards mechanisation claimed that the possibility of expansion in terms of quantity of production depended on their ability to break into the market for higher quality soap—which, in its turn, was possible only through the adoption of mechanised techniques.

All this is not to deny the fact that the government policy of restriction on large scale mechanised units has in several industries created a sharper cleavage between the 'superior' and 'inferior' markets. In soap, the excise duty, based on the tonnage of soap (which was imposed on the mechanised sector) clearly provided an impetus for the firms in this sector to increase the quality level of their products so as to reduce the burden of excise duty per unit value of soap produced. The physical restriction on the capacity of the factory sector (mills) in the textile industry meant that they moved towards specialisation in higher grade cloth to increase the value of output per unit of capacity.

Some Notes on Welfare Implications

In the traditional literature on the choice of techniques, co-existence of firms with different techniques is usually traced to the existence of different factor price ratios facing firms of different types—say, different sizes. More mechanised techniques will be used by firms facing a higher ratio of wages to interest cost of capital. Moreover, such differences in factor price ratios are normally thought to be due to 'distortions' in labour and/or capital markets created by institutional interference. A simple policy prescription is that economic welfare would be improved if one removed these distortions or, if such a course were not possible, intervention may be justified to encourage firms to adopt techniques more appropriate to the 'real' factor price ratio (reflecting the true opportunity cost of capital and labour).

Our discussion of the very substantial wage differentials existing between the different segments of the Indian manufacturing industry suggest that not all the differentials can be ascribed to institutional 'distortions'. There is no obvious cut-off point for the high wage sector. Instead, there is a wage ladder showing that wage levels increase continuously from the casual labour sector, through non-factory establishments, small factories and being the highest in factories employing 500 workers or more. The jump in wages in the larger units within the factory sector is quite sharp and seems to come in factories in the employment size group of 100 workers or more. Evidence was presented to show that *some* (but not all) the high wages in the larger factories could be due to the influences of trade unions-cum-state supported wage legislation, which became important after Independence. At the same time, there are substantial economic reasons which explain a part of the wage differential between the large factories, on the one hand, and the rest on the other, and also between different segments of the manufacturing labour market.

While, as discussed, it is impossible to give a precise estimate of the extent of the wage differential which is due to 'distortions,' an important qualitative conclusion seems to emerge clearly. Insofar as economic forces are responsible for a part of the wage differentials, the difference in the efficiency wages for the different classes of firms will be much less than the differences in actual wages which are observed. Accordingly, the inefficiency from 'distortions' in a neo-classical allocative sense will be less than what might be expected. The choice between large and small firms may, on the other hand, involve the more important issue of distribution of income—a choice between a small volume of employment at high wages against a larger volume of employment at low wages.

Turning to the results on product market segregation, the tentative conclusion of the research is that in some industries the degree of mechanisation could be more significantly related to product quality than to wage differentials. For such industries, the case for the subsidisation of the less mechanised process will depend not just on the social opportunity cost of the factors of production (relative to their market prices), but also the welfare consequences of promoting the consumption of goods of a particular quality.

Coarse handloom cloth is mostly bought by the lowest income classes in India. With a significant rise in real income, the market for this type of product will, probably, tend to disappear. But so long as per capita income stagnates, it is possible to argue that subsidisation of handloom is justified on distributional grounds. The case of laundry soap is different. The prevalent opinion in the industry is that much of the growth of the labour-intensive sector has been due to a new demand from a growing class of consumers who previously used very little soap. Demand for labour-intensive soap probably would have grown anyway because of rising urban incomes in the post-Independence era. But the establishment of the industry in northern India was helped by the migration of entrepreneurs after Partition from Punjab and Sind (Pakistan) where the industry had taken root. The industry in Delhi seems to have been started by these migrants before the restrictions on large-scale soap production, but was clearly helped in its growth by this policy of the government.

Protection against technologically advanced domestic factory production is analogous to the infant industry argument for protection against foreign competition. The non-mechanised soap industry is a case where protected infants have made some progress, for there was ample evidence of product improvement despite the fact that improvement by using power was ruled out. While this may be held to have justified such protection, it is doubtful whether it should become a permanent feature.

There are good distributive reasons for retaining an excise tax on superior soap. But it should be ad valorem, not specific, for the latter gives an artificial inducement to large scale producers to move further up the quality range. Given such an excise tax, is there any ground for retaining the restrictions on the productive capacity in the power-using sector? Our examination of the history and technology of the industry suggests that it is unlikely that the power-using sector would seriously invade the low-cost territory, though the latter might eventually shrink as incomes rise. The main reason to fear such an invasion would be the resultant decline in the demand for low wage labour. This would certainly be the direct effect in the soap industry itself. But we have not evaluated the claim of the technologically advanced units that the production of their material inputs is far more labour-using than that of the non-power sector.

The machine tool industry offers a marked contrast to the two preceding examples. There is no sharp break in the technique of production associated with small and large firms; rather, there appears to be a continuous substitution along a range of factor intensities. This continuity of technical choice is accompanied by a similar continuity in product quality. Small and large firms compete in essentially the same market for machine shop lathes and produce equipment with similar dimensional characteristics. Superior product quality and price are determined primarily by superior design characteristics, which entail a greater degree of technological mastery in production. These characteristics are exhibited primarily by firms in the size range 100–199 employees, which are superior to both smaller and larger scale competitors.

It is difficult to advance any argument on distributional grounds in favour of the capacity restrictions on large firms in this producer goods industry. Lower cost machines embody lower quality characteristics which can be objectively evaluated by purchasers. The fact that firms across the full size range of the industry produce machines of varying quality indicates that there is no potential benefit to be gained from restricting the output of any size class of producers.

12 V.S. Patvardhan

Financial Assistance to the Small Scale Industry Sector: An Appraisal

Introduction

The information base of the industry sector in India is very weak, particularly in regard to the small scale and the household and cottage sectors. The available data on the small scale industry (SSI) sector are, at best, informed guesses and there is no single, continuous source of information which can claim to be reliable and accurate. Moreover, the term 'small scale sector' is often used in an omnibus fashion, encompassing the relatively modern small scale enterprises, also known as light engineering industry mainly located in and around the metropolitan and urban centres, consumer goods units in both rural and urban areas and the vast scattered traditional household industry comprising the artisan and cottage sector. The term small sector is amorphous and imprecise. For administrative and policy implementation purposes, the Government of India entrusted the development of khadi and twenty-two industry groups

mainly operational in rural areas—village industries—to the statu-
torily set-up Khadi and Village Industries Commission (KVIC) at
the national level and the Khadi Boards at the state level. The
Handicrafts Board is responsible for the promotion and development of and assistance to certain traditional industries. Similarly,
the development of handloom and powerloom operator units is
assigned to the Textile Commissioner. All the remaining manufacturing and processing units having their original value of plant
and machinery up to one million rupees[1] are under the purview of
the Development Commissioner, SSI, Government of India; in the
states, the respective Departments of Industries are the authorities
enjoined with the task of registration, promotion and development
of small scale industries.

In the discussion on the assistance to the small scale sector in this
paper, attention is mainly devoted to the last segment of 'small
industry' which is under the charge of the Small Industry Development Organisation (SIDO) and the State Directorates of Industries.
In the second section an assessment is attempted of the aggregate
financial assistance by the Industrial Development Bank of India
(IDBI) and the State Financial Corporations (SFCs). In the third
section the credit to small units according to the Reserve Bank of
India Survey (RBI), 1977, is examined. In the last section, relevant
data from a field survey carried out by the author during 1981–82 in
two industrial centres in Maharashtra state are used.

The term small scale sector has been used in the second and third
sections according to the official definition of small scale—namely,
those enterprises which have a gross original value of plant and
machinery below the specified limit. However, in the RBI Survey of
Small Industry 1977, even household or cottage activities were
included, as is evident from the lowest bracket of the value of plant
and machinery (namely, up to Rs. 1,000), in which a sizeable (about
35 per cent) number of units were reporting. In the fourth section
we deal with units in Pune and Aurangabad cities, where the sample
was selected on the basis of the number of employees reported in
the Economic Census, 1977. Though in the original census slips,
information about the value of plant and machinery was recorded,
this information was not found to be quite reliable. The sample was,
therefore, drawn on the basis of the number of employees. The

[1] Till July 1980, when this limit was raised to Rs. 2 million. Earlier, this limit was
Rs. 750,000 until 1976. In April 1985, this limit was further raised to Rs. 3.5 million.

units covered in the Pune and Aurangabad survey were from a universe in which the number of employees was 49 or below. However, the change in the criterion for selection of the small scale units in the survey did not effect the sample, as of the total number of 370 units only six had crossed the small scale limit of Rs. 1 million for the value of plant and machinery.

Small Scale Industry in Perspective

The information concerning the small scale industry as available with the SIDO is quite deficient. The data do not cover all the small scale units as it is not obligatory for the units to register with the Industries Department. Another limitation of the data is the change in the definition of small units that took place from time to time; for instance, units having a gross value of plant and machinery up to Rs. 750,000 were considered small until 1976. This limit was revised to Rs. 1 million in 1976, and again to Rs. 2 million in July 1980. Evidently, units which were not earlier eligible to be considered as small became so in the subsequent period. Strictly, therefore, the figures and information for the period 1969 to 1982–83 are not comparable.

As regards financial assistance to the small scale industry, it is necessary to distinguish the two types of credit: short term credit for working capital purposes and medium/long term finance for the creation or acquisition of fixed assets; the latter are known commonly as term loans. The State Financial Corporations have all along been granting term loans for the creation of fixed assets; though technically they are authorised to grant working capital assistance, the latter type of assistance has been negligible. In recent years, particularly in the 'eighties,' some SFCs have started giving composite loans up to Rs. 50,000 to small borrowers; nevertheless, in the aggregate, the number of such loans has remained extremely small and has not been separately reported. The IDBI grants refinance to the State Financial Corporations of funds already disbursed to the small scale enterprises. Thus, the assistance by the IDBI and the SFCs is, by and large, in the nature of term loans. The commercial banks do give both types of assistances—the short term and the long term—separate figures for which are not readily available. Consequently, there is considerable difficulty in indicating the extent of the working capital credit granted by the commercial banks, though it can be presumed that over two-thirds of the assistance granted by the commercial banks is for working capital needs. Moreover, the commercial banks' data give figures of loans outstanding at a point of time, while the SFCs data give figures of the amount disbursed during a specified year. The addition of the two, therefore, is not possible. What follows is a broad perspective about the total assistance granted by the commercial banks and the State Financial Corporations.

Let us briefly look at the status of the small scale sector. According to the Report of the Department of Industrial Development, Government of India, 1983–84, it was estimated that during the year 1982–83, the value of goods and services produced in the SSI sector was Rs. 350 billion, it provided employment to about 7.9 million persons, and the exports amounted to Rs. 20.9 billion. The progress of the small scale enterprises (excluding the KVIC industries, and the household/traditional enterprises enumerated earlier) in recent years is seen from the figures in Table 1 as estimated by the Ministry of Industry. It should be mentioned that the number of registered units does not tell us anything about the functioning units, as the former can include closed units, whose number is not reported.

Table 1
Progress of Small Scale Industry Sector

	1979–80	1980–81	1981–82	1982–83
No. of units registered ('000)	392	454	572	596
Value of production (Rs. billion)	216.3	280.6	326.0	350.0
Employment (million)	6.7	7.1	7.5	7.9

Note: The figures of the value of production are at current prices and the figures of employment relate to hired labour only (excluding self-employed proprietors). However, whether the hired employees are full time or part-time workers is not known.

Since the nationalisation of fourteen major private banks in 1969, the small scale industrial sector has been accorded priority status in the banks' lending programme. In 1969, the bank loans outstanding with 50,850 small scale units stood at Rs. 2.51 billion; by 1980 these figures had risen to 800,000 units and Rs. 27.50 billion, respectively, while the banks' outstanding gross credit with the SSI sector had further risen to Rs. 54.12 billion at the end of March 1984.[2] It is clear that bank credit to the small scale sector has registered a phenomenal growth since 1969. The growth in the number of small scale enterprises has been mainly the result of the government's policy thrust in favour of the small sector which included following measures: (*i*) reservation of an increased number of products for the small units to the exclusion of medium and large sectors, (*ii*) reservation of a number of items for supply to government and semi-government organisations, (*iii*) price preference for specified items produced in the SSI sector by government purchasing organisations, even if the price is 15 per cent above that of the corresponding items produced in the medium and large sectors, provided their standard and quality compare with those of the latter; (*iv*) concessional credit and finance on liberal terms to the small sector units, and (*v*) marketing assistance and supply of scarce raw materials (like steel, coal, aluminium and certain chemicals) through the state level Small-Scale Industries Development Corporations.

Financial Assistance by IDBI and SFCs

While the nationalised and other commercial banks are encouraged to give liberal credit assistance to the small scale units through the operation of the credit guarantee scheme and the targets laid before them under the priority programme, the SFCs have been compelled to give liberal term finance to the small units through the grant of refinance from the IDBI at concessional rates of interest. The IDBI, since its inception in 1964, has been granting refinance to the SFCs and the banks to enable them to assist the SSI units on concessional terms but the size of such refinance markedly increased in the latter half of 'seventies' (see Table 2).

The IDBI's refinance assistance to the small scale sector, moreover, assumed an increasing share in the period. The number of small units benefiting from refinance also rose during the period,

---

[2] The inadequacy of the reporting system becomes evident here as the banks reported the number of borrowing units to have been over 800,000 in 1980 while the Ministry of Industry's report cited earlier puts the number of registered SSI units at 454,000.

Table 2

Assistance Sanctioned by IDBI to Small Scale Sector (1964–65-1983–84)

Year (ending June)	Total Assistance to SSI by Refinance and Bills Rediscounting (Rs. million)	Aggregate Assistance by IDBI (Rs. million)	Share of SSI in Total Assistance by IDBI (%)	SSI Units Assisted (No.)	Average Per Unit Refinance Assistance to SSI Units (Rs.)
1964–65 to 1969–70	94	2,989	3.2	1,012	92,885
1970–71 to 1975–76	2,204	11,503	19.2	19,042	115,744
1976–77 to 1981–82	20,390	63,000	32.4	225,492	90,424
1982–83 to 1983–84	15,517	46,403	33.4	121,645	127,559
Total	38,205	123,895	30.8	367,191	104,046

Source: IDBI *Annual Report*, 1983–84, Table 3.3.

particularly during the latter half of the seventies. Nevertheless, it is to be noted that the number of units benefiting from refinance was much below 100,000 during even the later years. If this number is juxtaposed with the total number of registered units (596,000) at the end of March 1983, it is obvious that the benefits of refinance from the IDBI have not been distributed widely. The number of units benefiting from refinance has also to be seen in relation to the total number of small scale units having borrowal accounts with commercial banks (about 800,000 in 1980). At the same time, it has to be borne in mind that at least about 25 per cent of the registered units would not be functioning and that refinance is provided selectively—more in backward areas than in metropolitan cities—and that not all units are eligible. Moreover, there is reason to believe that relatively developed states continued to secure a sizeable share in the IDBI's refinance assistance; in fact, the figures from 1979–80 to 1982–83 show that around one-third of the IDBI refinance was disbursed.in three industrially advanced states (Maharashtra, Gujarat and Tamil Nadu).

The State Financial Corporations have been, during the period under survey, the principal state level financial institution catering to the term loan requirements of the small scale enterprises. The commercial banks also have been supplying term loans to the small scale units, but this constitutes a small part of their total financial assistance to the SSI sector units. Total outstanding term credit to small scale units from the commercial banks stood at Rs. 5,542 million at the end of June 1981 (excluding term credit to small road transport operators). On the other hand, the gross bank credit outstanding to the SSI sector from fifty banks (which account for about 95 per cent of gross bank credit) was at Rs. 54,120 million at the end of March 1984 and at Rs. 34,060 million at the end of June 1981. The SFCs' assistance disbursed during the four years, 1980–81 to 1983–84, to the SSI (excluding SRTOs) was Rs. 1,533.9, Rs. 2,107.1, Rs. 2,911.0, and Rs. 3,161.2 million, respectively, their cumulative disbursements at the end of March 1984 having been Rs. 16,096.5 million. These figures are quite impressive, but the share of the SSI in aggregate financial assistance disbursed by all the financial institutions in the country just amounted to about 9.5, 10.2, 12.3 and 11.0 per cent respectively, in the four years 1980–81 to 1983–84.

Credit to Small Units—The RBI Survey, 1977

After the general review of the assistance from the financial institutions towards term loans for creation of fixed assets and from the banks for working capital, we will now examine the position regarding the individual units. The Reserve Bank of India conducted a country-wide survey[3] of all bank assisted small scale industrial units during 1977–78, the results of which throw a good deal of light on the situation of the small scale units generally and vis-a-vis the institutional supply and availability of credit. This is, perhaps, the only reliable study of small scale industrial units carried out systematically in the country, though it is a little out-dated and covers only bank assisted units.

The survey covered a sample of 12,356 units with an original investment not exceeding Rs. 1 million in plant and machinery (against an estimated population of 233,218 bank assisted units in the country). Some important features were (*i*) 46.7 per cent of the

[3] Reserve Bank of India, Department of Statistics, 'Survey of Small Industrial Units, 1977,' *Statistical Report*, Volumes I & II, Bombay, 1979.

units were located in backward districts, so notified by the Planning Commission for purposes of concessional finance. The average per unit value of gross output was Rs. 172,879 in the backward districts as against Rs. 662,000 in other districts. Correspondingly, the average market value of all fixed assets was Rs. 43,924 and Rs. 141,184, respectively. The average value per unit of all loans outstanding was Rs. 34,802 in backward districts, as against Rs. 138,897 in other districts; of these, the institutional loans constituted 72.5 per cent and 70.5 per cent respectively. (ii) A little less than 17 per cent of the units were registered under the Factories Act. The average value of their gross output was Rs. 1.68 million against Rs. 0.17 million in respect of the unregistered units; the average market value of all fixed assets was Rs. 368,000 and Rs. 40,087, respectively. The average value of outstanding loans from all credit agencies was Rs. 352,117 for registered units and Rs. 36,830 for unregistered units, respectively, of which the loans outstanding from institutions constituted 70.2 per cent and 72.2 per cent, respectively. (iii) There were wide inter-state and also intra-state variations with respect to the units located in the metropolitan centres and elsewhere. At the all-India level, 28.2 per cent of the units reported to have non-institutional borrowings resulting in an average outstanding of Rs. 26,313, whereas in Maharashtra, a relatively developed state, 48.1 per cent units had non-institutional outstanding loans of the order of Rs. 61,665 per unit. For Bombay metropolis these figures were 63.9 per cent and Rs. 97,381, respectively. In the industrially backward states of Bihar and Madhya Pradesh, the proportion of units reporting non-institutional outstandings was 15.77 per cent and 22.98 per cent, with the per unit average amount outstanding at Rs. 17,692 and Rs. 9,050, respectively. It is thus evident that access to non-institutional agencies also was restricted in underdeveloped areas of the country. (iv) The wide spectrum of the small units covered in the survey becomes obvious from certain indicators of their size and operations, as brought out in Table 3 based on the classification of the surveyed units according to type of organisation. Clearly, sales-wise, the partnerships were ten times larger than the proprietary units and private limited companies had more than three times the sales of the partnership concerns. Such differences and variations are noticed more vividly by glancing at some selected financial ratios by the classification of units according to the original value of plant and

Table 3

Indicators of Size Variation of Surveyed Units According to Type of Organisation
(Average in Rs.)

Selected Indicators	Proprietary	Partnership	Private Limited Company	All Units
Percentage distribution	68.23	27.74	3.15	100.00
A.1 Capital and reserves	16,780	137,675	307,514	61,617
A.2 Borrowing: total	21,141	169,616	720,464	87,691
from financial institutions	2,671	10,738	47,309	6,778
B.1 Sundry creditors	9,861	103,966	620,445	57,944
B.2 Net fixed assets	19,327	121,007	475,307	63,840
C.1 Net sales	90,504	954,951	2,963,564	436,577
C.2 Gross profit	8,056	61,836	120,617	27,374

Source: Reserve Bank of India, Department of Statistics, 'Survey of Small Industrial Units, 1977,' *Statistical Report*, Vol. II, Tables 1.4 and 3.4, Bombay, 1979.

machinery (Table 4). It is seen that the ratio of short-term bank borrowings to inventories, the proportion of total bank borrowings to total net assets, total outside liabilities as a percentage of net worth as also the debt as a percentage of net worth show an unmistakable steady increase with size in terms of the value of plant and machinery. The units thus have a definite advantage as regards access to banks or outside agencies as they grow in size. Similarly, the units' ability to secure long-term funds increases from the lower to higher size, as witnessed from the steady rise in the percentage of long-term borrowings from banks and financial institutions together and from financial institutions separately to net fixed assets.

What is equally important is the somewhat limited dependence of the small unit on the whole, at about 10.6 per cent on financial institutions, in the context of the value of their net fixed assets. The poor reach of the financial institutions and their less than satisfactory contact with the small scale units is obvious from the fact that though they can advance up to 75 per cent of the value of fixed assets (that is on a 25 per cent margin), their advances on a long-term basis were merely 10.6 per cent against the value of net fixed assets of the small units. Evidently, neither the financial institutions nor the banks were fully meeting the long-term requirements of the small units (as seen from the difference between percentage shown against items 5 and 7, which was obviously met by borrowings from sources other than banks and financial institutions).

Small Scale Units and SFCs

The size-wise data on loans sanctioned by the different SFCs to the SSI sector are not available but the data for their total sanctions reveal the position (as shown in Table 5). Overall, a little over 5 per cent of the amount sanctioned by the SFCs went to loans below Rs. 50,000 each, even though 51 per cent of the total number of loans were sanctioned in this range. In fact, during the last four years (1980–81 to 1983–84), the amount of loans sanctioned in this size group as a proportion of total loans registered a steady fall; on the other hand, the share of the largest size group of loans above Rs. one million recorded an increase. Evidently, in the SFCs' portfolio, small loans up to Rs. 50,000 did not figure much. Contrary to expectation, the SFCs' thrust towards a relatively small size among the SSI enterprises has not yielded satisfactory results. Indeed, the

Table 4

Financial Ratios for Bank Assisted Units Classified According to Original Value of Plant and Machinery (1976–77)

Financial Ratios	Original Value of Plant of Machinery				
	Up to Rs.1,000	1,000 to 10,000	10,000 to 20,000	20,000 to 50,000	50,000 to 100,000
Percentage distribution of the units	34.75	21.15	11.70	13.71	7.69
1. Short-term bank borrowings as % of inventories	28.91	47.60	51.11	48.60	62.82
2. Total bank borrowings as % of total net assets	15.10	18.56	19.97	19.61	22.75
3. Total outside liabilities as % of net worth	220.7	155.7	170.4	172.8	234.8
4. Debt as % of net worth	37.25	27.75	36.46	43.95	51.71
5. Long-term borrowings from banks and financial institutions as % of net fixed assets	11.41	13.77	14.69	22.58	23.92
6. Long-term borrowings from financial institutions only as % of net fixed assets	—	2.28	3.48	6.32	7.34
7. Long-term borrowings as % of net fixed assets	70.50	28.87	27.57	37.17	38.29
8. Institutional loans outstanding as % of total amount of loans outstanding	61.14	65.05	70.28	68.65	68.86

	100,000 to 200,000	200,000 to 500,000	500,000 to one million	Above one million	All Units
Percentage distribution of the unit	5.03	3.87	1.79	0.27	100.00
1. Short term bank borrowings as % of inventories	64.00	68.19	78.64	65.56	61.12
2. Total bank borrowings as % of total net assets	22.93	26.29	29.07	24.48	23.62
3. Total outside liabilities as % of net worth	370.1	363.8	401.6	570.9	288.8
4. Debt as % of net worth	67.96	93.40	101.22	81.85	63.62
5. Long-term borrowings from banks and financial institutions as % of net fixed assets	27.36	36.55	33.44	22.48	28.09
6. Long-term borrowings from financial institutions only as % of net fixed assets	11.37	15.03	13.71	8.90	10.61
7. Long-term borrowings as % of net fixed assets	45.26	47.84	42.78	26.86	41.17
8. Institutional loans outstanding as % of total amount of loans outstanding	68.63	75.22	72.86	71.23	70.86

Source: Reserve Bank of India, Department of Statistics, 'Survey of Small Industrial Units, 1977,' *Statistical Report*, Vol. II, Tables 1.4 and 3.4, Bombay, 1979.

Table 5

Size-Wise Distribution of All SFCs Sanctions (Percentages)

Loan Amount Sanctioned	Amount				Cumulative up to March 1984	
	1980–81	*1981–82*	*1982–83*	*1983–84*	*No.*	*Amount*
Up to Rs. 50,000	7.78	5.58	4.57	4.42	51.22	5.10
50,000 – 200,000	18.42	15.58	19.24	18.70	29.88	19.42
200,000 – 500,000	19.27	20.47	18.14	16.18	11.08	19.63
500,000 – 1 million	15.95	14.98	16.07	14.70	4.17	17.38
Above one million	38.58	43.38	41.96	46.00	3.65	38.45
Total (Rs. million)	3,705	5,095	6,115	6,429	202,368 (No.)	35,674

Source: IDBI, *Report on Development Banking in India, 1983–84*, Appendix Table 72.

average amount of sanctions by all SFCs has been going up, which may in part be due to the falling value of the rupee. In the case of the Maharashtra SFC, the share of loans up to Rs. 50,000 was above 20 per cent in 1970–71 and 1971–72 but dropped to about 5 per cent in 1974–75 and thereafter fluctuated around 5–6 per cent till 1981–82 to rise a little to 7.5 per cent in 1982–83. The number of loans below Rs. 50,000 sanctioned by all SFCs consistently fell from 19,603 in 1980–81 to 14,930 in 1983–84, even though the total number of loans had increased up to 1982–83 and recorded a fall in 1983–84. Clearly, the SFCs' assistance to the smaller among the small scale sector has not been significant.

As between the different states, the SFCs' overall average assistance sanctioned varied markedly. During 1983–84, it was the highest in Madhya Pradesh (at Rs. 730,000) and lowest (at Rs. 130,000) in Uttar Pradesh. In Bihar, Delhi, Punjab and Himachal Pradesh it was over Rs. 500,000. One possible reason for the generally high overall average size of SFCs' sanction per unit is their limited penetration in rural areas. Except for Maharashtra and Gujarat, the SFCs do not have a wide network of branches; even in Maharashtra, though all districts are covered by the SFCs' branch offices, not many taluka centres have its offices. The limited branch office network of the SFCs may be due to historical reasons, but this would seem to be an important reason for their limited coverage of smaller or tiny[4] industrial units. Another possible reason may be the difficulties encountered by the tiny or smaller units in approaching more than one lending institution.

Whereas the SFCs meet the term loan needs, they are not equipped to handle the working capital credit requirements of the borrower, for which he has to approach the commercial bank. True, some of the SFCs have started a composite loan scheme for small borrowers, but this scheme has not apparently picked up. For the small industrial unit, its more urgent need is for working funds for which it would more likely tend to approach first the commercial bank and often would go without term loan assistance just to save the bother of approaching another specialised financial institution. As is known, the commercial banks' branch office network is much wider than that of the SFCs. The commercial bank's rural branch network has considerably deepened in the decade-and-a-half since the major bank nationalisation of 1969, with over 44,500 offices at the end of March 1984, as against hardly a few hundred offices of the SFCs. Consequently, the SFCs' capacity to reach the small (and particularly the tiny) and rural industrial enterprises is extremely restricted. It may be recalled that the gross bank credit outstanding to the SSI sector was Rs. 34,060 million in June 1981, of which term credit was of the order of Rs. 5,542 million; at about the same time in March 1981, all the SFCs' cumulative disbursements to small scale units (excluding small road transport operators) stood at 7,917 million. If it is borne in mind that regarding commercial banks, the data on outstandings exclude accounts with a credit limit up to Rs. 10,000 each, and that in case of SFCs, the figures represent their cumulative disbursements—and not outstandings which would be much smaller after deducting the recoveries—the performance of the SFCs in their assistance to the SSI units becomes poorer. To sum up, though the SFCs are designed as a specialised financial institution to cater mainly to the small sector, their penetration and reach has been much more limited than that of the commercial banks.

It may be pertinent to note here another feature of the SFCs and the banks—almost their entire assistance takes the form of loans. Of their cumulative disbursement of Rs. 24,707 million till the end of March 1984, Rs. 24,367 million (or 98.6 per cent) was in the form of loans, Rs. 141 million, Rs. 2 million and Rs. 197 million having

---

[4] 'Tiny' units are defined as those with an investment in machinery and equipment up to Rs. 150,000 and located in towns with a population up to 50,000.

been in the form of equity and preference, debentures and guarantees, respectively. It needs to be mentioned that these latter three forms of assistance operate invariably in favour of limited companies which are, more often than not, medium scale units. Proprietary and partnership units are not legally eligible for support of equity and preference, debentures and guarantees and the small scale units are most unlikely to be beneficiaries of this type of assistance. Consequently, small scale units have little possibility of availing funds from the capital market in any form other than loans.

The geographical spread of assistance sanctioned by many SFCs has substantially improved over the years. This can be illustrated by the position in Maharashtra. During the Third Plan period, 51.6 per cent of the sanctioned assistance in Maharashtra was accounted for by Greater Bombay metropolitan districts. Their share declined to 38.5, 21.2, 13.4 and 9 per cent during the Annual Plan years, Fourth Plan, Fifth Plan and the four years of the Sixth Plan ending 1982–83, respectively. The developing regions of Marathwada and Vidarbha correspondingly increased their shares in the state sanctions from 3.2 per cent to 11 per cent and 4.4 per cent to 17.7 per cent, respectively, from the Third to the Sixth Plan. In spite of this, in the last four years, there were four districts of the Marathwada region and three of the Vidarbha region where their share of the state's total sanctions was less than 1 per cent. It should be noted that these data pertain to all sanctions (including those to the non-SSI units). Thus, the thin geographical spread of assistance is still evident in the case of one of the leading states like Maharashtra as far as the SFCs are concerned.

Small Units in Pune and Aurangabad

It may be useful to cite some relevant information gathered in a field survey which I carried out during 1981–82 in Pune, a developed industrial centre and Aurangabad, a notified backward centre in Maharashtra. The report of this study is yet unpublished.[5] In all, 124 units in Aurangabad and 246 in Pune were covered. Loans from institutional sources as a percentage of total capital employed formed less than 50 per cent in 36 per cent of the units in Aurangabad as against 53 per cent units in Pune (Table 6).

[5] 'Role of Small Scale Industries in the Process of Industrialization,' under the Indo-Dutch Programme of Alternatives for Development, submitted to ICSSR, New Delhi, in December, 1983.

Table 6

Loan from Institutional Sources as Per Cent of Total Capital Employed in Specified Number of Units

Range of % Share of Institutional Loans in Capital Employed	Aurangabad	Pune
Up to 25 per cent	4	25
26 to 50 per cent	19	43
51 to 75 per cent	26	40
75+ per cent	14	19
Total no. of reporting units	63	127

Overall, it is seen that the institutional support was a little better in Aurangabad than in Pune. This could be explained by the fact that in the Aurangabad area, the emergence of the units has been recent since 1971–72, and mostly due to the spurt in concessional finance available from the banks and the financial institutions; on the contrary, in Pune, industrialisation started in the mid-fifties and a large number of small units apparently had not approached or had no access to banks and financial institutions and had been running without much of institutional support. This is also supported by the other set of recorded data. In Aurangabad, of the 62 units reporting, 51 had borrowings from the MSFC and 32 from the Marathwada Regional Development Corporation; in Pune, of the 91 reporting, 28 had borrowings from the MSFC and 12 from the Regional Development Corporation. It was noticed earlier in the RBI survey that non-institutional borrowings were relatively more common in developed states and centres, which corroborates the situation in Pune and Aurangabad during 1981–82.

It would seem that, generally, small scale enterprises have to rely largely on their own funds, as access to institutional as also non-institutional sources is quite limited to them. This observation is substantiated by the fact that the interest paid by them during 1976–77 as percentage of the value of their produce, according to the RBI survey of bank assisted units, was as low as 2.86 per cent. In contrast, this percentage was 3.49 for 1976–77 in the case of 415 large public limited companies in the RBI sample in its study of finances for public limited companies. The interest as a percentage of the value of production was seen to rise from units in the lower range of original value of plant and machinery to the higher ranges in the RBI survey; it was 1.96 per cent in the range of Rs. 1,000–10,000 and rose steadily to 4.15 per cent in the range of Rs. 500,000–1 million.

Other Sources of Funds

Obviously, as the size of operations becomes large, the entrepreneur has better chances to borrow both in the organised and the traditional capital or money markets. Technically, it is possible to argue that these low interest payments might be due to non-payment of interest or default among small units. But there is no evidence to suggest that default in smaller units is more than in large units. Secondly, as seen earlier, total outside liabilities as a percentage of net worth were less in the lower value of plant and machinery ranges. One would normally expect that the cost of borrowing will be high in the small scale (which is in the unorganised sector) because of the risk that would be associated with lending to the small operators by the lenders. This was precisely the reason why the Government of India had to initiate the Credit Guarantee Scheme in 1960 under which banks were to be persuaded to assist the small scale units. In spite of the CGS, the advances of banks to the small sector remained almost negligible till bank nationalisation in 1969. Thus, the supposed high risk associated with small borrowers continues to be a factor influencing bank lendings.

The experience of recent years as regards mopping of savings of the community by large reputable companies in the form of even unsecured deposits suggests that funds are available with less difficulty to the large and established manufacturing companies. It is common knowledge that unsecured deposits with proprietary and partnership concerns in the small scale sector usually are available from a limited circle of friends and relatives, at rates of interest which compare favourably with the rate of dividend of reputable companies. Quite often it is possible that deposits with the proprietary and partnership concerns (or even private limited companies for that matter) are the own funds of the promoters or proprietors, placed under the category of 'deposit' with the firm so that interest on it can be charged to revenue. The other source of funds in the unorganised market for the small scale industry is unregistered money-lenders—professionals whose money is available at very high rates of interest (usually at least twice the banks' lending rates of interest). Unfortunately, no reliable data on the volume of such funds and the rates of interest at which these are availed of by the small scale units (both at the macro and micro levels) are available. Chit funds and finance corporations, which operate in important industrial and trading centres in south India, usually make their funds available to wholesale and retail traders as also to road transport operators but very small amounts, if any, are lent to small scale industrial units. To sum up, the non-institutional sources of funds for the small scale enterprises are first, the friends and relatives of the enterpreneurs and secondly, the unofficial unregistered money-lenders; in the former case, the funds are available on relatively easy terms while in the latter case, funds are advanced selectively but on much higher rates of interest, the cost of these funds often being prohibitive.

Summing up

We may now briefly highlight the general observations meriting attention. (*i*) The IDBI's refinance to the small scale sector has grown rapidly in recent years; nevertheless, the proportion of beneficiary units is small in relation to the registered units and the number of those having borrowal accounts with the banks. (*ii*) Drawing upon the results of the RBI's 1977 survey of the bank assisted units, wide variations between the size and operations of units are perceived as between backward districts and others, different states, registered and unregistered units, and so on. It is, nevertheless, clear that reliance on institutional sources increased with an increase in the size of units which is also true for non-institutional sources of funds. (*iii*) The State Financial Corporations have expanded their loaning activity, yet the smaller among the small scale units do not seem to figure prominently in the SFCs advances portfolio, probably because of less than adequate branch office network. The commercial banks, on the other hand, have been relatively better placed as regards assistance to the small scale sector. (*iv*) The small scale sector is obliged to rely considerably on non-institutional sources of funds at high rates of interest; the small units, moreover, have difficulty in access to even the non-institutional sources because of their weaknesses.

13 S.R. Hashim

Nature of Small Scale Industry and its Developmental Role

I

It has been widely believed, over a long period of time, that small scale industry, in its wider sense (including rural industry) has a special place in the Indian economy and its development. Of course, the role perceived for small scale industries and the nature of industries it refers to has been changing over time, but the importance attached to it in the developmental process remains.

In the late nineteenth and the early part of this century, the main concern of the Indian economic thinkers was protection of the artisan class from the onslaught of British industry, and indigenous industry was described as 'indigenous arts and manufactures'. Indigenous manufacturers were based on traditional technology and had lost ground against the products of large-scale mechanised British industry. British industry competed with indigenous industry not only on the strength of its superior technology but also on the powerful support of colonial rule which, through discriminatory fiscal and transport rate policies, encouraged the imports of manufacturers. In the light of this experience it was natural that protection and encouragement to the indigenous industries became an important item of the agenda of self-rule. And existing Indian industries were mostly traditional and comprising of small scale units. M.G. Ranade advocated 'state action in creating agro-industries like sugar refining, oil pressing, tobacco curing, silk rearing, etc., for which both the climate and the traditional skilled labour were available.'[1]

The Swadeshi movement was mainly directed towards the encouragement of Indian industries. Besides protection and encouragement to existing industries, Gopal Krishna Gokhale also emphasised modernisation of technology, and hence, 'training of selected Indians abroad and the promotion of industrial and technical education at home' was a very important item of his agenda of economic reforms.[2] It is worth noting here that till the early years of this century there was no effort at drawing a distinction between the small and the large units, traditional and modern units, and so on. The dichotomy was simple, i.e., indigenous vs. foreign industries. It so happened that indigenous industries were mostly in small units, and predominantly based on traditional technology, Gopal Krishna Gokhale had visualised that the growth of indigenous industries could not be brought about without modernising the technology.

The emphasis later shifted somewhat towards khadi and village industries (industries with traditional and manual techniques) with Mahatma Gandhi's ideal of a decentralised economic system and a self-reliant and self-contained village community and a more philosophical insight into the relation between man and machine. However, it was during this period (during and after the First World War) that some large scale industries, based on imported technology, came to be established in India—particularly in the area of sugar, textiles and steel. This gave rise to a continuing debate on small vs. large scale industries. The Sub-Committee on Manufacturing Industries, National Planning Committee, noted:

> In India... one school of thought lays greater emphasis on the development of large-scale industries on grounds of higher efficiency, low costs, uniformity of products, etc., while another school of thought lays greater emphasis upon the development of

[1] M.G. Ranade, *Essays on Indian Economics*, Madras, 1916 as quoted in V.B. Singh, From *Naoroji to Nehru*, New Delhi, Macmillan 1975, p. 49.
[2] Gopal Krishna Gokhale, Budget Speech of 1906 as quoted in V.B. Singh, *ibid.*, p. 84.

cottage industries for humanitarian and social reasons.[3]

The National Planning Committee resolved: 'We feel that by judicious adjustment it may be possible to establish a mutually beneficial cooperation between large scale and cottage industries as a whole.... We recommend that there should be a permanent Board of Research to go into the changing economics of large scale and cottage industries.'[4]

It may be noted from these quotations that the dichotomy adopted till then was 'cottage industries' (representing traditional technology) and large scale industries (representing modern technology), and there came to exist somewhat of an apologetic approach towards cottage industries, the justification for them being sought mainly on humanitarian and social grounds. Soon cottage and small scale industries came to be spoken of together and the emphasis shifted to 'scale' rather than 'technology'. The Industrial Policy Resolution of 1948 emphasised the importance of 'cottage and small scale industries' as these industries offered scope for individual, village or cooperative enterprise and a means for rehabilitating displaced persons. The Industrial Policy Resolution of 1956 sought to ensure, through state policy, that the small scale (or decentralised) sector acquired sufficient vitality to be self-supporting and its development was integrated with that of large scale industry. Considerable emphasis was given to the improvement and modernisation of the techniques of production. Thus we see a positive change in outlook. It was no longer the Gandhian question of man vs. machine but simply a technical question of small vs. large scale, where small scale had the distinct advantage of the possibility of diffusion of ownership.

In the Mahalanobis model, which became the basis of the Second Five Year Plan, the role of small scale industries was visualised as that of meeting a large part of the demand for consumer goods with little investment, on the assumption of a very low capital-output ratio for this sector. The induced demand, which was to be generated through large investments in heavy and large scale industries, was expected to be met by the additional output generation in the small scale sector. In the process of additional output generation, a high

[3] *Report of the Sub-Committe on Manufacturing Industries*, National Planning Committee, Bombay, Vora & Co., 1947, p. 55.

[4] *Ibid.*, Resolution No. 22. p. 82.

employment multiplier effect was also expected under the assumption that labour-output ratios in small scale industries were much higher. The Second Five Year Plan adopted protective measures and also emphasised constant efforts at upgrading the technology and improving the competitive strength of this sector. Accordingly, reservation of certain areas of production for village and small scale industries, differential excises, gradual and guided technological advance, organising village artisans and industrial units in co-operatives, and the establishment of industrial estates formed part of this programme. In the words of D.R. Gadgil:

These ideas were worked out most fully in relation to cotton textiles industry.... A factor which has emerged in unexpected strength, in the meanwhile, has been that of powerloom. In a sense this provides now an important link in the programme of technological and economic transformation.[5]

Gadgil made this observation in 1968. This trend, especially in powerloom, has gained even more strength since then.

Thus, there came to exist a mixed outlook on the small sector in industry. The need for protective measures was emphasised, clearly with reference to the cottage industries and traditional arts and crafts, which still employed a substantially large number of people. The assumptions of low capital and high labour intensity of the small sector led to the belief that we could have large scale capital-intensive industries for producing capital and basic intermediate goods and small scale labour-intensive industries for producing most of the consumer goods (Mahalanobis model). There was yet another justification for the small sector, and perhaps a stronger and much more valid justification in the context of development, though often overshadowed in discussions about the other two. This was repeatedly emphasised by D.R. Gadgil:

Creation of a small number of centres of advanced industry in a country fails to have any significant impact on the bulk of the rural masses and areas in the rest of the country and does not

[5] D.R. Gadgil's speech on 'Role of Handicrafts in the National Economy in Developing Countries' (1968) published in *Writings and Speeches of Professor D.R. Gadgil on Planning and Development*, Gokhale Institute of Studies No. 62, New Delhi, Orient Longmans Ltd., 1973

initiate a process of transformation which embraces within any reasonable time-span the whole of the country. In addition, it...often leads to the development of a phenomenon often described as dual economy.... Everything thus points to the desirability, nay, urgency, of initiating widespread industrial development in all regions of the country which will prevent accentuation of dualistic features.... This I take to be the justification and purpose of any programme of rural industrialisation.[6]

The factor intensity and economic efficiency assumptions about the small scale sector have been more systematically examined. Dhar and Lydall[7] came to the conclusion that small factories used more capital and more labour per unit of output than larger factories. From the point of view of saving capital, medium or large multi-shift factories gave the best results and small factories usually the worst. On the issue of decentralisation, their opinion was that small modern (i.e., modern technology based) factories could not be forced out into rural areas, where the necessary facilities of trade, communications and finance were lacking, and where enterprise and skilled labour were scarce. They thought that the pioneers in decentralisation should be larger enterprises—smaller firms would follow when a favourable environment was created.

On economic efficiency considerations, J.C. Sandesara came to conclusions similar to those of Dhar and Lydall: 'Small units have lower output, lower wage and lower surplus each per worker; and also that they have lower output and lower surplus each per unit of capital than large units'.[8]

Thus, we are able to trace three clear lines of thought about the place of small scale industries. One stems from protectionist ideology, and emphasises the need for protection, particularly to rural industries and traditional handicrafts (industries mostly based on traditional technology). In spite of the emergence of an organised modern industrial sector over the last three decades, enough employment has not been created to move people significantly away from agriculture and traditional industries. And, hence, there is still a place

---

[6] D.R. Gadgil, 'Notes on Rural Industrialization' (1963), in *Planning and Economic Policy in India*, Gokhale Institute of Politics and Economics, Poona, 1972, p. 346.

[7] P.N. Dhar and H.F. Lydall (1961), pp. 84–85.

[8] J.C. Sandesara (1969), p. 63.

for this line of thought. The second views the place of the small scale industries sector in terms of production function efficiency, i.e., capital saving, employment generation, resource utilisation, etc., and draws negative conclusions for small scale industries vis-a-vis the large scale industries sector. Sometimes there is an attempt to fuse these two approaches together in the framework of social benefit-cost analysis,[9] but then, given the assumptions involved in measuring various non-quantifiable benefits and costs, the conclusions are of a mixed nature. The third line of thought, relatively less explored empirically, relies on the spread-effect potential of small scale industries and this is an important developmental role which the small scale sector could play.

It is also clear from this brief review that the perception of the role of small scale industries depends very much on the perception of the nature of small scale industries.

II

From the point of view of identifying the growth potential and developmental linkages of the small scale industry sector, two of its characteristics are important—the technology (modern or traditional) and organisation (formal or informal). In fact, the technology and the form of organisation are mostly related. The production units with modern technology are also, by and large, those which belong to the organised (formal) sector.

A broad identification of the 'modern' and 'traditional' technology could be made with 'mechanised' and 'non-mechanised' technology, like powerloom and handloom technology. Another identification could be in terms of the nature of products. Modern technology-based small scale units would be producing almost the same products which large scale units could also produce—for example, cycle tyres or sewing machines. The only difference would be that of 'scale'. The traditional technology based industries would be producing very different products, for example, *gur* instead of sugar, or khadi instead of mercerised cloth.

The small scale industries, based on traditional technology, can

[9] For example, the study Small Scale Sugarcane Processing Industry in India, by H.H. de Haan, Centre for Development Planning, Erasmus University, Rotterdam (unpublished).

be divided into two distinct groups. One group is of those industries which are based on traditional art and craft. Examples of industries in this group are papier-mache and embroidery work, carpet weaving, brass work, sandalwood work, silk, zari, chikan work, etc. This is the group of industries which is highly labour-intensive. Technology is, by and large, traditional, though the use of electricity may have improved the technique in some cases. The workers have a skill which is inherited from family traditions or is acquired through a long period of training. The product is artistic, has high value in elite circles and has export markets. But the workers in the industry earn a living only marginally above the subsistence level.[10] Production is mostly organised on a household basis. The organisation of marketing is a crucial factor, which accounts for a rather large differential between the purchaser's price and the producer's price. The middleman plays an important role. Government-sponsored organisations have not succeeded in replacing the middlemen. Cooperatives have not succeeded. The Khadi and Village Industries Board has helped in sustaining some of these industries, both by easing the supply of raw-materials and by creating some extra marketing channels. Though these industries can be sustained and there is no threat of their extinction, the growth inducing potential of these industries is limited.

Then there is the less fortunate group of traditional industries which mostly supplied the consumer products of local needs. Examples are *gur* and *khandsari*, shoe-making, pottery, traditional weaving, and so on. Their products have to compete with the products of modern technology. Most of them have become extinct or are near extinction (like pottery). A few which have survived have done so by crossing over to the modern technology sector (textiles, for example) or due to certain special advantages, subsidies and concessions. Shoe-making, for example, revived in the traditional sector because the bigger shoe companies started marketing these products under their own brand names, while also imposing on these household units a certain degree of standardisation and quality control. This has happened mainly because the economies of scale of production in large scale organisations were offset by the unmanageability of organised factory labour. This is now happening in textiles also where the scale effect is not so important and dis-

---

[10] See, for example, T. S. Papola (1982), pp. 40–42.

persed powerlooms can produce as fine a product as the factories, thus avoiding the cost of large scale organisation and enjoying the concessions and privileges of small scale units. Their products can still be marketed under well-known brand names. Except for those traditional small scale industries which have either transformed or modernised their technology (and thus become a part of modern small scale sector) or have come under the umbrella of the organised sector, the rest have hardly any growth potential or even the capacity to survive.

In the sequence of industrial development, the industries based on traditional arts and crafts and other rural industries using traditional technology preceded the development of large scale industries based on modern technology. For some time the development of technology and enlargement of scale of production went hand-in-hand, in the sense that every advancement in technology was accompanied by an increase in the most efficient size. In the course of time, scale and technology, together, produced another trend of vertical disintegration of industrial processes and higher and higher levels of specialisation under different establishments. Thus, from the stage of raw materials to the stage of finished products, numerous specialised processes are involved and are handled by different plants. With this development, the scale advantage has shifted more and more towards the basic processing, i.e., lower order processes (processes which are nearer to raw materials than to finished products). Examples are smelting of metallic ores, cracking of naphtha, and so on. Thus we have basic processing industries (like basic metal, basic chemicals, fertilisers and petrochemicals), where scale advantage in production is tremendous. In the category of industries with a high degree of scale advantage, we should also include heavy engineering industries and electricity generation.

Proceeding from the lower order processes to higher order process, the scale advantage seems to diminish. Sometimes the highest order process involves mere assembly, as in electronics, and here the scale advantage is insignificant. This has created a new scope for modern technology based small scale industries.

If the sequence of development described above is broadly accepted, then it is clear that the modern-technology based small industry sector is not just a modernised version of the traditional industries, but has its genesis in the modern technological and industrial development as a whole and, as such, has vast potential for expansion. What can be organised on a small scale can, of course, also be organised on a large scale, perhaps, with certain advantages in financial and market management. But the point is that at a stage of processing where production technology is neutral to scale, the developmental objective is better served by organising the production at smaller scale, as it has two great advantages: (*a*) diffusion of ownership—thus involving a larger number of people in entrepreneurial efforts, and (*b*) dispersion in space—thus inducing growth processes over a larger area. But to achieve these objectives, a deliberate push to the small sector will have to be given and maintained for quite some time, partly to counter the financial and trading advantages of the larger organisations and partly to facilitate the provision of basic infrastructure specially in the rural areas.

III

A number of propositions have been made in the foregoing discussion. While these propositions are based on a general understanding of the nature of small scale industry sector in India, it would be interesting to consider some empirical evidence. What follows is based on a study of the modern technology based small scale industry units in districts Vadodara and Kheda of Gujarat.[11] While all the details of the study cannot be presented in this paper, summary results reflecting some of the propositions are presented here.

The study was based on data pertaining to low voltage industrial consumers of electricity obtained from the records of Gujarat Electricity Board (GEB). These industrial consumers cover small scale industrial units with installations of around 100 horsepower or less. The data were available for the years 1961–80. Information pertaining to the year of connection, load connected, nature of activity, annual consumption of electricity and location of the unit were available from the GEB records. In total there were 3,320 electrified small industry units in Vadodara and 6,615 units in Kheda. Information for Vadodara district excluded the municipal limits of Baroda city, as the units within the city were not supplied electricity

[11] S.R. Hashim, M.M. Dadi, Atul Sarma and Avtar Singh, *Small-Scale Industries—Their Role in Development*, A Research Project sponsored by ICSSR under Indo-Dutch collaborative Programme of Research (Final Report, 1985).

by GEB directly. Another source of primary data on the nature and the working of these industrial units was a field investigation of sample units out of the GEB population. The sample covered 110 units in Vadodara and 200 units in Kheda. As far as the two districts are concerned, Vadodara is more urbanised, but the urban population is largely concentrated in and around the city of Baroda. Vadodara also has a heavy concentration of large-scale industries, mainly around Baroda city. Kheda is less urbanised, but the urban population is more evenly distributed over a larger number of small and medium towns all over the district. Kheda is also more densely populated and its agriculture is highly developed. In fact, it is the best agricultural district of Gujarat.

A proposition was made that it would be more useful to identify and classify small scale industries on the basis of technology. In this context modern technology could be identified with reference to the use of electrically operated machines. For electricity using industrial units, the load connected in terms of horsepower (HP) also seems to be a stable and easily identifiable measure of size. The coefficient of correlation between the value of machinery and equipment and HP connected was found to be significant for both the districts. Thus, even if it was important to give representation to value of capital in defining the scale, the HP of the connected load would be a good proxy to that value.

The spatial distribution of small scale units in Vadodara district was highly concentrated, while it was even in Kheda. Between 1970 and 1980, there was a tendency for the units to spread out in both the districts. Thus, it was concluded that where the development of small scale industries was based on agricultural development, it had a tendency to be more evenly spread.

In the context of development, the role of small scale industry is also visualised as that of encouraging first generation entrepreneurs. As a part of the sample survey, questions on whether the specific business was hereditary or started by the present owner, and on reasons for starting the business were asked. In district Vadodara, nearly 83 per cent of the units reported that the business was started by the present owners, and in Kheda the corresponding percentage was 68. Excluding the 'food' group in Kheda, for other groups of industries the percentages of self-started units varied between 70 to 100. Thus, a majority of industrial units in both the districts were started by the present owners, and this tendency was stronger among the non-traditional industry groups. It conforms to the hypo-thesis that the small scale industry encourages first generation entre-preneurs. In majority of the cases, the reason for going into the business was that 'business' was the hereditary profession. Keeping in mind the role of family traditions in the country, it is significant that nearly a sixth of the units reported special training or an artisanship background as the reason for going into the business. This, too, is an important developmental role which small scale industries can perform.

A higher proportion of hired workers is characteristic of a formally organised modern technology-based small scale sector, while a larger proportion of family workers is characteristic of the traditional sector.[12] The case of powerloom textiles is an exception as, in terms of technology, it is a modern sector, but has mostly emerged due to the entrepreneurship of the traditional weavers, and still retains the traditional characteristic of a work force consisting mainly of family members. The overall average number of workers per unit, in our sample, was 7.6 for Vadodara and 12.4 for Kheda, and the range was between 3 to 32 workers per unit for various industry groups. The proportion of 'hired workers' in both the districts varied be-tween 62 to 97 per cent, with the only exception of a textile group in Kheda where over 80 per cent of the workers were family members. The small number of workers in the units, who were counted as family workers, were in fact the owner-managers, generally at the rate of one per unit.

In both the districts, the wages of unskilled workers varied bet-ween Rs. 200 to Rs. 300 per month. The reference year was 1980. Skilled labour got wages a little over Rs. 300 per month and clerical staff mostly between Rs. 400 and Rs. 500. One single exception in case of skilled labour was that of diamond-cutters who netted, on an average, Rs. 1,500 per month. Diamond cutters are paid on a piece-rate basis.

It is generally assumed that the small scale units operate in a localised market. However, in the modern small scale sector, firms are coming up which have access to a state level or national market. Out of 108 units in Vadodara, a significant number of units reported district level (20), state level (25) and national level (13) markets. Similarly, out of 188 units in Kheda, significant numbers reported

---

[12] For these and other characteristics in respect to wage-rate, the nature of problems faced, etc., in the traditional small scale sector, see T.S. Papola, *op. cit.*

district level (34), state level (35) and national level (28) markets and three units even reported export markets. The market channels for disposing of their products and for purchasing the main inputs may reveal interesting characteristics about the methods of business operation of these units. In terms of the number of units, the dominant channel for the disposal of the product in Vodadara was the trader-wholesaler, followed by cooperatives, producer-processor and ultimate consumer, in that order. The pattern in Kheda was different, where the dominant channel was the ultimate consumer. In terms of the value of the product, the dominant channel in Vadodara became cooperatives followed by the trader-wholesaler, whereas in Kheda the dominant channel was the wholesale-trader followed by the ultimate consumer. Thus, on the whole, the dominant channels appeared to be the wholesale dealer and cooperatives, though local agro-based demand seemed to play an important role in Kheda. In the case of purchase of main inputs, cooperatives and wholesale dealers in that order emerged as the most important channels in both the districts.

In order to know the problems faced by small-scale units, the entrepreneurs were asked to list the problems in the order of priority. Shortage of power emerged as the most important and dominant problem faced in both the districts (55 per cent of the units in Vadodara and 64 per cent in Kheda). Significantly, a shortage of skilled labour was reported to be an important problem in Vadodara (14 per cent of the units). The problem seemed to be more of the high rate of turnover of skilled labour in Vadodara. Significantly, 'finance' and 'market'—which are generally assumed to be the most acute problems of small-scale units—did not appear to be important. Power is a problem which even the larger scale industrial units face.

Thus, on the whole, it may be concluded that the modern technology based small scale industry sector has a significant role to play in development. Particularly when small scale industry development follows the lead of agricultural development, then the industries are more widely spread in space. The small scale industry sector does encourge first generation entrepreneurs, particularly those who have special training or an artisanship background. The modern small scale sector is more formally organised and mostly depends on workers employed from outside the family. Wages paid to workers are above the statutory minimum. These industrial units have access to wider markets, and use the well-established market channels. Marketing and finance do not appear to be significant problems. Thus, this sector has the potential of involving in the development process, those rural areas and towns which do not benefit from large-scale industrial complexes, and those sections of the population which are not capable of undertaking large-scale entrepreneurship.

V Government Policy

14 J.C. Sandesara

Small Industry Development Programmes in India—Efficacy, Explanations and Lessons: Some Field Studies

I. Introduction

The Government of India, the state and Union Territory governments, and the agencies and institutions sponsored by them have for long been pursuing a policy of protecting and promoting small industry. Over time, these programmes have become more numerous, more varied and more detailed. These relate to information, consultancy, entrepreneurship development, training, modernisation and technology support, industrial estates, raw materials, marketing, finance, reservation, ancillary development, and so on.[1]

[1] For the latest information on these programmes, see D. Nagaïya, *Small Industries Development Programmes in India*, Hyderabad, National Institute of Small Industry Extension Training, 1982.

The objective of these programmes is to help improve the efficiency and viability of the small industrial units, and their rationale stems from their qualifications to subserve one or more of the various socio-economic objectives of society (such as, promotion of employment, saving of capital, dispersal of industry, diffusion of entrepreneurship, and so on). A number of these programmes have been evaluated, some of them repeatedly. The industrial policy statement of the Government of India announced on 23 July 1980 has this to say on this subject:

> In the past, numerous incentives had been provided to industries from time to time. It is government's considered view that all incentive given to industry must be performance oriented. It is, therefore, proposed that a regular periodic assessment be made of the impact of these incentives, to the extent to which they have fulfilled their initial purpose. Unless it is apparent that the purpose is being served, government will review the system of incentives.

This is an essay in such an evaluation. The programmes dealt with here include long-term finance (Section II), reservation (Section III), use and significance of incentives, (Section IV) and industrial estates (Section V). We also deal with one related issue, namely, the aggregate value of incentives (Section VI). The last section (VII) contains policy suggestions to reorient the programmes.

This paper is based largely on the studies of small scale units at Bombay, Hyderabad and Jaipur which we organised and conducted during the late seventies. It draws heavily on them for which, in general, no references are made here.[2] As this paper is confined to presenting a summary view, for details reference to those (as also to other original sources cited in the notes) will be necessary. All the same, a brief sketch of the scope and method of the field studies (see Note 2, Publication 1) is appended.

[2] These studies are J.C. Sandesara (1982), (hearafter Publication 1) and *Small Industry in India*, Ahmedabad, Gujarat Economic Association, 1980 (hereafter Publication 2). The material for Sections II, III, IV and VII is taken from Publication 1 and that of Section V mostly from Publication 2. The latter, in turn, is taken from a number of sources. These sources, as well as the source on which Section VI is based, are specified in the respective sections. It may be added that a summary of Publication 1 had appeared under the title 'Incentives and their Impact—Some Studies on Small Industry,' in *Economic and Political Weekly*, Bombay, 27 November 1982.

II. Long-Term Finance

Here, we examine two hypotheses. The first is that the units which have received long-term finance from the State Financial Corporations (assisted units) might be expected to show better performance than other (non-assisted) units at a point of time.

This hypothesis is examined in terms of seven ratios of profitability, productivity and capital intensity (specified in Table 1). The details regarding coverage of units and the definitions of the terms employed are also given there.

We may infer that while the assisted units had higher labour productivity, higher surplus per worker and higher average wage than non-assisted units in a majority of industries, the latter had higher profitability, higher capital productivity and higher surplus per unit of capital than the former in a majority of industries. Thus, in general, while the assisted units showed more efficient use of, and better rewards to, labour, the non-assisted units showed a more efficient use of, and better reward to, capital. Also, on four or more of the total of seven ratios, only in four of the twelve industries did the assisted units show better performance than the non-assisted units.

Our second hypothesis is that the assisted units may be expected to show improved performance over time, and that this performance may be expected to be better than that of the non-assisted units.

This hypothesis is examined in terms of growth rates on five indicators, namely, total assets, fixed assets, equity capital, output and value added. The growth rates are expressed in terms of per cent per annum (compound) with reference to the first and the last years of the four/five year period. Details are given in Table 2.

It is seen that the assisted units showed positive growth rates on two or more growth indicators of total assets, fixed assets, equity capital, output and value added in all the ten industries for the last four-five years. In five industries for which a relative picture of growth of the assisted and the non-assisted units could be attemped, the growth rates in three were lower and in two higher in the assisted as compared to the non-assisted units.

How do we explain these findings? First, we must remember that the small industry market is a leading species of a genius of what Joe S. Bain calls the 'atomistic market'. In such a market, the suppliers compete with one another, rather fiercely, and apart from actual

Table 1

Financial and Economic Ratios of Assisted and Non-Assisted Units

City/Year/Industry	Number of Units	Profits to Equity Capital (%)	Value Added to Total Assets	Value Added Per Worker	Surplus to Total Assets	Surplus Per Worker	Wages Per Worker	Total Assets Per Worker
1	2	3	4	5	6	7.	8	9
I. Bombay (1976–77)	39							
1. *Metal Products*								
Assisted	8	14.25	0.21	9,198	0.11	4,793	4,073	44,470
Non-Assisted	5	6.46	0.22	6,454	0.04	1,258	4,603	28,891
2. *Machinery and Spare Parts*								
Assisted	9	21.39	0.40	14,090	0.09	3,194	10,582	35,450
Non-assisted	4	–114.59	0.06	1,088	–0.19	3,530	4,296	18,316
3. *Paper and Paper Products*								
Assisted	9	–3.19	0.13	5,244	0.04	1,601	3,506	40,433
Non-assisted	4	42.26	0.23	6,217	0.12	3,279	2,471	27,338
II. Hyderabad (1977–78)	59							
1. *Industrial Fasteners*								
Assisted	4	8.62	0.18	9,445	0.10	5,508	3,893	53,476
Non-assisted	3	20.44	0.31	6,798	0.14	2,969	3,414	21,582
2. *Printing Press*								
Assisted	2	–8.73	0.36	3,975	–0.03	–299	4,174	10,985
Non-assisted	6	6.36	0.21	6,147	0.07	2,131	3,784	29,223

3. *Chemicals and Pharmaceuticals*								
Assisted	7	23.90	0.21	11,100	0.14	7,039	3,969	51,820
Non-assisted	7	24.12	0.32	11,465	0.11	3,905	7,426	35,554
4. *Machinery and Spare Parts*								
Assisted	14	25.93	0.36	9,348	0.12	3,241	6,044	26,357
Non-assisted	16	48.31	0.35	9,684	0.13	3,718	5,731	28,006
III. **Jaipur (1978–79)**	40							
1. *Industrial Fasteners*								
Assisted	4	−1.37	0.16	5,520	0.06	2,237	3,270	34,410
Non-Assisted	2	32.20	0.27	12,905	0.17	7,950	4,850	48,032
2. *Metal Products*								
Assisted	5	20.68	0.28	16,174	0.14	7,776	8,245	57,343
Non-assisted	9	36.27	0.31	9,062	0.16	4,740	4,164	29,685
3. *Electricals and Electronics*								
Assisted	3	45.06	0.24	15,990	0.19	12,746	3,184	67,700
Non-assisted	5	80.23	0.41	9,079	0.27	5,949	2,974	21,878
4. *Plastic Products*								
Assisted	2	45.48	0.28	27,738	0.24	23,252	4,411	97,989
Non-assisted	3	5.19	0.19	4,109	0.05	1,192	2,909	22,155
5. *Chemicals*								
Assisted	4	−15.52	0.15	6,088	.0330	1,138	4,403	41,945
Non-assisted	3	−12.87	0.10	5,561	.0336	1,812	3,688	54,004

The items included in the terms used here and the other tables are briefly described.

(a) *Assets side*: The term fixed assets used here includes land, building, plant, and machinery, furniture and fixtures and other assets (such as office equipment and vehicles). They relate to net fixed assets, arrived at after deducting accumulated depreciation from their value at the time of installation or purchase. *Total Assets* relate to the net fixed assets, total current assets and other assets, such as deposits for water and electric connections.

(continued)

(b) *Liabilities:*   *Equity Capital* includes proprietary funds—paid up capital and reserves.

(c) *Profits and Loss side:*   Output is arrived at by adding to net sales (gross sales less value of goods received, allowance, discount and excise) the differential value of closing and opening stocks of finished and semi-finished products, other income and work done for others. Value added is the net income produced by the units, and is arrived at by deducting the expenses of basic raw materials, power, other materials, miscellaneous expenses, depreciation and work done for others from the value of output. *Wages* include wages and salaries, benefits paid to employees as also It is thus the sum of rent, wages, interest and profits. It is thus the sum of rent, wages, interest and profits, and it thus includes interest and management remuneration. Surplus is defined as value added less rent and less wages, and it thus includes interest and management remuneration. Surplus is defined as value added less rent and less wages, and are inclusive of taxes and provisions profits. Profits are the residual item arrived at by deducting interest from surplus, and are inclusive of taxes and provisions for taxes.

(d) *Workers:*   Includes all workers, including owners and members of the family along with workers receiving wages and salaries in cash or kind.

Table 2
Growth Rate of Continuing Assisted and Non-Assisted Units (Per cent per annum, Compound)

City/Years/Industry	Number of Units	Total Assets	Fixed Assets	Equity Capital	Output	Value Added
1	2	3	4	5	6	7
I. Bombay (1972–73 to 1976–77)	23					
1. *Metal Products*						
Assisted	7	6.7	1.7	3.6	–1.41	–5.7
2. *Machinery and Spare Parts*						
Assisted	6	2.5	–0.7	10.2	8.9	4.9
3. *Paper and Paper Products*						
Assisted	7	16.3	14.0	11.3	9.4	11.2
Non-assisted	3	16.3	34.2	12.9	14.1	–5.2
II. Hyderabad (1974–75 to 1977–78)	19					
1. *Chemicals and Pharmaceuticals*						
Assisted	2	14.9	1.9	15.6	125.8	*
Non-assisted	4	3.3	—	–3.0	6.0	5.6
2. *Machinery and Spare Parts*						
Assisted	8	5.6	8.0	6.5	13.1	12.8
Non-assisted	5	32.3	16.9	6.7	37.3	33.8

* Here the rate of growth could not be worked out because of the data problem.

(continued)

City/Years/Industry	Number of Units	Total Assets	Fixed Assets	Equity Capital	Output	Value Added
1	2	3	4	5	6	7
III. Jaipur (1974–75 to 1978–79).	21					
1. *Industrial Fasteners*						
Assisted	2	3.6	−2.4	−0.9	6.2	0.3
2. *Metal Products*						
Assisted	2	3.7	−4.5	1.0	20.5	10.5
Non-assisted	5	9.7	3.0	5.6	14.1	17.0
3. *Agricultural Implements*						
Assisted	4	4.6	−4.5	8.3	−7.6	−32.4
4. *Casting and Rolling*						
Assisted	3	12.6	5.1	10.9	23.7	−3.0
5. *Chemicals*						
Assisted	3	5.3	5.3	16.9	24.8	2.1
Non-assisted	2	4.2	1.8	−2.6	−16.9	−24.2

competition, they are also exposed to potential competition—thanks to easy entry. Secondly, people are also known to enter this sector for non-pecuniary reasons. Some may prefer the status of an independent worker or even an employer with a low income to that of an employee with a higher income on the consideration that it is better to rule in hell than to serve in heaven. Some others are known, even at some personal, pecuniary sacrifice to provide employment to members of the family who are otherwise unemployable or could be employed less profitably outside the family business. Third, some others may be there transitionally as if in ante-room waiting for a job in the organised sector.

To this list must be added the weight of certain well-known facts that mark the present scene of the small industry which is saddled with considerable excess capacity. Not all of the small industry is growth-prone. Nor is it efficient in the market sense or in the sense of being capital-saving in relation to income/employment.

The assistance programmes tend to make the entry easier in an area where even otherwise, for the above reasons, there may already be too many cooks in the kitchen. And, the point is not met by saying that this may not happen if assistance is restricted, at least for some time, to the existing units. For the improved profitability or reduced losses of such units, consequent upon the assistance, may tend to make this sector more attractive so that it becomes more conducive to entry than before. Moreover, often the criteria employed by the assisting agencies to judge their own effectiveness is the number of units assisted and the amount of assistance given so that there is temptation to assist new, rather than the established, units; and to give the units once selected more assistance than what may be absolutely necessary.[3]

[3] In this context, the following quotation is of interest: 'Some of the state authorities—and their associated small industries' officers—have felt it their responsibility not only to give advice to entrepreneurs looking for a suitable line of investment, but also to go out and recruit new entrepreneurs from amongst people who were not at present in industry, so as to claim that they have established entirely "new" small scale enterprises. This is, in part, a reflection of the idea that there are too few small firms. But it is also a reflection of an actual shortage of local entrepreneurs in the more backward areas. In these areas we have found entrepreneurs in the industrial estates who were previously local shopkeepers or cultivators who had been persuaded by the local small industries' officers to move into industry. As an inducement to do this, such people had usually been offered every possible assistance. The amount of effort put in by officials in order to create new entrepreneurs is sometimes out of all

As a corollary, we may note that very often assistance, given easily and without proper and rigorous scrutiny, excessively or cheaply, tends to be 'wasted' by the recipient units in the sense that it is used excessively not merely in the sense of being employed more than absolutely necessary, but also as a substitute for some other factor. Thus, for example, when capital is so available it may be used as a substitute for labour. Such a substitution runs counter to the objective of promoting employment. It is all the more regrettable when it is not accompanied by superior performance of assisted units even on private account.

The 'waste' of scarce resource may manifest itself in one or more of various ways. Units getting better facilities in respect of finance, for example, may suffer from excess capacity. On the criterion of capital employed, their size may be large. They may employ more capital-intensive techniques of production. They may have large proportions of borrowed funds, and in spite of a fair rate of interest, interest costs may be high.[4]

There is yet another way in which 'waste' of assistance arises. Assistance may make room for 'ghosts'. The 'ghosts' are not 'formless'. They have some sort of shed to shelter the junk that is their plant and machinery. On the strength of this workshop, they qualify as 'small industry' and get assistance. These 'ghosts' have no interest in manufacturing. So they 'sell' this assistance (raw materials, price preference and so on), in one way or the other, to traders and small and large manufacturers. Not being manufacturers themselves, the 'ghosts' do not compete directly with other small manufacturers. But they may have received assistance in preference to other genuine small manufacturers. To the extent this assistance flows back, via 'ghosts' or traders, to the genuine small manufacturers it would only be at a higher price, defeating the basic purpose of alleviating the hardships of the small industry sector. And, to the extent it finds its way to the large scale producers, it reinforces the already weak position of the small manufacturers in the market.[5] The number of

---

proportion to their potential usefulness to the community.' P.N. Dhar and H.F. Lydall (1961), pp. 82–83. This was written in a book published in 1961. Since then, this kind of 'responsibility' has only increased. Quoted from Publication 2, pp. 39–40, fn. 25.

[4] For details, see Publication 1, pp. 113–14.

[5] On this point, K. Bandopadhyaya has observed in the context of the industrial estates programme: 'Sometimes it happened that the entrepreneurs took occupation

such 'ghosts' in the small industry sector, we understand, is not inconsiderable, nor their impact insignificant.

However, it is extremely difficult to form even a tentative estimate of the number of such units, and even more difficult to assess their impact. It is a common experience that of the units approached at their recorded addresses, a few are found closed, not located at the addresses recorded, not traceable, or giving no or inadequate response. It is possible that the number of units in these categories may be fewer if the investigators exerted more. But it may not be a wild guess that a sizeable proportion of such units may be 'ghosts'.[6]

We have already referred to the relatively superior position of the assisted units in general on labour productivity and wages. This may be due to their relatively large size in terms of capital and high capital intensity. However, this position has not led to better performance on other criteria. On the other hand, while the non-assisted units have not, in general, given a better account of themselves on labour productivity and wages, on other criteria they are ahead of assisted units. This may be explained by the former extracting more out of the scarce as well as the plentiful factors (like capital and labour) than the latter. And they may well be headed by men of superior entrepreneurial mettle—a quality not quantifiable.

III. Reservation

As the impact of competition on the small scale units in the category of reserved products/industries from large scale products/industries may be expected to be less, the small units in the reserve categories may be expected to give a better account of themselves than those in the other, general categories. More specifically, the 'reserve' industries may be expected to show a better performance than other industries at a point of time as well as over a period of time.

---

of the sheds and tried their best to obtain raw material quotas and machinery, etc., on easy terms, but as they are men with small means they become impatient on considering the time they would require to get started in business and quit the estate. Besides, in two cases, it has been found that the chosen entrepreneurs quit the estate after making easy money by blackmarketing their plants and equipment and essential raw materials.' *Industrialisation through Industrial Estates*, Calcutta, 1969, p. 145, quoted from Publication 2, p. 40, fn. 32.

[6] For hints on a possible proportion of 'ghost' units, see Publication 1, p. 115.

The data concerning the assisted and the non-assisted units have been used to throw light on the performance of the reserve vs. other industries, with reference to the above two hypotheses. We examine these hypotheses city-wise for these two categories of industry; and in this examination we use the same seven financial and economic performance ratios and the same five growth indicators as the ones used in the previous section. The relevant data are given in Tables 3 and 4.

Of the three industries in Bombay, metal products is in the reserve list. Of the six ratios, this industry was first only on surplus/ total assets and surplus/workers, and had, in fact, the highest capital intensity. On growth indicators, it ranked second on total assets and fixed assets and was the last on others.

Of the four industries in Hyderabad, industrial fasteners is in the reserve list. Of the six ratios, this industry was first on none and second on one (surplus/workers). It had the second-highest capital intensity.

Of the seven industries in Jaipur, three (namely, industrial fasteners, metal products and agricultural implements) are reserve industries. On five of the first six ratios, excepting surplus/total assets on which there was no reserve industry in the first three places, there was only one reserve industry in the first three places. As for capital intensity, the first, the third and the fifth places went to the three reserve industries. On growth indicators in the first three places, on fixed assets there was no reserve industry, and on total assets, equity capital and output there was one, and on value added there were two such industries.

Thus, the performance of reserve industries does not outshine that of others.

The basic idea underlying the reservation policy seems to be that once the door is shut for the large scale producer, generally believed to be more efficient in the 'market' sense, the field is left open for the small scale sector and the small man should produce goods/ services in that branch, earning better rewards for himself, and also helping to subserve socio-economic objectives. This may not, however, necessarily happen. The economic health of the small industry sector, like that of other sectors, hinges on the balance of the demand for and supply of its products. While closing the additional supply of competing products produced by the large industry sector, reservation increases the demand for the products of the small

Table 3
Financial and Economic Ratios of 'Reserve' and Other Industries

City/Year/Industry	Number of Units	Profits to Equity Capital (%)	Value Added to Total Assets	Value Added Per Worker	Surplus to Total Assets	Surplus Per Worker	Wages Per Worker	Total Assets Per Worker
1	2	3	4	5	6	7	8	9
I. Bombay (1976–77)	39							
1. Metal products	13	13.05	0.21	8,451	0.10	3,830	4,217	40,226
2. Machinery & spare parts	13	14.08	0.37	12,377	0.07	2,308	9,753	33,192
3. Paper & paper products	13	–1.09	0.14	5,361	0.05	1,804	3,381	38,852
II. Hyderabad (1977–78)	59							
1. *Industrial fasteners*	7	14.56	0.22	8,027	0.11	4,148	3,636	36,390
2. Printing press	8	5.94	0.22	5,906	0.07	1,861	3,828	27,197
3. Chemicals & pharmaceuticals	14	23.93	0.24	11,219	0.13	6,011	5,102	46,488
4. Machinery & spare parts	30	32.55	0.35	9,384	0.13	3,374	5,891	26,693
III. Jaipur (1978–79)	51							
1. *Industrial fasteners*	6	11.71	0.20	7,449	0.10	3,729	3,683	37,969
2. *Metal products*	14	26.97	0.29	12,943	0.14	6,397	6,391	44,779
3. Agricultural equipment	5	–15.74	0.08	4,960	0.02	1,223	3,429	62,852
4. Casting and rolling	6	30.88	0.38	8,765	0.14	3,212	5,542	23,300
5. Electricals & electronics	8	62.81	0.33	10,760	0.23	7,601	3,025	33,016
6. Plastic products	5	26.38	0.24	9,925	0.16	6,622	3,279	40,822
7. Chemicals	7	–14.24	0.12	5,828	0.03	1,595	4,050	47,898

Note: Reserve industries are shown in italics.

Table 4

Growth Rates of Continuing Units of 'Reserve' and Other Industries
(Per cent per Annum, Compound)

City/Years/Industry	Number of Units	Total Assets	Fixed Assets	Equity Capital	Output	Value Added
1	2	3	4	5	6	7
I. Bombay (1972–73 to 1976–77)	25					
1. Metal products	8	5.8	0.9	3.1	–1.4	–5.8
2. Machinery & spare parts	7	2.8	–0.6	9.8	8.2	0.6
3. Paper & paper products	10	16.3	21.9	11.4	10.1	7.9
II. Jaipur (1974–75 to 1978–79)	24					
1. Industrial fasteners	2	3.6	–2.4	–0.9	6.2	0.3
2. Metal products	7	4.9	–2.2	2.6	19.5	12.2
3. Agricultural implements	4	4.6	–4.5	8.3	–7.6	–32.4
4. Casting and rolling	3	12.6	5.1	10.9	23.7	–3.0
5. Electricals and electronics	3	16.3	13.8	11.8	18.9	–1.8
6. Chemicals	5	4.7	4.0	5.5	–2.8	–15.9
Ranking: Bombay Industry No.		3,1,2	3,1,2	3,2,1	3,2,1	3,2,1
Jaipur Industry No.	5,4,2,6,3,1	5,4,2,6,3,1	5,4,6,2,1,3	5,4,3,6,2,1	4,2,5,1,6,3	2,1,5,4,6,3

Reserve industries: In Bombay No. 1 and in Jaipur Nos. 1, 2 and 3.

industry sector. This increase enhances profits or reduces losses of the already established small units. But this very betterment induces, in the second round, additional production both by the established producers and new entrants (especially because of easy entry here), resulting in less profits or more losses than in the first round. From that perspective, it becomes basically a question of the rates of increase in the demand for and supply of the products produced by the small industry sector. Whether, as a result, the net position in terms of the viability of the small scale units and the health of the small industry sector as a whole in 'reserve' industries would be better or worse is anybody's guess, as it may lead to increased competition from within the sector. At any rate, our findings suggest that as judged by the relative performance of 'reserve' and other industries, reservation does not seem to have rendered any special benefit to the industries in this sector. One may, therefore, have to be even more cautious on this policy.

In the context of our discussion in Section II, we have inferred about the 'waste' of easily available resources. Of the criteria used there, some (like size and capital intensity) may not be relevant here, as those are conditioned by the nature of the product/industry. However, other criteria—excess capacity, borrowed funds, rate of interest and interest/value added—are of some value to illustrate the point in the present context of reserve versus other industries by city, and on these, we have some evidence.[7]

IV. Use and Significance of Incentives

We now mention the findings on the use and significance of incentives. The incentives in our questions related to land/shed, finance—long/medium and short term, machinery, raw material, marketing and technical assistance.

First, regarding the reasons for not having taken the benefit of one or the other type of assistance, some had no knowledge of the existence of the incentive schemes and some (varying from a few to a large majority), had no need of assistance. Others needed assistance, but of these some did not get it while the remaining stayed away from even attempting to get it for various reasons. The main

[7] See Publication 1, pp. 110–17.

reason was that too many formalities were associated with the processing of assistence.

A majority of the units had availed of the government/institutional finance in respect to land/shed and long/medium term and short term finance. As regards other types of assistance, in each case only a minority of the units reported having availed of them.

Of the units which had availed of assistance in respect to long/ medium term finance, short term finance, machinery on hire-purchase and raw materials, we had asked a further question as to whether they would have started the units without this assistance. Nearly half (of a total of 206 units) said that they would have done so. In respect to other assistance, such units formed between three-fifths to three-fourths.

To the question whether the timely availability of different facilities in adequate measure was more important than concessional terms, 150 (out of 166, i.e., 90 per cent) answered in the affirmative while 16 (10 per cent) were negative. Among the reasons given by the former were better utilisation of men and machines, greater turnover and good customer relations. The reasons given by the latter include lower cost and fixed tenure, especially in the case of finance.

It is most surprising that in spite of the fact that the programmes of assistance have been in currency for long—some of these for over a quarter of a century—and that the aid-giving agencies as also the units under reference are located in the same city, we should have discovered units claiming to be in the dark. One would imagine this situation in respect of the units located in remote areas other than the state capitals. Not that the aid-giving agencies do not publicise their activities but, clearly, there is something wrong somewhere with programmes for the dissemination of information.

Secondly, we have no comments on the finding that some units had no need of assistance. We may, however, reflect on the finding that some needed assistance, but did not get it. It is all to the good if they did not deserve assistance. It would, however, be unfortunate if they did not get it because, given other things, they could not prepare their projects as per the technical and other requirements, or could not formally satisfy the institutions on one or the other of the several formalities. The aid-giving agencies need to strengthen their efforts at proper counselling on such matters, so that requests for assistance do not get turned down for minor, avoidable and less important considerations.

We have then, in the third place, the finding that some stayed away simply because of procedures and formalities associated with the receiving of assistance. And it is not that others who had received assistance were happy or satisfied. In response to another question in a different context, some units suggested that even where the assistance was adequate, procedures and formalities were 'a big bother'. While underlining that in all non-small organisations—private or government—formalities and procedures are inescapable, 'like the act of God,' our respondents were not convinced that all that went in that phrase was vital or very necessary. We have little doubt that the impact of the assistance programmes would be increased if formalities could be reduced, procedures streamlined and decisions in practice as well as in principle taken quickly. The moral is: Time is money. Only some bold and imaginative reforms in this area can remove the widely-held unfortunate belief that people in industry and government live in different worlds. A bridge of understanding that they are working for a common end needs to be built expeditiously.

Further, had our investigation been based on the units selected from the lists other than the list of units assisted by the SFCs, we would surely have got a larger number of units which received other types of assistance—raw materials, marketing, machinery, technical advice, and so on. But, then, considering the fact that we have also the non-assisted units and also the possibility that the assisted units located in the big cities are likely to have received other types of assistance, we are surprised that we should find such a small number of units receiving assistance in respects other than land/shed, and long/medium and short term finance. We understand that even otherwise, the number benefiting from other schemes of assistance is not likely to be large, nor their impact substantial. If so, it is questionable whether it is necessary to continue other schemes of assistance. If a sufficiently large number of units do not need or seek one or the other of these types of assistance for reasons such as inconvenient location, inadequate quantity, poor quality, and so on and, further, if, of those who seek it, a sufficiently large number may not be found worth encouraging, it is legitimate to ask: whom are these programmes expected to benefit? Our findings underline the need for a proper assessment of assistance programmes related to raw materials, machinery on hire-purchase, technical assistance, and preferential purchase scheme. On the other hand, the data on the assistance programmes relating to land/shed, long/medium and short term finance establish the point that on the criterion of the number of units which have availed of the assistance, the need for such programmes is established. In view of this, there is perhaps a case for strengthening the assistance programmes on these fronts.

Fifth, it is clear from the replies that assistance might have gone to the units which did not need it badly or in the quantum they got. The replies suggest that government assistance was perhaps more substantial and less supplemental, replacing the resources they would have raised from elsewhere—other agencies in the private field, diverting their resources from other investments or sparing some of their current incomes for investment through more austere living (as some of the first generation entrepreneurs are known to have done).

This also raises the question as to whether, in the context of the limitation of resources, the aid-giving agencies by giving more to some than what they really needed, have not denied it completely or partially to other units. If this has happened, it is all the more regrettable in case the latter were really more needy and, at the same time, at least as worthy as the former.

Finally, the importance of concessional terms on which the various facilities are given appears to be highly exaggerated, and the government and the aid-giving agencies may be losing on this score, perhaps avoidably. Our units seem to value far more the timely availability of different facilities in adequate measure than the concessional terms on which they are made available.

V. *Industrial Estates*

We now consider the industrial estates programme. A major hypothesis on this incentive is that the units located in industrial estates might be expected to show better performance than outside units. The principal findings on this hypothesis as summarised by various investigators will now be presented.

A conclusion in the study of the programme in Rajasthan by Bhati states: 'Comparison of estate-units with similar units outside, with respect to rate of surplus, shows that in a majority of cases, outside units have performed better than inside units.'[8]

[8] G.S. Bhati, 'Industrial Estate—An Evaluation (A Case Study of the Programme in Rajasthan),' Ph.D. Thesis (unpublished), University of Bombay, 1976, p. 247.

We now refer to the findings which we have summarised in Publication 2. Specific references to this publication are also given, wherever necessary.

Sanghvi found that the small textile units located in the Udhna estate had a higher rate of return than those located in Surat.[9]

The bench-mark and the follow-on studies of industrial estates in Karnataka by Somasekhara reached more or less identical conclusions. As to the former, he states:

All the industrial estates, except the Harihar Industrial Estate and the Mysore Industrial Estate, were less viable economically compared to their controls. The Mysore Industrial Estate had higher economic efficiency in spite of lower technical efficiency: the value productivity was higher even though technical productivity was lower. The Mysore Industrial Estate did not display consistently higher efficiency.

On the whole, the industrial estates in Mysore had not been a great success. They had not achieved many of the objectives for which they are intended . . . . This study was not alone in reaching this conclusion. Other studies had come to similar conclusions.

Comparing the units at the bench-mark and the follow-on dates, he observes:

It appeared that the real efficiency of units as measured by both the technical and economic indicators in both industrial estates and control groups had gone down consistently in the last decade . . . . An important contrast between the industrial estates and their controls was in the last decade, i.e., between the bench-mark and the follow-on, the former had become more capital-intensive in output, whereas the latter had improved its capital-output ratio by reducing it . . . . Since both the industrial units and control groups have deteriorated in terms of efficiency indicators, it was interesting to examine which group had deteriorated more . . . . It appears that the units in the industrial estate group deteriorated more than their peers. This was

[9] R.L. Sanghvi, *Role of Industrial Estate in a Developing Economy*, Bombay, 1979, pp. 175–76.

consistently so for all the industrial estates in respect of all indicators.[10]

A study of the Kerala small industries by Oomen has made the following observations on this aspect:

An analysis of the working of several units has led to the conclusion that the objective of creating more output and employment has not been achieved satisfactorily in the industrial estates of Kerala. The capital-output ratio in the estate of Kerala was higher than that of the small factory sector and in certain cases even exceeded that in the large-scale sector. The capital-labour ratio was also of a higher order in the estates compared to the small-scale sector, approximating to that in the large-scale sector in some cases.[11]

A study of West Bengal industrial estates by Bandopadhyaya observes: 'in general, the outside industries . . . are more efficient than the Howrah estate industries in the sense that the outside industries produce more output per unit of rupee invested and use less capital per unit of labour engaged.' Further, as to the Kalyani industrial estates, 'the outside industries show a much better performance so far as the output-capital and capital-labour ratios are concerned, than the estate industries. The Kalyani estate industries require on average more capital per unit of labour engaged and produce less output per rupee invested than the outside industries.'[12]

Finally, Dhar and Lydall observe: 'Factories in industrial estates do not have a particularly advantageous output-capital ratio, indeed upto the present they have shown even more unsatisfactory results than might have been expected.'[13]

It is seen from the foregoing that only Sanghvi's study strikes a different note. Other studies conclude that the performance of estate small units is inferior to that of non-estate units; the former make more economical use of labour, and less economical use of capital than the latter.

[10] N. Somasekhara, *The Efficacy of Industrial Estate in India*, Delhi, 1975, pp. 45 and 68–71.

[11] M.A. Oomen, *Small Industry in Indian Economic Growth—A Case Study of Kerala*, Delhi, 1972, p. 190.

[12] K. Bandopadhyaya, *op. cit.*, p. 215.

[13] P.N. Dhar and H.F. Lydall, *op. cit.*, p. 86.

Some of the above-mentioned studies have also pointed to wastes of different types. Sanghvi's study shows that the units located in industrial estates were less labour-intensive and, therefore, had limited employment potential.[14]

After noting that the industrial estates have not been economically viable, Somasekhara writes:

All these in spite of the fact that the industrial estates had superior command over finance from both institutional and non-institutional agencies. But, unfortunately, this led to over-capitalisation which became a curse on the industrial estates. It resulted in higher inventories and large fixed investments. There was a slower turnover of financial assets in the industrial estates and a greater blockade of working capital resources. They had a higher cushion against sales which meant greater interest cost. The industrial estate units were less liquid, less productive and less profitable. The findings of the economic analysis with regard to the performance of industrial estates were corroborated by financial analysis and it reinforced that there were intrinsic financial reasons for the unsatisfactory performance of the industrial estates. They have not been financially viable.[15]

Dhar and Lydall have noted:

The average amount of capital employed per person in the estates, barring Sanatnagar, is within the range of Rs. 5,000–8,000. This is high compared to about Rs. 2,000 per worker obtaining in the Delhi light engineering industries using power and employing less than 20 workers.[16]

VI. Aggregate Value of Assistance

Small industry receives assistance from a number of sources and in a variety of ways. In view of this, it becomes difficult to know the aggregate value of assistance in absolute terms or in relation to the total capital, output, and so on, even in respect of programmes

[14] R.L. Sanghvi, *op. cit.*, p. 121.

[15] N. Somasekhara, *op. cit.*, p. 109.

[16] P.N. Dhar and H.F. Lydall, *op. cit.*, p. 56.

where assistance is quantifiable. In this context, we refer here to an effort by S.K. Tulsi [17] to evaluate the value of subsidies/incentives of nine selected programmes with reference to six industries in seven states. The nine programmes included in this study are exemption from excise duty and price preference (both Central government), power subsidy, electricity duty exemption, interest subsidy on seed capital, sales tax subsidy, octroi exemption, water concessions, additional price preference (all by state governments). The six industries are cosmetics and toilet preparations, rubber and rubber products, paints and varnishes, glass and glass products, handtools and gases. The seven states are U.P., Orissa, Rajasthan, Andhra Pradesh, Punjab, Madhya Pradesh and Maharashtra.

The value of the subsidy/incentive for each industry in the state is expressed as a percentage of the ex-factory value of output. The author warns that this percentage represents the maximum to which the industry is eligible; in practice, the value of incentives availed of will be smaller. All the same, it would seem that assistance can be very substantial indeed, as can be noted from the general findings that the value of incentives/subsidies varied from 70 per cent of the ex-factory value of output in cosmetics and toilet preparations in units with output of less than Rs. 5 lakhs to 33 per cent in gases. Further, the bulk of incentives came from two principal concessions given by the Central government, namely, excise duty exemption and price preference. Thus, for example, for cosmetics and toilet preparation industry, excise duty exemption formed nearly 71 per cent of the total value of the incentives to which that industry was eligible.

VII. Concluding Remarks—Some Lessons

Do the above findings and the explanations suggest that the schemes of assistance and incentives for small industry have, by and large, failed? Can we infer that the game is just not worth the candle and that the schemes be scrapped?

There can be the other view that but for these schemes, the performance of the small industry sector could have been worse. To elaborate: profitability and productivity would have been lower,

[17] S.K. Tulsi, *Incentives for Small Scale Industries—An Evaluation*, Delhi. The figures reported in the following paras are from pp. 97 and 98.

fewer small units would have existed and the employment and output of this sector would have been less than what has presently been the case.

While there is some point in this line of speculation, the temptation to overdraw on it must be resisted. It may as well be argued that the void otherwise left by the assisted units could have been filled, at least partly, by other units which would have sprung forth—an event prevented by the pre-emption of resources and the markets by the assisted units.

There is perhaps no end to this type of speculative arguments. We may as well begin by presenting our own judgement on this general question, in the light of the experience and insight acquired by us during the course of our work.

We do not subscribe to the view that small industry *per se* is an unproductive activity nor to the view that the incentive schemes be scrapped. To be sure, there are quite a few areas where small scale production is feasible and where it may be able to hold its own. Also, there would be other areas in which it may pass muster on social cost-benefit criterion. It is also readily agreed that a vigorous small industry is vital for industrial and economic growth. At the same time, its handicaps are rooted in the very smallness of its operations and, therefore, left to itself the market will not permit this sector to play its rightful role. There is, therefore, a case for preferential treatment of this sector by the state.

While fixing the quantum of assistance for small scale industries, the following perspective, however, needs to be kept in view: (*a*) resources of the government/agencies are limited, (*b*) productivity of resources on private/social counts may be higher elsewhere (for example, in family planning, health, primary education, public utilities, large manufacturing, etc.), (*c*) growth of demand for the products of small industry may be limited by growth elsewhere (in agriculture and large industry, in particular).

In view of the foregoing, as also because of the current situation concerning the efficacy of incentives and the health of the small industry sector, the government and its agencies have to be extremely careful before strengthening the existing programmes or starting new programmes. The small industry is an easy entry sector, and further assistance makes entry easier. Overcrowding in this sector may nullify the impact of assistance, or what is worse, make assistance counter-productive. To be sure, we do not favour regulation of entry by the state. People with the best of faith in the license/permit system and in the administrative capability of our bureaucracy would also, we hope, agree that the licensing for the small sector is a hopeless, well-nigh impossible, proposition for reasons too well known to merit elaboration.

The adverse effect of easy entry on the viability and health of the small units needs to be borne in mind, though it is realised that any assistance *per se* would make entry easier. Also, of the large number in this sector, only a tiny minority may grow to the station of a large unit. Of the rest, some will grow a little, perhaps a majority will remain small and some will die. It is difficult, from this mix, to identify in advance the first two types, more difficult to do so without inviting further entry. It is still more difficult to design and operate programmes of sufficient sensitivity to benefit each type of these units. This is a challenge—to be met squarely—and an opportunity to be exploited for a more productive functioning of these agencies.

It cannot be said that the wide variety of assistance programmes which have been in operation for long have come anywhere close to the sensitivities referred to earlier. In fact, a number of studies suggest that they may have been wide off the mark. Of our survey units, to repeat, some were in the dark about even the existence of assistance programmes. Some had availed of assistance though they might have done as well without it. Some fought shy of the procedures and did not attempt to get it. Some others who crossed these hurdles did not do even as well as others which had not availed of the assistance for one reason or another.

It goes without saying that a wider publicity of the aid-giving agencies is called for. Also, a more discriminating programme of assistance needs to be designed and operated for better allocational needs. The principle of discriminating assistance entails the following three requirements:

(a) favouring growth-prone and viable types of units and avoiding others;

(b) relying exclusively or principally on assistance related to land/shed and finance, and having or using other assistance programmes related to raw materials, marketing machinery, technical advice, etc., sparingly; and

(c) giving timely and adequate assistance and avoiding giving it belatedly and excessively or deficiently.

While (b) and (c) are self-explanatory, the phrase growth-prone and viable types of units perhaps needs elaboration. As noted earlier, the number of such units in the vast multitude of small scale establishments would only be small, and it is difficult to spot them. While a measure of risk is inevitable in all aid-related policies, it is, perhaps, much higher with respect to the small manufacturing sector. The risk can, however, be reduced or contained if the units are selected for assistance by applying objective criteria of private and social returns or net benefits. This might entail a consideration of factors such as demand and supply balance, economies of scale, priority accorded to efficiency and social objectives.

A policy of indiscriminate assistance, while it may appear 'fair' on some vague notion of 'justice,' is 'wasteful' in the sense of resulting in the excessive assistance rendered to some. It is also 'wasteful' in the sense that in view of the overall resource constraint, it cannot spare resources for other units which may, at least, be as deserving as the units already helped, or for other purposes which are as important as the purpose already served by the existing programmes of assistance. Finally, we may reiterate the point made earlier that streamlining of procedures and expeditious decision-making would make the assistance programmes have greater impact.

APPENDIX

Scope and Method of Field Studies

During the late seventies, we carried out a number of fact-finding field investigations of small scale industrial units. The objective, in the main, was to evaluate one of the assistance programmes, namely the long term finance by the State Financial Corporations (SFCs). The evaluation was conducted in terms of its impact on the assisted units—that is, as judged by their financial and economic performance juxtaposed against that of the non-assisted small scale and medium scale, otherwise broadly comparable, units, cross-sectionally and on a time-series basis. The focus in the field investigation was, therefore, on the collection of detailed data on assets and liabilities and output and on the opinions of the respondents on different types of incentives.

In view of the necessity of permitting some time between the receipt of assistance and its utilisation, only the units which had received assistance for at least three years at the time of investigation were selected. As regards the non-assisted small and medium units, only the units which were otherwise comparable with the assisted units were selected. This principle was observed by applying the following criteria: the units belong to the same product/industry group, are located in the same/neighbouring locality, and have been in existence for at least three years at the time of investigation. The definition of the small industry was as it was then prevalent, namely, units having investment in plant and machinery not exceeding Rs. 1.0 million and with ancillaries not exceeding Rs. 1.5 million (installation/purchase prices). The field studies were designed to cover the three cities of Bombay, Hyderabad and Jaipur. In view of the close proximity and high economic linkages, Thane was included in Bombay and Secunderabad in Hyderabad. The selection of industries in each city was guided principally by the importance of the industry as judged by the number of units assisted by the respective SFCs in the city. Accordingly, we picked up three, four and seven products/industries for Bombay, Hyderabad and Jaipur, respectively, as listed in Table A. Of these, first product/industry each in Bombay and Hyderabad and the first three in Jaipur belong to the reserve category as of 1973. We planned to cover around ten sample units, and five each of the non-assisted small and medium units in each product/industry.

On the assumptions that some of the units listed in the SFC records of relevant dates (31 March 1974 for Bombay and Hyderabad and 31 March 1975 for Jaipur) used for sampling may turn out to be 'non-existent' or 'non-traceable' in the field and that some may not respond or respond adequately, we had decided to build a measure of largeness in the initial selection itself. As it turned out, the number of units in twelve of the fourteen industries was rather small, so that all of them were selected. Of the remaining two industries (namely, metal products and machinery and spare parts, both in Bombay) where we had 130 and 70 units respectively, we drew a random sample to get twenty units in each, the respective fractions being 15 and 29 per cent. The non-assisted units were selected without any scientific procedure on the basis of considerations listed earlier, through contacts of assisted units, industry/ trade associations, banks, and so on. The response from the non-assisted medium units was very poor, so that they do not figure in this paper.

The paper is thus restricted to assisted and non-assisted small scale units. The details of the coverage of this paper are given in Table A.

Table A: Statement

Sample Design of Field Studies Showing Number of Assisted and Non-Assisted Units at Bombay, Hyderabad and Jaipur—1976–79

City/Year/Industry	Assisted	Non-Assisted	Total
1	2	3	4
I. *Bombay (1976–77)*			
1. Metal products	11	8	19
2. Machinery and spare parts	11	4	15
3. Paper and paper products	11	6	17
Total	33	18	51
II. *Hyderabad (1977–78)*			
1. Industrial fasteners	4	4	8
2. Printing presses	3	9	12
3. Chemicals & pharmaceuticals	8	8	16
4. Machinery and spare parts	17	20	37
Total	32	41	73
III. *Jaipur (1978–79)*			
1. Industrial fasteners	6	5	11
2. Metal products	7	13	20
3. Agricultural implements	4	1	5
4. Casting and rolling	10	2	12
5. Electricals and electronics	4	9	13
6. Plastic products	4	8	12
7. Chemicals	4	5	9
Total	39	43	82
TOTAL (I, II & III)	104	102	206

Of the 206 units, only 149 could give financial and economic data for the latest year, and 72 for the last four or five years continuously. These years are as specified in Tables 1 to 4. Here, in a number of cases, the data of assisted and/or non-assisted units at the product/industry level related to only one unit or there were no units at these levels. It was, therefore, decided to ignore such cases. Accordingly,

Tables 1 to 4 are restricted to the categories where the number of units in each category was two or more. The details of coverage can be seen from these tables. The items included in the headings of columns 3 to 9 of these tables are specified in the footnote to Table 1.

15 Arun Ghosh

Government Policies Concerning Small Scale Industries— An Appraisal

I. Evolution of Government Policy

In order to appraise government policies concerning the development of small scale industries, it may be useful to start with a brief sketch of the evolution of government policy relating to this sector. Interest in small scale industries in India can be traced back to the national movement and to Mahatma Gandhi's stress on village industries, especially the handloom weaving industry. In retrospect, while the Swadeshi movement and the decision to boycott British goods before the Second World War led to a major spurt in the growth of the large scale cotton mill industry in India, the movement did not lead to the growth of small scale or cottage industry; if anything, the handloom industry continued to decline and languish, in the face of competition from the large mill industry. One reason for this development was that the Congress party did not have the authority or the state power to actively encourage the growth of cottage and village industries, and its influence was limited only to a suasion of the large body of consumers.

In retrospect, yet another point seems to be relevant in this context. While khadi and village industries have always had an emotional appeal for the Congress party, the National Planning Committee (NPC), set up with Pandit Jawaharlal Nehru as the Chairman (in 1938), had two distinct and entirely divergent strands of opinion regarding the future growth of the small scale sector. One group favoured the growth of modern small scale industries, while another looked at decentralised production as a means for achieving the political and economic salvation of the country. There was, however, no clear conception as to what constitutes decentralised production. In his introduction to the volume prepared by the National Planning Committee (NPC) on rural and village industries, K.T. Shah suggested for the first time a definition of small scale industries:

> A small scale or cottage industry may be defined to be an enterprise or a series of operations carried on by a workman skilled in the craft on his own responsibility, the finished product of which he markets himself. He works in his own home with his own tools and materials . . . . These workers work mostly by hand labour and personal skill . . . . He works, finally, for a market in the immediate neighbourhood, that is to say in response to known demand with reference to quality as well as quantity.

It would be seen that K.T. Shah's definition of small scale industry related only to the sector now falling within the ambit of khadi and village industries. This point is worth emphasising here because, while the basic concern of the Congress party, at least in the early years of planning, was to encourage the village artisan, the handloom weaver (the worker who worked mainly with his own skill and without the aid of much equipment), the policy adopted by the government from about the end of the First Plan was to encourage the growth of modern small scale industry.

In contrast to K.T. Shah's definition, Pandit Jawaharlal Nehru submitted a note to the NPC in May 1940 wherein he suggested a three-tier definition of cottage, small scale and large industries.

Cottage industries, he suggested, are those which have either no mechanical power and no hired labour, or no mechanical power and hired labour under ten persons. In contrast, small scale industries may be deemed to be made up of those units which have either no mechanical power but hired labour over ten persons, or mechanical power under 10 BHP but no hired labour.

Pandit Nehru thus clearly differentiated between the cottage and the small scale sector, and he also provided for capital intensity in small scale units provided there was no hired labour. It would appear that as far as Pandit Nehru was concerned, the small scale sector was an intermediate step between cottage and large scale industry.

The historical background is highlighted here because, over the years since the formulation of the First Five Year Plan, there has been considerable dichotomy in the thinking within the government and the Congress party regarding the precise role of the small scale sector in the evolution of Indian industry. An important group of Congressmen has consistently emphasised the importance of traditional village industries. In contrast, the dominant or prevailing opinion both in the government and the Congress party was that village and cottage industries were essentially a clog to progress. They favoured the growth of modern small scale industries as a means to achieve both decentralised employment as well as efficiency in production.

The NPC resolution on cottage and small industries reflected mainly the Gandhian view. Soon after Independence, however, an Industries Conference was convened in December 1947, wherein there was representation from a variety of interests, including industrialists. The Conference considered the case of small industries and divided them into three categories: (*i*) those which are auxiliary to large scale industries; (*ii*) those which are engaged in repair services; and (*iii*) those which are engaged in the production of finished goods (such as, brass, copper and aluminium-ware, cutlery, iron foundries, hosiery, soap-making, coir rope, preserved foods, and so on).

This delineation of small industries is in sharp contrast to the NPC definition. It would be seen that the Industries Conference visualised the small scale sector to be made up essentially of modern, mechanised industries. This was in conflict with the Gandhian concept—

reflected in K.T. Shah's definition—of small scale industry. Shah envisioned small industries as a means not only for securing fuller employment but also for ensuring equitable distribution and regional balance in the growth of industry, a concept which was lost in the thrust for the growth of small scale units either as ancillaries to large units or as modern, mechanised units.

In fairness, it must be stated that the government was not unmindful of the role and importance of the cottage industry sector. Government policy on cottage and small scale industry was concretised in the Industrial Policy Resolution (IPR) of April 1948. The approach in the IPR on village and small scale industries is reproduced in the Appendix. Briefly, the IPR reflects an amalgam of traditional thinking, laying emphasis on cottage industry, and the emerging view in the Industries Conference that the future growth of small industries should be on modern lines (much in the tradition of Japanese small industry). This 'dualistic' approach has informed government policy on small scale industry ever since.

Following from the approach outlined in the Industrial Policy Resolution, an All India Cottage Industries Board was set up in 1948. In due course, it was found necessary to bifurcate this Board, and by the end of the First Five Year Plan, six All India Boards were set up. These were the All India Handloom Board, the All India Handicrafts Board, the Central Silk Board, the Coir Board, the All India Khadi and Village Industries Board (later converted into a statutory commission), and the Small Scale Industries Board. While the first five were to be concerned with traditional (village) industries, the Small Scale Industries Board was to be concerned with modern small scale industry.

Government policy on industry was further elaborated in the Industries Development and Regulation Act (IDRA) of 1951. The Act laid down that all undertakings in industries listed in Schedule I annexed to the Act, with a size larger than a specified minimum, would need to be registered with an agency to be notified by the government. More importantly, the setting up of new units of a size larger than the specified minimum in the 'scheduled industries,' or substantial expansion (above 25 per cent of existing capacity) of the existing units in the scheduled industries, would require the prior approval of the Government of India in the form of industrial licenses.

The IDRA was the main instrument of government policy for regulating industrial growth. Thus, by implication, the IDRA defined the small scale sector to be constituted of industrial units (at least in the scheduled industries) which were exempted from the registration/licensing requirement. The IDRA exempted from registration all units employing less than 50 workers and using power, or less than 100 workers when not using power. For certain specified industries (like cotton weaving and matches), the Act laid down that no new units (except in the cottage industry sector) would be set up without prior approval, thus extending the scope of the Act to units employing less than 50 workers.

The First Plan document stressed the need for the proper development of small industries. An important plank of policy in this connection was to be the concept of a common production programme with reference to large and small scale industry. The concept of the common production programme was employed, first, for the reservation of certain spheres of production for small scale units; secondly, for the regulation of the expansion of capacity of large scale industry; third, for the imposition of a cess on large scale industries where necessary; fourth, for making proper arrangements for the equitable supply of scarce raw materials to both large and small industry; and, finally, for coordination of research and training in the sphere of industry. In retrospect, it can be stated that little attempt was made to implement the last two elements of the policy relating to the common production programme.

During the First Plan it was also decided that in a number of industries, all future expansion would be in the small scale sector. In these industries, the capacity of existing large units was to be restricted to the best year's production up to the year 1954. Differential excise duties were also imposed on various products, in respect to which the government desired to encourage the growth of small scale industries. The First Plan period also saw the listing of a number of commodities for which government purchases were to be made only from the small scale sector. The state governments were also advised to relax the rules and conditions governing the grant of loans to small scale industries, and to simplify the procedures for making such loans.

Even before the completion of the First Plan, the Government of India invited a team of experts to look into the policies and procedures for small scale industries. This team of foreign experts, sponsored by the Ford Foundation, reported in March 1954 that the measures adopted in the First Plan for the development of small scale industry were inadequate. The team also felt that the methods of management in small scale industries fell short of the modern demands for efficiency. The team felt that better marketing, better financing, better finish, better equipment for manufacture and better power facilities were not separate remedies but required simultaneous attention in order to solve the problems of the small scale sector. The team suggested the establishment of a multipurpose institute of technology for the service of small industries; the establishment of a customers' service corporation to take care of marketing of products of small industries; the establishment of credit facilities; the strengthening of trade associations and cooperatives; the establishment of a small industries corporation to serve small industries in regard to government purchases from industries; the establishment of centres equipped with machinery and other facilities to serve as training centres for small industrialists; and the establishment of a marketing service corporation.

Following this report, the government decided to establish four regional institutes of technology (in Bombay, Delhi, Madras and Calcutta) for small industries. These were to serve as service agencies and to assist small industries in improving their techniques of production and management. The National Small Industries Corporation (NSIC) was also set up at this time, partly to provide equipment to small entrepreneurs on a hire purchase basis and partly to act as a service corporation. No independent marketing service corporation was established, it being assumed that the NSIC would perform this function.

To supplement these, the Small Industries Development Organisation (SIDO) was formed under the Ministry of Industry, with the Development Commissioner of Small Scale Industries as its head. The SIDO was quickly expanded; by 1956, twelve major institutes and sixty Extensive Centres were set up. The NSIC, which was originally registered with an authorised capital of Rs. 1 million was expanded, and its authorised capital raised to Rs. 5 million.

The government's promotional measures for the development of small scale industry were thus modelled essentially on the recommendations of the Expert Team (financed by the Ford Foundation).

The organisational framework for promoting small scale industry was generally completed by the end of the First Five Year Plan. With minor changes and with further expansion of the type of facilities already initiated, the SIDO and its constituent units (and services provided by them) have remained the main instruments of government policy for promoting the growth of modern small scale industry.

When the Second Plan was under preparation, a Committee on village and small scale industries was set up under D.G. Karve to recommend programmes for the development of small industry in the Second Plan. The Karve Committee adopted as its main focus three objectives, namely, (i) to avoid technological unemployment; (ii) to increase employment as much as possible through village and small industries; and (iii) to provide the basis for the structure of an essentially decentralised society. The ultimate objective of policy, insofar as the Karve Committee was concerned, was to develop industry based on a progressive rural economy. The Committee clarified that its emphasis on avoiding technological unemployment did not preclude the improvement of techniques of production in village industries. The Committee's main suggestions were to improve finance and marketing for small scale industries.

Thus, the Karve Committee's focus was mainly on village and cottage industries as against modern small scale industries (which had so far generally attracted the attention of the government). The Karve Committee viewed this sector as the principal means of decentralisation, as also for the avoidance of technological unemployment. The focus was on self-employment, on improved techniques for the village artisan, and on decentralised economic activity.

It is worth reiterating that all through this period, there were clearly two separate and widely divergent streams of thought, in regard to the role and the precise manner of the development of small scale industry. One school of thought regarded the modern small sector as deserving the focus of government attention, while the other emphasised the importance of decentralised village industries.

Since the basic policy thrust during the Second Plan—formulated by P.C. Mahalanobis—was to give priority to the production of capital goods and basic materials through large investments in the public sector, by inference, the requirements of consumer goods were supposed to be met from the efforts of the private sector. There was thus a large area of consumer goods which was to be met substantially from the small scale sector. The Second Five Year Plan document observed that small scale units 'provide immediate large scale employment, they offer a method of ensuring a more equitable distribution of the national income and they facilitate an effective mobilisation of resources of capital and skill which might otherwise remain unutilised.'

This approach to small scale industries was reiterated in the Industrial Policy Resolution (IPR) of 1956. To the extent that the IPR of 1956 was the basis of industrial policy over the coming decades, the IPR was to inform the government approach in regard to small scale industry, until the late seventies.

At the beginning of the Second Plan it was also announced that the small scale sector would be defined as composed of 'units employing less than 50 workers employing power, and less than 100 workers if not using power, and having capital investment of less than Rs. 0.5 million.' While the financial limit of investment (in plant and equipment) has been revised several times—the present limit being Rs. 2.0 million—the twin criteria of employment and investment were applied for the first time from the Second Plan onwards, for defining small scale industry.

Many promotional measures for small scale industry which have become a part of the scenario today were initiated for the first time during the Second Plan. The major plank of policy in this connection was the reservation of certain products for manufacture exclusively by small scale units. Existing large units in these industries were allowed only to maintain their current rate of production (at the best year's level) and not to expand capacity any further. Other policy measures adopted were protection of small industry through a common production programme; differential tax treatment (more specifically, exemption of several small industries from excise duty); and direct subsidy in the form of concessional credit. A programme of construction of industrial estates was also initiated to provide built-up factory space and other infrastructure facilities at a subsidised rate. Increased technical assistance, training, tool-room and extension services were extended to more centres throughout the country. Over the years, the promotional measures have improved both quantitatively and qualitatively, though the thrust has broadly been in the directions indicated above.

At the end of the Fifth Plan, there was a change in the political power structure in the country, and the new political party which came to power professed to adopt a Gandhian policy in regard to industrial development. The industrial policy of the new government stated, *inter alia,* that 'the main thrust of the new industrial policy will be on effective promotion of cottage and small industries widely dispersed in rural areas and small towns.'

The specific measures adopted by the new government to achieve the above-stated objective were, first, to pay special attention to the 'tiny' sector, that is, small scale units with investment in plant and machinery up to Rs. 0.1 million—lately raised to Rs. 0.2 million—and situated in towns with a population of less than 50,000; secondly, the setting up of District Industries Centres in all districts (throughout the country) to provide under a single roof all services and support assistance required by small entrepreneurs; and, finally, the setting up of a special unit in the IDBI to deal exclusively with the credit requirements of small village and household industries, and to coordinate, guide and monitor the entire range of credit facilities offered by diverse institutions to the small scale sector. The new government also increased, in a very significant manner, the number of items reserved for the small scale sector from about 180 to more than 800. However, as transpired in reality, many of these products were no more than sub-divisions or components of products already reserved and, thus, the number of items technically reserved for the small scale sector increased enormously without any really significant change in the nature and content of the reservation programme.

The thrust of the policies adopted by the government in 1977 remained unchanged. After yet another political change in 1980, the new government greatly stressed the strengthening and build-up of the District Industries Centre for rendering comprehensive assistance and support to small scale industries. Certain additional facilities were announced. In particular, the 'nucleus industry' programme was initiated, the idea being that there should be emphasis on the development of a core unit around which a nucleus of small units can grow in each area, hitherto deprived of industrial activity. The core units were to offload at least 50 per cent of the total manufacturing programme to ancillaries, to be developed within the area.

At this juncture, perhaps some reference is necessary to the latest policy thrust in regard to the functioning of the District Industries Centres, and to the support being extended by the government today, through diverse agencies, to small scale industries. As per the Annual Report of the Department of Industrial Development for 1983–84, the SIDO now has a network of twenty-six small industries service institutes, twenty-five branch institutes, forty extension centres, four regional testing centres, one product-cum-process development centre, two footwear training centres and four production centres. The 1983–84 proposals, when they materialise, would lead to further strengthening and extension of the area of activity of the SIDO, particularly in backward areas. The list of items reserved for production by small scale units now stands at 872. The number of products for which price preference is extended by the government (for DGS&D purchases) to small scale units now extends to 404. (The value of DGS&D purchases from SSI units during 1981–82 was, however, only Rs. 2.07 billion out of a total of Rs. 16.57 billion.) The total number of District Industries Centres (DIC) sanctioned till 1983–84 was 395, covering 408 districts out of a total of 413 districts in the country; and the DICs are supposed to identify and assist new entrepreneurs, artisans and workers engaged in hand crafts. As far as credit is concerned, the balance of commercial bank credit outstanding with small scale units, as of December 1982 was Rs. 40.86 billion.

The somewhat long discourse in regard to the evolution of policy on and the actual development of the small scale sector just described, and the broad thinking over time in regard to the instruments of policy to be used to encourage the growth of the small scale sector, provide the basis for an evaluation of the policies adopted, and an assessment of their impact on the growth of the small scale sector, with special reference to the major objectives of policy (namely, employment, dispersal and growth rate of economic activity).

II. Facts Regarding Growth of Small Scale Industry

It must be stated at this juncture that there is generally a paucity of data in regard to the small scale sector. There is also some confusion in regard to definitions, the jurisdiction of different authorities and, therefore, data on the results of the promotional measures adopted by the government. Data on industries are generally compiled either under the Annual Survey of Industries by the Central Statistical Organisation or under the Factories Act by the Labour Bureau. The latter cover all industrial units employing 10 or more persons using power or 20 or more persons and not using power. Thus, all data pertaining to the 'registered' factories sector would encompass not only large and medium industrial units but also a very substantial part of modern small scale industry. In fact, the small scale sector straddles both the 'organised' manufacturing sector—covered under the Factories Act—and the unorganised sector (employing less than 10 persons). Indeed, some units even under the purview of the Development Commissioner, Small Scale Industries, may technically fall within the ambit of 'unorganised' industry, by virtue of the fact that the total employment may be less than 10 persons.

Many capital intensive units have, in fact, been started in recent years, with employment below 10 persons, thus evading the Factories Act. Likewise, the Annual Survey of Industries may miss out much of the modern small scale sector. On the other hand, data compiled by the DC (SSI) or specialised agencies like the Khadi and Village Industries Commission in regard to their areas of control are sporadic and incomplete. National Income Accounts data distinguish only between the registered manufacturing sector and the unregistered manufacturing sector, where the distinction is the same as under the Factories Act: units employing 10 or more persons with power or 20 or more persons and not using power being part of the registered manufacturing sector. The DC (SSI) does collect data on units registered with the SIDO (as small scale units) but, as indicated earlier, these data are sporadic and incomplete. Data on traditional small industries, i.e., those belonging to the unregistered manufacturing sector, are woefully inadequate, the only estimates available in regard to this sector being either 'guesstimates' prepared by the National Income Division of the CSO (with the decennial population census as the frame of reference), or scattered data compiled by specialised agencies like the Khadi and Village Industries Commission, the Handlooms Commissioner, the Coir Board, the Silk Board, and so on.

Table 1 gives the employment and net output in 'organised' and 'unorganised' manufacturing industry in India, as per the population census and National Income Accounts statistics. The estimates of net output per worker derived from these data are obviously in-accurate (and indefensible for any statistical presentation), and are of value only for *inter-se* comparison between the two types of manufacturing activity.

Table 1
Employment and Output in Organised and Unorganised Manufacturing Sectors in India

Item	Organised Manufacturing	Unorganised Manufacturing	Total
Employment in 1971 (thousand)	4,777	12,146	16,923
Net value of output 1975–76 (Rs. billion)	60.08	35.77	95.85
Net value of output per worker (annual) (Rs.)	12,577	2,945	5,664

As indicated earlier, the 'organised' sector of the manufacturing industry would encompass not only large and medium scale industries but also, very substantially, the modern small scale sector under the purview of the DC (SSI), while the 'unorganised' sector would cover artisans and other traditional industries which are the res-ponsibility of specialised agencies like the KVIC, the Handloom Board, the Silk Board, the Coir Board, etc. (powerlooms, which usually employ less than 10 persons, would also get covered under 'unorganised' manufacturing industry).

The point that emerges is that the new output per worker in 'unorganised' manufacturing activity in 1975–76 was considerably less than Rs. 3,000 per annum (since the estimate given earlier is based on the 1971 work force figure) which is less than one-fourth of the output per worker in 'organised' manufacturing industry. On the other hand, employment in such 'unorganised' industry was nearly three-fourths of the total employment in manufacturing industry.

This point has important implications for policy, which will be examined later.

For the modern small scale sector—on which government policy has largely been focused since the Second Five Year Plan—we have to depend on scattered data compiled from time to time by the SIDO.

The following figures, which are readily available, may be cited here (Table 2) even though they are somewhat out of date.

Table 2
Growth of Small Scale Industries—1972 to 1978

Indicator	1972	1974-75	1975-76	1976-77	1977-78
Number of units (thousand)	140	216	239	260	287
Employment (million)	1.65	2.16	2.40	2.68	2.90
Fixed investment (Rs. million)	10,450	14,480	16,730	19,240	21,440
Gross output (Rs. million)	26,030	49,320	57,420	67,000	75,000
Value of gross output per worker (Rs.)	15,776	22,833	23,925	25,000	29,310

Source: For 1972, *All India Census of Small Industries, 1972*, Vol. 1. For the other years, see SIDO Annual Report, 1978-79.

According to the Annual Report of the Department of Industrial Development for 1983-84, as of end-March 1983, the number of units registered with the DC (SSI) had grown to 0.596 million. The figures of employment and output as given, however, include the unregistered sector also, and hence these figures are not comparable with the estimates given by the SIDO.

The SIDO does not indicate whether the figure of gross output represents the total value of output or the gross value added. *Prima facie*, it appears to be the former, since the output per worker (in 1975-76) would be seen to be Rs. 23,925 which would be nearly twice the figure of net value of output per worker in large, medium and modern small scale industry (i.e., all registered factories), as given earlier.

As per the Annual Survey of Industries, the net value added by manufacturing industry is of the order of 20 per cent of the gross sales value of output (ex-factory), and this ratio has remained more or less constant over a number of years. If we assume the consumption of raw materials, fuel and other materials by modern small scale industry to be approximately the same (i.e., on an average, 80 per cent of the gross sales value of output), the net output per worker in small scale industry, as per SIDO figures, would be approximately Rs. 4,800 in 1975–76 (i.e., nearly 63 per cent more than in unorganised manufacturing, and around 38 per cent of the figure for the entire registered manufacturing sector, encompassing large, medium and registered small scale industry).

In other words, as may be expected, the organised small scale sector, which is the focus of attention of the SIDO, stands somewhere midway in the scale as between unorganised industry and large and medium industries, insofar as net output per worker is concerned.

If the SIDO figures of the number of establishments, employment, investment and output are accepted, this sector has shown a fairly rapid growth rate in regard to all these variables during the seventies. Indeed, this growth rate has been considerably higher in respect to small scale industry than in respect to large and medium scale industry, and very much higher than cottage and village industries.

However, when we examine independent studies conducted by experts, the picture that emerges in respect to the modern small scale sector is not very flattering. As far back as 1961, P.N. Dhar and H.F. Lydall had concluded that modern small scale industry (employing between 10 and 49 persons) is fairly capital-intensive; that is, these units do not generate more employment per unit of capital than large scale industry.[1] Dhar and Lydall also found that these units pay lower wages to workers and are usually concentrated in large, urban areas. They concluded that there was no case for giving preferential treatment to modern small scale industry. In recent years, J.C. Sandesara has tried to summarise all available evidence (as of 1981), and has concluded that though some small scale units are labour-intensive, available evidence casts considerable doubt on the policy premise that small units are capital saving and employment promoting.[2]

In a well-argued paper, C.T. Kurien has observed that 'there is no *a priori* theoretical reason why a unit operated on smaller scale should be more labour-intensive (or for that matter capital-intensive) than one operated on a large scale.'[3]

Bimal Jalan has done some welcome research from unpublished data compiled in the course of the Annual Survey of Industries (1975–76), and has found that while the 'tiny' sector (i.e., units with

[1] P.N. Dhar and H.F. Lydall (1961).
[2] J.C. Sandesara (1981a).
[3] C.T. Kurien (1978).

less than Rs. 0.1 million of capital) had the most favourable capital-output ratio in a number of industries, out of 16 groups of industries considered, in as many as 11 the small scale sector had a higher capital-output ratio than either the large scale sector or the tiny sector.[4] The figures in Table 3, culled from Jalan, are revealing.

Several interesting points emerge from Table 3. Apart from the point already highlighted—that in 11 out of the 16 groups of industries, the capital-output ratio in small scale industry is higher than the capital-output ratio not only in 'tiny' industries but also in large and medium industries, a fact that puts into serious doubt the premise that modern small scale industry provides more employment per unit of capital than large and medium industries—the value of output per worker in the three types of industrial units provides much food for thought. Except in a few industries (like edible oils and fats and knitting mills), the value of output per worker in small scale industry does not compare favourably with that in large and medium industry and occasionally even with 'tiny' units, particularly when reference is made to the capital-output ratio in these industries. This brings to mind a criticism made by the Estimates Committee (1965–66) of the Third Lok Sabha.

The Estimates Committee (1965–66) of the Third Lok Sabha, in its 105th, 106th and 107th Reports, had attempted an evaluation of the progress of small scale industry, and made several critical references to the extant government policy on small scale industry.[5] It observed that the growth of small scale units had been mainly in urban areas, and noted that there had been no substantial state effort or support for the dispersal of industries. In regard to the common production programme, the 106th Report of the Estimates Committee lamented that the government had merely enunciated the programme, but had not paid due attention to it. Among the reasons for the failure of the common production programme, the Committee stated that proper research had not been undertaken to ascertain the possibilities of introducing such programmes, in particular, the suitability or otherwise of areas where such programmes are introduced, or industries which are reserved for the small scale sector. The Committee further noted that a major reason for the

[4] Bimal N. Jalan (1978).

[5] Estimates Committee, Third Lok Sabha 1965–66; Reports Nos. 105, 106, 107 on the Ministry of Industry (Organisation of the Development Commissioner, Small Scale Industry).

Table 3

Capital, Employment and Output in Selected Industries (1975–76) (Rs. '000)

Industry	Capital-Output Ratio				Value of Output Per Employee			
	'Tiny' Units	Small Scale Units	Large & Medium Units	Total Factory Sector	'Tiny' Units	Small Scale Units	Large & Medium Units	Total Factory Sector
Edible oils & fats (excl. hydrogenated oils)	0.41	0.57	1.25	0.60	11.6	178.9	219.6	149.0
Matches	0.24	0.93	0.51	0.45	16.4	21.7	36.5	21.8
Utensils & cutlery*	0.51	0.99	0.51	0.68	29.1	45.8	65.4	43.2
Handtools & general hardware*	0.66	1.09	0.80	0.85	23.4	31.2	44.7	36.3
Textile garments, weaving apparel, etc.	0.29	0.73	0.72	0.62	29.9	34.1	30.7	32.0
Electrical appliances, apparatus & parts*	0.79	0.96	1.57	1.39	23.7	35.0	48.2	40.8
Knitting mills	0.30	0.62	0.72	0.51	68.3	108.6	112.9	91.9
Bakery products	0.39	1.79	0.54	0.59	33.7	38.4	78.5	60.5
Rubber products (excl. footwear, tyres & tubes)	0.67	0.90	0.67	0.74	28.4	42.0	55.7	45.6
Soap & other toilet preparations	0.36	0.65	0.49	0.51	71.2	52.7	262.9	170.1
Bicycles, cycle rickshaws & parts	0.82	1.35	0.78	0.91	32.4	36.9	54.3	45.3
Footwear	0.49	1.81	0.33	0.51	32.0	46.5	33.7	35.5
Medical, surgical & scientific equipment	0.60	1.04	1.33	1.19	29.8	33.2	31.3	31.6
Radio, TV & allied electronic equipment	0.65	1.02	0.74	0.75	31.1	45.2	42.1	41.2
Stationery articles	0.63	1.51	0.90	0.97	18.3	22.9	69.2	37.4
Watches & clocks	1.11	1.01	1.24	1.21	9.9	25.2	46.2	38.0

Note: *Figures relate to 1974–75.

Source: Bimal N. Jalan, 'Production in Tiny, Small and Large Scale Sectors,' *Economic and Political Weekly*, Bombay, 20 May 1978.

failure of the common production programme was the inequitable distribution of scarce raw materials.

In regard to dispersal, according to the Sixth Plan (1980–85) document,

> the industrially developed states (including Delhi) accounted for nearly 67 per cent of the registered small scale units which had come up by 1976 and about 75 per cent of the employment generated by them. And within the developed states, there has been concentration of units in a few areas which are either metropolitan or large cities or industrial complexes. There has not been much improvement in the activisation of the idle capacities of the units either. It has been estimated that capacity utilisation in different village and small industries (VSI) has been ranging from about 45 to 60 per cent. Though there are varying estimates regarding the number of sick units in the VSI sector, there is general agreement about the enormity of the problem.

The Sixth Plan further states that according to a survey conducted by the RBI, of the units assisted by commercial banks up to June 1976, about 69 per cent of the total credit was availed of by 11 per cent of the (bigger) units in the small scale industries sector, which accounted for 55 per cent of the total production.

Harking back to the report on the All-India Census of Small Scale Industries, 1972, the picture which emerges in regard to capacity utilisation in the small scale sector in the industries/products reserved for the small scale sector, is shown in Table 4.

The figures speak for themselves. The point to note in this context is that the figures of capacity and its utilisation relate to industries reserved for the small scale sector; further, while capacity figures are frequently historical (i.e., at some base year prices), the value of output recorded is at current, and *prima facie* higher, prices.

Judging from the available evidence, including the remarks made in this context in the Sixth Plan document, there is no reason to believe that the situation today is very different from what was recorded for 1972 by the Census of Small Scale Industries.

The picture that emerges in regard to the khadi and village industries sector is no more encouraging. Again, to quote the Sixth Plan Mid-Term appraisal document, the 1984–85 targets (incorporated in the Sixth Plan) may be seen in comparison with the actual

Table 4
Capacity Utilisation in Small Scale Sector

Industry	Capacity (Rs. billion)	Output 1972 (Rs. billion)	Percentage Utilisation of Capacity
Mechanical engineering industries	63.38	29.93	47
Electrical equipment	9.79	4.89	50
Electronic industry	1.42	0.81	57
Automobile ancillary industries	1.87	1.09	58
Garage equipment	0.14	0.07	49
Chemical industries (incl. materials)	21.59	10.37	48
Glass & ceramic	7.10	3.61	51
Leather products	1.94	1.07	55
Plastic products	14.03	4.03	29
Rubber products	1.50	0.87	58
Wood products	1.88	0.95	50
Miscellaneous industries	7.00	4.03	58

output achieved during 1980–81 and 1981–82. It is to be noted that where value figures are concerned, the Plan targets are given at 1979–80 prices.

Table 5
Sixth Five Year Plan Targets and Actual Output in Khadi and Village Industries

Industry	Target for 1984–85 Output in Sixth Plan (value figures at 1979–80 prices)	Actual output (at current prices, where relevant)	
		During 1980–81	During 1981–82
Khadi (million sq. metres)	165	91	96
Village industries (value Rs. billion)	10.00	4.51	5.43
Sericulture (million kg.)	9.00	5.00	5.20
Handloom (million metres)	4,100	3,100	3,113
Handicrafts (value Rs. billion)	32.00	23.00	28.00
Coir (million tonnes)	0.263	0.159	0.107
Powerlooms (million metres)	4,300	3,369	3,603

It can be seen that where it is possible to compare the quantity of output with the target, the performance is not very encouraging. Indeed, there has been some stagnation in the output of most industries falling within the purview of the KVIC and other specialised agencies.

Again, in respect to khadi and village industries, the Sixth Plan document has observed that:

> low levels of technology resulting in poor productivity and inadequate returns have continued to characterise the traditional industries sector. Coupled with this, the problem of obtaining raw materials of desirable quality at reasonable prices and lack of marketing arrangements have deprived the artisans of a good part of the earning which should have accrued to them.

The Sixth Plan document goes on to note that the traditional sector continues to rely on non-institutional sources for its credit needs. In short, most of the problems which affected the traditional hand crafts at the time of Independence have continued to bedevil this sector, despite large sums spent on diverse specialised agencies like the KVIC, the Coir Board, and so on.

Indeed, if one may quote from L.C. Jain who has spent a lifetime championing the cause of the decentralised sector,

> There is no system instituted to clear industrial investments from the point of view of employment or their impact on existing employment in cottage and village industries .... Financing arrangements for small scale industries and modern cooperative agro-processing industries have been developed fairly extensively. But institutional finance for cottage and village industries is practically non-existent .... Even in Government purchases, the small sector has price preference and organisational back up, but not the cottage sector. The small sector also gets technical and organisational support through Small Industries Service Institutes, but there is no matching technical service for the village industries whose need is even greater .... The view that decentralised village industries can be aided and promoted bureaucratically from the top without participatory development and Government at decentralised levels continues to be held.[6]

6 L.C. Jain (1980).

The crucial point—apart from the failure to supply credit to village industries—is in the last sentence: government policy has been attuned to highly centralised direction and support for what is essentially decentralised activity, without any genuine participatory effort at the local level.

One point that emerges is that a great deal of government support has in the past been directed, with some success, in favour of modern small industry, while similar efforts to aid village industries have not succeeded in the same measure. As C.T. Kurien has pithily put it, 'If the policy of protection and support to the small sector is meant primarily for the small scale industrial units *why* should it be so? If it is meant for the village and household production units *how* is it to be made effective?'[7] Therein lies the crucial question in regard to government policy on the decentralised sector.

To sum up, the growth of the small scale manufacturing sector during the thirty-five years of planning has broadly taken the following pattern:

(*a*) There has been, since the sixties, a phenomenal growth in the number of units, investment and output of the (modern) small scale sector falling within the purview of the Small Industries Development Organisation (SIDO).

(*b*) This development, however, has been concentrated in a few metropolitan areas and large towns, and only a few of these units account for a substantial part of the total output of this sector; institutional credit has also very significantly gone to a small percentage of small scale units.

(*c*) For the rest, there is considerable under-utilisation of capacity, as well as sickness in this sector. By one reckoning, nearly a quarter of the new units registered every year fall by the way side, and do not survive, if annual figures of registration of new units and ex-post figures, after a few years, of the number of units in existence are any guide.

(*d*) While the modern small scale sector does show a fairly high overall rate of growth, the same cannot be said of the traditional crafts and village industries in the 'unorganised' sector. Except for a few selected areas and a few industries (like handloom weaving in West Bengal where the cooperatives have played a major part in the growth of output), the

C.T. Kurien, *op. cit.*

traditional cottage industry sector has been, by and large, stagnant. In any case, support by way of raw material supply, easy credit and marketing has not been available in any significant manner to traditional village industries.

(e) As a result, even though employment in the modern small scale industry has shown a steadily rising trend, this has not solved the problem of lack of employment opportunities—outside of farming activities—in the rural areas; and, even in urban areas, the employment opportunities in small scale industry have arisen mainly in metropolitan areas and a few other large towns and selected areas.

One of the promotional measures of the SIDO has been the construction of industrial estates for small scale units, where new entrepreneurs may get subsidised access to built-up sheds with diverse infrastructure facilities already provided. And yet, as of March 1981, the position—excluding Bihar, Madhya Pradesh and Himachal Pradesh, for which no information is available—was as follows:

Industrial estates sponsored	799
Industrial estates functioning	659
Sheds constructed	21,547
Sheds occupied	17,253
Plots occupied	24,006

In other words, out of 0.523 million registered small scale units as of March 1981, only some 21,000 had availed of sheds or plots made available in 659 industrial estates. There are many reasons why a number of industrial estates have not 'taken off'. Those located near major markets (e.g., at Okhla in New Delhi), have been a success story, whereas those located in remote areas have not succeeded, again because the provision of raw materials and the marketing facilities have not been adequately provided; the lack of an 'industrial tempo' has tended to push up repair and maintenance costs.

Certain Issues: Policy for the Future

As indicated earlier, some three-quarters of the total employment in industry today is in the traditional village industries and other hand crafts (including handloom weaving). And despite the efforts of the KVIC and other specialised agencies, these traditional industries have generally been stagnant, with only a few isolated bright spots where there has been growth of employment and output. In fact, the only sectors (among the industries not controlled by the DCSSI) which have grown phenomenally in the last two decades are the manufacture of gems and jewellery in Gujarat, where large capitalists have successfully made use of skilled craftsmen to build up a flourishing export business; and the powerloom sector, in regard to which there is considerable doubt as to ownership, a common surmise being that the powerlooms are very largely owned by big magnates and their associates, each owning large numbers of powerlooms but being operated in tiny units, which are nonetheless concentrated in a few areas.

Considering the resources of men and money bestowed through the SIDO on the modern small scale sector, it must be admitted that this effort has not been able to attack even the fringe of the problem of rural unemployment and, indeed, even of urban unemployment. Since, apart from the effort of the SIDO, there is a fairly large Central subsidy to this sector by way of excise duty concessions, concessional commercial bank loans, and state government subsidy by way of sales tax exemption, several questions arise, which are briefly listed below:

(a) Can the process of industrialisation (leading to increasing industrial employment) really take off without a groundswell in regard to demand for variegated industrial products from the rural areas, where the bulk of the Indian population lives?

(b) The policy of reservation for, as also the subsidies currently available to, the modern small scale sector apply only to small units which continue to fulfill the twin criteria of employment and capital investment. In other words, in order to obtain the facilities available to the small scale sector, a small unit must necessarily remain small, and must never expand. Is this a desirable or an economically viable proposition?

(c) It is common knowledge that many small units have decided to split their location and to remain within the definition of small scale industry, and yet expand (either by splitting operations vertically or horizontally) thus effectively increasing the scale of operations, in order to avail of diverse concessions available to the small scale sector. To cite one example, as of today, the production of television sets is almost entirely in the small scale sector, as also of other entertainment electronics, like tape-recorders, hi-fi music systems, cassettes, etc. In many instances, such units have availed of the liberal import policy in force for small scale units, and have reaped a bonanza merely by assembling imported components and selling them in a highly protected market, with no competition either from imports or from large units in the same industry. The question that arises is: does this represent a desirable pattern of industrial growth? And do these units really deserve the large concessions granted to small scale units?

(d) Impressive as the growth of the small scale sector—looked after by the SIDO—is, can one say that the concentration of government attention and resources (including the subsidies given) to this sector are fully justified by the growth of employment and output in this sector? Or should one apply certain correctives, and if so, in what manner?

(e) Finally, what are the specific problems in regard to the growth of the traditional (village and) cottage industries, and how can they be tackled? In particular, what framework of policy would one recommend in the future, in order to attain the objective of rapid growth in industrial employment, dispersed over as large an area as possible?

To go back to the first issue raised, obviously, sustained industrialisation requires a sustained demand for industrial products, and such a demand is not a function of population but of income. Hence, one cannot really solve the problem of increased industrial production and employment without a general improvement in incomes in rural areas where the bulk of the Indian population lives. The distribution of income in India today is highly skewed, in tune with the skewed distribution of capital assets (including landholdings in rural areas). It is this factor which makes for the presence of abject poverty among 40 to 50 per cent of the population.

A more broad based ownership of land, coupled with the supply of inputs like irrigation water—for which exploitation of groundwater resources would be both quick as well as economical in many parts of the country—can provide higher incomes to the farming community, and increase the rural demand for industrial products. Incidentally, the West Bengal experience has been that the yield rate is the highest in respect to small holdings, possibly because what the small and marginal farmer lacks by way of capital is more than offset by the input of concentrated effort. That being so, a re-distribution of landholdings is likely to simultaneously increase output and make for a better distribution of income.

Such developments create their own demand for industrial products. For instance, groundwater exploitation may create a demand for pumpsets, so that there would arise not only an increased demand for industrial consumer goods but also for diverse types of capital equipment. But the process calls for land reform as the starting point, a better distribution of the productive assets in the rural areas, and a better distribution of income which may lead to higher effective demand for industrial products.

Public policy, therefore, needs to be geared to promoting such conditions in rural areas as would automatically foster a higher demand for industrial products. Many of the emerging requirements of consumer goods can be met locally, by village industries, which are languishing today because of the absence of local demand.

But village industries can be of two types: those that cater to local demand, and those that meet the needs of a larger market. Industries like handlooms, silk, coir and matches constitute the latter. There are many others: and for these, the limitation of the local market does not pose any insuperable difficulty. But, even in regard to these industries, government support and assistance is necessary by way of easy access to raw materials, credit and assistance in marketing.

Concessional credit has been one of the instruments adopted by the government for the promotion of the modern small scale industry. An important point to note in this context is that while a handful of units get concessional credit, the bulk of small producers do not get any commercial bank credit at all. The need, therefore, is not so much for concessional credit—since such concessional credit needs to be subsidised by someone—as easy access to credit for meeting the genuine credit needs of all producers.

Herein lies a major weakness in government policy, namely, the failure to reach raw materials of reasonable quality, to meet the credit needs, and to assist in the marketing of the products of village industries. Such promotional effort, coupled with policies calculated to raise the level of demand in the rural areas, can help to promote the growth of rural industries, both those which cater to local demand and those which meet the requirements of a wider market.

The second policy issue raised earlier relates to the policy of reservation of industries for small scale units. It has been hinted earlier that this policy is calculated to keep 'infant' industries in a permanent state of infancy. In fact, data cited earlier also indicate considerable under-utilisation of capacity in industries whose products are reserved for the small scale sector. What is required is a bold policy of generous assistance initially, gradual withdrawal of all forms of special assistance, but continued support for the supply of raw materials and credit, as well as for marketing where necessary.

Unfortunately, the policy of reservation has come to stay as one of the major instruments of government support, and has also become an emotive issue. It would, however, be better by far to adopt policies such as that of price preference for government purchases in respect to small industries, and not to stand in the way of the natural growth of industrial undertakings—a principle which has now come to be accepted in respect to large and medium scale enterprises, in respect of their licensed capacities.

This may be a good point at which to stop, except that there is need for some degree of realism while prescribing policy changes. We are not starting from scratch; and we are constantly adding new parameters in a scenario where past policies have given birth to many activities which cannot be allowed to die. A major achievement of the extant policy has been to encourage the growth of a new breed of entrepreneurs, most of whom have graduated from commerce to industry, while some have come from the professions (like engineering, accountancy and the like). Preservation of the entrepreneurial upsurge would be a vital desideratum while considering any policy change, and the momentum of entrepreneurial growth should not be dampened. Hence, what is required is, first, a careful study of the long term viability of different industries by size—involving a careful reappraisal of the common production programme, the lack of which had been noted by the Estimates Committee of Parliament as far back as 1965–66; secondly, an 'adjustment period' for existing units which have so far been propped up undeservedly; third, a new thrust for the proper supply of raw materials and credit to all units, in particular the tiny, village industries and hand crafts (through cooperativisation of small producers where possible); and, finally, and most importantly, the stimulation of demand for industrial products on a wide front, by re-ordering the distribution of landholdings in rural areas (through conscious implementation of land reform measures which are already part of legislation), leading to a better distribution of rural incomes.

APPENDIX

Industry Policy Resolution, 1948: (Excerpt on Small Scale Industry)

Cottage and small scale industries have a very important role in the national economy, offering as they do scope for individual, village or cooperative enterprise and a means for the rehabilitation of displaced persons. These industries are particularly suited for the better utilisation of local resources and for the achievement of local self-sufficiency in respect of certain types of essential consumer goods like food, cloth and agricultural implements. The healthy expansion of cottage and small scale industries depends upon a number of factors, like the provision of raw materials, cheap power, technical advice, organised marketing of their products and where necessary, safeguards against intensive competition by large manufacture, as well as on the education of the worker in the use of the best available technique. Most of these fall in the provincial sphere and are receiving the attention of the governments of the provinces and the states. The resolution of the Industries Conference has requested the Central government to investigate how far and in what manner these industries can be coordinated and integrated with large scale industries. The Government of India accept this recommendation. It will be examined, for example, how the textile mill industry can be made complementary to, rather than competitive with the handloom industry, which is the country's largest and best organised cottage industry. In certain other lines of production, like agricultural implements, textile accessories and parts of machine tools, it should be possible to produce components on a cottage industry scale and assemble these into their final product at a factory. It will also be investigated how far industries (at present highly centralised) could be decentralised with advantage.

The resolution of the Industries Conference has recommended that government should establish a Cottage Industries Board for fostering small scale industries. The Government of India accept this recommendation and propose to create suitable machinery to implement it. A cottaʒe and small scale Industries Directorate will also be set up within the Directorate General of Industries and Supplies.

16 Dipak Mazumdar

Indian
Textile Policy

This paper summarises the main findings of a larger study called
'The Issue of the Small Versus Large in the Textile Industry: An
Analytical and Historical Survey,' which has been issued as a World
Bank Staff Working Paper No. 645.[1]

In India we do not need to apologise when talking about the
government policy on textiles. This is a major industry on which
government policy has had a tremendous impact for a very large
number of years. In fact, it was probably the first industry that was
selected for small scale protection in 1950, just after Independence.
Textile policy and its impact on the industry has ramifications in a
number of directions. However, I shall pinpoint two aspects of
government policy that will be particularly useful as illustrations of
the practical implementation of small industry policies.

The first is the difficulty of supporting substantively, in practical
terms, the household sector, which was the ostensible aim of government policy. Second, the way the different branches of government policy-making, pursuing separate sets of objectives, did not
get related to each other and in some ways produced results which
are not entirely consistent.

The early decision on handlooms was taken in 1950 by an-
nouncing a list of items to be reserved for this sector. At that time,
or soon after, there was within the textile context the same debate

[1] Another somewhat different abstract of findings of the study is to be found in
Chapter 6 of I.M.D. Little, D. Mazumdar and J.M. Page (forthcoming).

that has been referred to by Arun Ghosh, in another paper in this volume.

A view expounded by the Kanungo Committee that powerlooms would be the obvious next step for handlooms, that powerlooms with intermediate technology should be encouraged, and that handlooms should be given all assistance to graduate to this sector through gradual mechanisation over time. At the time this committee was meeting, there was another committee called the Karve Committee which put forward a completely different set of recommendations, adopting a Gandhian kind of approach for the support of handlooms.

Whether these two points of view were ever debated seriously in government circles is not clear. Anyway, policies went ahead and as far as the Second Five Year Plan was concerned the latter view won the day as far as planning was concerned. The government banned the installation of new looms by the mills, except for replacement or for export production. In 1956 the Second Plan envisaged that powerlooms would account for only 10 per cent of increased cloth production, and handlooms were to take up the rest of the demand for cloth.

Incidentally, this particular formulation owed a lot to the Mahalanobis model, which concluded that the capital goods sector would be the growth point for industrialisation and the under-utilised household sector was expected to meet the demands for consumer goods that will be generated with the development of the capital goods sector. The general view was that there was so much idle capacity in handlooms that we could expect a kind of perfectly elastic supply of handloom goods from this sector and, therefore, there was no need to divert investment resources to consumer goods production, particularly cloth. All investments should be in the capital goods sector and handlooms should respond automatically by supplying cloth to meet the additional demand expected.

What the exponents of the Mahalanobis model (or anybody else in government policy-making) did not ask at that time was this. Presumably the development of the capital goods sector was meant ultimately to produce machines to produce consumer goods, but how would this transition from domestic production, particularly handlooms, to consumer goods produced by more mechanised methods take place and what would happen to handlooms in this process of transformation?

In any event, the policy of protection of handlooms was in place. But the actual turn of events was very different. Mill cotton cloth production fell from its peak of 4.9 billion metres in 1956 to 3.1 billion metres in 1981, while total cloth production rose from 6.5 to 8.1 billion metres. But powerlooms accounted for 74 per cent of the small scale sector output of 3.3 billion metres. These are statistics which I have estimated from various sources detailed in the Bank Staff Working Paper. So the lion's share of the increase in output came from powerlooms. There were several reasons for this remarkable unanticipated growth of powerlooms.

To begin with, powerlooms were free of excise taxes and had a much shorter list of restrictions on items they produced with respect to mills. The second point I will come to later because it relates better to the discussion on the economics of powerlooms. But the other important point is that the growth of the powerloom sector was essentially the growth of unlicensed units and they did not have to pay any income tax at all. So the entire taxation system was geared to helping the growth of powerlooms, which was not anticipated.

Powerlooms used the same type of technology with probably somewhat cheaper non-automatic looms than used in the mills. It used twice as much labour per loom but had wage levels significantly less than half the mill wages, so that labour costs were lower in powerlooms than in mills. Clearly, employment per loom was higher. There is one point which needs special attention. The larger organisation of the mills would have given them a potential advantage in terms of working more shifts. But this could not be done because of the power problem. Mills which had to operate more than one shift had to have investment in generators so that capital investment per unit of labour had to be correspondingly higher.

At the other end of the scale, handlooms had much lower productivity but the earnings of an adult male worker, which defined the wage cost from the point of view of the entrepreneur, was not all that different (at least in our survey data) from that in the powerlooms. Thus, the labour cost of handlooms was much higher although capital cost per unit of output was considerably smaller.

The upshot of these observations is that, on the basis of the data that we collected and the cost structure of handlooms, powerlooms and mills as given in Table 1, we found that the private profitability of the powerloom sector was enormous. At the given market

Table 1

*Inputs Required to Produce Value Added of Rs. 10,000 Per Annum
in the Three Sectors of the Weaving Industry*

	Handlooms	Powerlooms	Mills
Number of workers or adult male equivalents	3.36	1.76	0.51
Fixed capital costs:			
(a) Machinery	534	3,426	
(b) Land & Buildings	5,155	4,480	
Total	5,689	7,906	
Working Capital	3,024	2,600	
Total Capital	8,713	10,506	19,000

wages, powerloom was the most profitable sector for a wide range of shadow interest rates between 13 and 46 per cent. If we make allowance for the taxes on mills, which the powerlooms escaped, the profitability range would be even wider. No wonder that the powerlooms expanded so much, and I venture to guess that they would have expanded even in the absence of the physical control of mills.

Now we shall look at social profitability. The reader must be warned that we are going on the basis of very shaky data. Powerloom and handloom cost data come from a small survey which we undertook in Mau, a little textile town in Uttar Pradesh. We could not survey the mills sector because they are mostly composite mills and it is difficult to get costs on the weaving industry without a great deal of trouble. So we culled various secondary sources—Planning Commission report by Raj Krishna, reports by various textile commissioners, and a Bombay doctoral thesis—and we gave our best estimates of the average costs of cloth production in mills, which is given in the Appendix Table.

Incidentally, this data problem surprised me. It is mind-boggling to think that a major industry of India, when such major policies were being enunciated affecting the fortunes of millions of people in the different sectors, did not have any data on costs. No government commission collected economic data. The last report that gave cost figures was the Handlooms Enquiry Commission published in 1942. There is no official cost data given in any of the reports or surveys made since then. Decisions were taken in an atmosphere of complete lack of information.

We tried to do a social profitability calculation on the basis of our limited data. The first adjustments one had to make were, of course, to wages. Mill wages, as mentioned earlier, were twice that of powerlooms, maybe more. Handloom earnings per adult male worker were equal, more or less, to the powerloom wage. The powerloom wage, we thought, could represent a kind of free market wage. The shadow wage for handlooms had to be smaller because a handloom adult male worker was helped by other family members and because he had the flexibility of hours, working at home. As far as mills were concerned—this is carrying over from the discussion on the labour markets—there is a big differential, partly due to economic reasons and partly due to institutional reasons, and it is hard to know how much is what. So we did various trials assuming the shadow wage to be equal to the powerlooms in the mill sector and also trying out various shadow wages for mills.

I will summarise the results. As far as the powerloom-mill comparison is concerned, ignoring the distributional consideration, if we adopt the powerloom shadow wage for the mills, the social rate of return, assuming a 25-year life for all equipment, was 30 per cent. The reader will recall that the private switch-over interest rate from powerlooms to mills was seen to be 13 per cent. At an interest rate less than 13 per cent it was profitable for the techniques to be switched over to mills. But if you took social profitability into account then the switch-over rate of interest went up to 30 per cent. A similar result was obtained at the other end of the spectrum. If we adopted the shadow wage of powerlooms, then the social rate of return—the switch-over interest rate from handlooms to power-looms—fell from 46 to 35 per cent. The strong conclusion emerges that on the basis of market wages we have an enormous range in shadow interest rate between 13 per cent and 46 per cent in which powerlooms are seen to be profitable. If you adopt the shadow wage of powerlooms, then this range is reduced from 35 to 30. So we can see that the social profitability of powerlooms is considerably reduced if we allow for the shadow wage calculation.

Here we have the first lesson, I think, given tentatively, having the data problem in mind, that the enormous expansion of power-looms was in some sense a social loss. Either the handloom or mills sector would have been socially profitable, given your view of the shadow rate of interest.

Given this high profitability of powerlooms, how did the other two sectors manage to exist at all? I think the answer is specialisation by product lines. You can talk about different types of cloth being produced by the different sectors only on the basis of the counts of yarn that were being woven in the different sectors. I have done that in the Working Paper. The rough specialisation that has existed in the Indian economy is that handlooms produced predominantly coarse cloth for the rural market. The powerloom has competed for the middle and lower-upper type of yarn. The mills have tried to compete with the powerlooms by producing not just cloth making use of finer counts of yarn, but by producing superior cloth. This specialisation by the quality of the product led to the possibility of the coexistence of the three sectors. The handloom sector of course increased, as the mill sector decreased in absolute size, but they both survived.

I will make one other point about handlooms. The slow rate of growth in handlooms that is observed in the post-Independence period is nothing new. I have produced data in the Working Paper going back to the beginning of the century. The startling result, for which I was not prepared, was that handloom output increased continuously since the turn of the century. There was not a single year in which the output of handloom showed a decrease. The handloom sector really has been growing, based on a market essentially related to the growth of the rural population and income, and it has competed successfully in the past against both the coming of Lancashire and the rise of the domestic mill industry, and it has competed successfully since Independence against the growth of the powerloom sector.

The lesson that I draw from this point is that the effect of the government policy that was supposed to mainly increase the growth of the handloom really seems to have been redundant. Probably handlooms would have increased in the post-Independence period at the same rate as before Independence. The policy of government protection of handlooms had only a marginal effect on the growth of the handloom sector as against the startling effect on the growth of the powerloom sector.

The unintended and disproportionate effect of government policy on the powerloom sector was helped by a couple of points of inconsistency in the policy package. One has to do with excise taxes. Direct tax on handloom has been non-existent. It was also non-existent on powerlooms for some time, but was introduced in 1974.

But excise tax on the final product is not the end of the story. There is a very complicated tax structure on the raw material and inputs of various kinds going into the production of cloth. Nicholas Stern and his colleagues have worked out the net burden of excise tax on the three sectors within a general equilibrium framework.[2] Their conclusion, rather spectacular, is that the net burden of taxation per unit of value added was 30 per cent lower for powerlooms than for mills, but as far as handlooms and powerlooms are concerned, there was no difference, both bearing the same net burden of excise taxes.

The second point I will make is that one of the aspects of the attack on mills was the directive that mills should produce a certain amount of coarse cloth and sell it at subsidised prices. This is odd because coarse cloth, in any case, was supposed to be produced by handlooms and you are encouraging the mill sector to produce a type of cloth for which you are protecting the handloom sector. The other aspect is of course that this policy of interference with the output-mix of the mills was instrumental in producing the large sector of sick mills which had to be nationalised. As it happens, the nationalised mills (in their attempt to achieve high productivity) pursued the idea of producing coarse cloth with the help of modernised automatic equipment—a policy which was encouraged by the fact that the existing labour force in the units could not be depleted when they were nationalised. We seem to have come full circle in contradictory aims. The demand for coarse cloth in the economy was expected to be met by the projected non-mechanical handloom, on the one hand, and the highly capitalised (but equally protected) nationalised units, on the other. It is not known how far the latter were competing with the former, and thwarting the aims of supporting handlooms.

What was the net effect of all this on the economy? I have already discussed the almost certain socially undersirable excess growth of the powerloom sector. What about employment? The way the policy worked out certainly increased employment because, as I said, powerlooms employed more people per loom than the mills. But what was the cost of achieving this extra bit of employment? The major cost, as I see it, is stagnation in textile output. We know that cotton output declined continuously during this period. At the same time, the slack could not be taken up by man-made fibres

[2] M.N. Murty and N.H. Stern, 'Price and Tax Policies for Cotton Textiles in India,' Development Economics Research Centre, University of Warwick, October 1982.

because of another unrelated set of policies of the government. As we know, the most dynamic sector of the textile economy in the world is man-made fibres. Everywhere in the world, man-made fibre is the poor man's cloth. In India, due to a set of policies, unrelated to the protection of small scale industry or the creation of employment, but based on some rather different considerations, huge burdens of taxation were imposed on the production and consumption of man-made fibres. In January 1981, the international price of polyester fibre was Rs. 12 per kg; the ex-factory price of fibre produced in India was Rs. 34 per kg, the higher cost of production partly reflecting the fact that the government would not allow the capacity of the plants established to be higher than a particular size. The excise duty was Rs. 45 per kg. to be added to the ex-factory price, and that made the price of the fibre in the Indian market six times the international price. Available data on consumption by income levels show that the consumption of man-made fibre cloth in India is very much a feature of the higher income groups.

So, in fact, because of the twin-pronged policy—the attack on the mill sector for the ostensible reason of protecting handloom and, secondly, the high tax cost imposed on man-made fibre—the cotton industry in India never had a chance to produce a commodity that seemed to be a mass consumption product in the textile field in the rest of the world. The contrasting picture with Indonesia is relevant. Since the abandonment of Sokarno's policies of protection of handloom, and the adoption of a policy of active encouragement of man-made fibres and of capital-intensive production, the consumption of textiles per head has gone up considerably in the last couple of decades. To some extent, of course, the difference in experience of the two countries can be traced to the higher rate of growth of income in Indonesia. But, a part of the difference is certainly due to different sets of policies adopted by the government.[3]

In effect, the employment increase in the powerlooms has been achieved but, taking cotton and man-made fibres together, textile consumption has stagnated. The cost of achieving employment increases has been substantial.

Finally, I will conclude with a point which brings us close to some of the findings of H.H. de Haan on the sugar industry. Why was the

[3] For a summary of the Indonesian experience, see Hall Hills, 'Choice of Technique in the Indonesian Weaving Industry,' Ph.D Thesis, Australian National University, December 1979.

powerloom sector allowed to flourish in the way it did? The Kanungo Committee had originally thought that the right way to tackle the handloom weavers was to make them slowly graduate to becoming powerloom weavers and increase their income that way. However, if they were to go back to their report and view the situation today, they would be sadly disappointed. Hardly any handloom weaver has entered the powerloom sector. The powerloom sector has been created essentially by a new entrepreneurial class, in the same way that the *khandsari* sector has been created by a new entrepreneurial class. The difference is that the promotion of the *khandsari* sector was a deliberate government policy; the promotion of powerloom sector is unintended, or at least so it seems. But there is no question that it is a new entrepreneurial class which has attracted investment from somewhere. The rate of profit is enormous. I have given you the private profitability figures. Even looking at our survey data, we get rates of return on capital of 40 per cent or so in powerlooms. I have not looked personally at the political economy of the formation of this new entrepreneurial class. H.H. de Haan has in the *khandsari* case. In that case, it is quite clear that this new entrepreneurial class came from the rural kulaks and the investment in *khandsari* came from the rural surplus produced by the middle and larger landlords. I rather suspect a similar sort of thing has happened in powerlooms.

APPENDIX TABLE

Machine Productivity in the Three Sectors

	Handlooms	Powerlooms	Mills
Output per loom shift (metres)	11	27	34
Number of shifts	1	1.5	2.5
Number of workers per loom	2.02	1.60	0.8
Capital costs per loom			
Machinery	321	3,358	13,435
Land and building	3,100	4,392	—
Working capital	1,818	2,652	—
Total	5,239	10,402	57,000

Bibliography

Anderson, D., and **F. Khambata**. 1981. 'Small Enterprises and Development Policy in the Philippines: A Case Study,' *World Bank Staff Working Paper*, No. 468.

Asher, Ramsinh. 1978. 'Small-Scale and Cottage Industries in India,' in J.S. Uppal, (ed.).

Bagchi, A.K., and **N. Banerjee** (eds.). 1981. *Change and Choice in Indian Industry*, Calcutta, Bagchi & Co.

Balasubramanyam, V.N. 1984. *The Economy of India*, London, Weidenfeld and Nicholson.

Banerjee, B. 1977. 'Growth of Industrial Employment in India and the Structure of Manufacturing Industries in Uttar Pradesh 1961–1971,' World Bank mimeo.

Banerjee, Nirmala. 1981. 'Is Small Beautiful?' in A.K. Bagchi & N. Banerjee (eds.).

Banerji, R. 1978. 'Average Plant Size in Manufacturing and Capital Intensity: A Cross Country Analysis by Industry,' *Journal of Development Economics*, Vol. 5, No. 2, June.

Bautista, R.M. 1981. 'The Development of Labor Intensive Industry in the Philippines,' in Rashid Amjad (ed.), *The Development of Labour Intensive Industry in ASEAN Countries*, ILO, ARTEP.

Bhagwati, J.N., and **P. Desai**. 1970. *India: Planning for Industrialisation*, London, Oxford University Press.

Bhalla, A.S. 1965. 'Choosing Techniques: Handpounding *Versus* Machine Milling of Rice: An Indian Case,' *Oxford Economic Papers*, No. 17.

Bhatt, V.V., and **Alan R. Roe**. 1979. 'Capital Market Imperfections and Economic Development,' *World Bank Staff Working Paper*, No. 338, July.

Bhavani, A. 1980. 'Relative Efficiency of the Modern Small Scale Industries,' M. Phil. Dissertation, University of Delhi, January.

Boon, G.K. 1980. *Technology and Employment in Footwear Manufacturing*, Alphen a/d Rijn.

Boswell, J. 1972. *The Rise and Decline of Small Firms*, London, George Allen and Unwin.

Bowden, R.J., and **D. Mazumdar**. 1982. 'Segmentation and Earnings Profiles in LDCs,' *Discussion Paper*, No. 4, World Bank, Development Research Department, November.

Briggs, G.W. 1920. *The Chamars*, Calcutta.

Child, F.C. 'An Empirical Study of Small Scale Rural Industry in Kenya,' *IDS Working Paper*, No. 127, Kenya, University of Nairobi.

Child F.C., and **Hiromitsu Kaneda**. 1975. 'Links to the Green Revolution: A Study of Small Scale, Agriculturally Related Industry in the Pakistan Punjab,' *Economic Development and Cultural Change*, Vol. 23, No. 2, January.

Cornelisse, P.A., **F. Bishay**, **S.I. Cohen** and **P. Terhal**, 1980. 'Agricultural Processing Industries in the International Division of Labour,' *Discussion Paper*, No. 49, Rotterdam, Centre for Development Planning, Erasmus University, January.

Dhar, P.N. 1958. *Small-Scale Industries in Delhi*, New Delhi, Asia Publishing House.

——————. 1979. 'Some Observations on Small-Scale Enterprise Development,' in C.H. Rao and P.C. Joshi (eds.).

Dhar, P.N., and **H.F. Lydall**. 1961. *The Role of Small Enterprises in Economic Development*, New Delhi, Asia Publishing House.

Datta, Bhabatosh. 1978. 'Small to Big: A Critique of the Industrial Policy Statement,' *Economic and Political Weekly*, 21 January.

Dorfman, Robert, and **Peter O. Steiner**. 1954. 'Optimal Advertising and Optimal Quality,' *American Economic Review*.

Goldar, B. 1982. 'Unit Size and Economic Efficiency in Small Scale Washing Soap Industry in India,' *Artha Vijñana*, March.

Fong, pang Eng, and **Augustine Tan**. 1981. 'Employment and Export-Led Industrialization: The Experience of Singapore,' in Rashid Amjad (ed.), *The Development of Labor Intensive Industry in ASEAN Countries*, ILO, ARTEP.

Freeman, C. 'The Role of Small Firms in Innovation in the United Kingdom Since 1945,' *Bolton Committee Research Report*, No. 6.

Gandhi, M.K. 1948. *The Economics of Village Industries*, Ahmedabad.

Ghosh, D. 1956. 'Techniques of Production and Employment in an Under-developed Economy,' *The Economic Weekly*, No. 8, August.

Gokhale Institute of Politics and Economics, Poona, and Central Leather Research Institute Madras, 1969. *Survey of India's Exports Potential of Leather and Leather Products*, four volumes.

Government of India, Central Statistical Organisation (Industrial Statistics Division). 1979. 'Wages and Productivity in Organized Manufacturing Sector, 1960–61 to 1976–77,' *Bulletin No. 15D/5*, New Delhi, August.

Government of India, Ministry of Commerce and Industry. 1954. *Report on Small Industries in India* (International Planning Team, sponsored by the Ford Foundation), New Delhi.

Government of India, Development Commissioner, Small Scale Industries, 1976–77. *All India Report on the Census of Small Scale Industries*, Volumes 1 and 2, New Delhi.

——————. 1982. *Small Scale Industries in India: Policies, Programmes and Institutional Support*, New Delhi, March.

Government of India, Ministry of Industry, 1963. *Development of Small Scale Industries in India: Prospects, Problems and Policies* (International Perspective Planning Team, Sponsored by the Ford Foundation), New Delhi.

——————. 1964. *Powerloom Enquiry Committee Report*, New Delhi.

——————. 1968. *Report of Khadi and Village Industries Committee*, New Delhi.

Government of India, Planning Commission, 1956. *Report of the Village and Small-Scale Industries Committee*, New Delhi.

——————. 1959. Perspective Planning Division. *A Study of Economic Co-efficients for Organised Industries in India*, Mimeo, New Delhi.

——————. 1960. *Capital and Labour Requirements of Small Enterprises*, Mimeo, New Delhi.

——————. 1978. *The Draft Sixth Plan for India*, New Delhi.

Gupta, N.S., and **Amarjit Singh**. 1978. *Industrial Economy of India*, New Delhi, Light & Life Publications.

Haan, H.H. de. 1980a. 'The Industrial Distribution of the Labour Force in India, 1961–1971,' Parts 1 & 2, *Discussion Paper* No. 55-A & B, Rotterdam, Centre for Development Planning, Erasmus University.

——————. 1980b. 'Rural Industrialisation in India. The Contribution to Labour Absorption and to Curbing Rural-Urban Migration,' *Discussion Paper*, No. 54, Rotterdam, Centre for Development Planning, Erasmus University.

Hajra, S. 1965. 'Firm Size and Efficiency in Manufacturing Industries,' *Economic Weekly*, 28 August.

Heemst, J.J.P. van. 'Choice of Techniques in Footwear Production and its Policy Implications: Some Further Evidence for the case of Ghana,' The Hague, University of Cape Coast/JJS, (mimeographed).

——————. 1977. 'Factor Intensities and Economic Efficiency in the Ghanaian Small Scale Footwear Industry,' *Research Report Series* No. 17, Cape Coast, Centre for Development Studies, University of Cape Coast.

——————. 1982. 'Scale, Organisation and Efficiency in Footwear Production: An Analysis of some Ghanaian Data,' *Occasional Papers*, No. 95, Institute of Social Studies, March.

Herman, Theodore. 1956–57. 'The Role of Cottage and Small-Scale Industries in Asian Economic Development,' *Economic Development and Cultural Change*, Vol. 5.

Ho, S. 1980. 'Small Scale Enterprises in Korea and Taiwan,' *World Bank Staff Working Paper*, No. 384.

International Labour Organisation. 1950. 'Handicraft and Small-Scale Industries in Asian Countries,' *International Labour Review*, December.

Jadavpur University. 1964. *Survey of Small Engineering Units in Howrah*, Reserve Bank of India.

Jain, L.C. 1980. 'Development of Decentralised Industries,' *Economic and Political Weekly*, October.

Jalan, Bimal N. 1978. 'Production in Tiny, Small and Large Scale Sectors: A Note,

Economic and Political Weekly, Bombay, 20 May.

Kaneda, Hiromitsu. 1980. 'Development of Small and Medium Enterprises and Policy Response in Japan: An Analytical Survey,' *Studies in Employment and Rural Development*, No. 32, World Bank mimeo, October.

Khan, R.R. 1979. *Management of Small Scale Industries*, New Delhi, Chand & Co.

Knight, J., and **R.H. Sabot.** 1982. 'From Migrants to Proletarians: Employment Experience, Mobility and Wages in Tanzania,' *Oxford Bulletin of Economics and Statistics*, Vol. 44.

Kulkarni, M.R. 1965. 'Small Industry in Two Big Cities: Delhi and Bombay,' *Indian Economic Journal*, April-June, Vol. 12.

Kulkarni, V.B. 1979. *History of the Indian Cotton Textile Industry*, Bombay.

Kurien, C.T. 1978. 'Small Sector in New Industrial Policy,' *Economic and Political Weekly*, 4 March.

Kuyvenhoven, Aries. 1980. 'Technology, Employment and Basic Needs in Leather Industries in Developing Countries,' *Discussion Paper* No. 51, Rotterdam, C.D.P., E.U.R.

Lakdawala, D.T., and **J.C. Sandesara.** 1960. *Small Industry in Big City: A Survey in Bombay*, Bombay, Vora and Company.

Lakshman, T.K. 1966. *Cottage and Small Scale Industries in Mysore*, Mysore.

Liedholm, Carl, and **E. Chuta,** 1976. 'The Economics of Rural and Urban Small Scale Industries in Siera Leone,' *African Rural Economy Paper*, No. 14, Michigan State University.

Lim, Chee Peng, Donald Lee, and **Foo Kok Thye.** 1981. 'The Case for Labour-Intensive Industries in Malaysia,' in Rashid Amjad (ed.), *The Development of Labour Intensive Industry in ASEAN Countries*, ILO, ARTEP.

Little, I.M.D. 1982. 'Indian Industrialisation 1857–1947,' in M. Gerowitz *et al.*, *The Theory and Experience of Economic Development: Essays in Honour of Sir Arthur Lewis*, London, Allen and Unwin.

——————. 1987. 'Small Manufacturing Enterprises in Developing Countries,' *The World Bank Economic Review*, Vol. 1, No. 2.

Little, I.M.D., D. Mazumdar, and **J.M. Page.** Forthcoming. *Small Manufacturing Enterprises: A Comparative Study of India and Other Countries*, New York, Oxford University Press.

Lynch, O.M. 1974. *The Politics of Untouchability*, Delhi.

Majumdar, A.G. 1963. 'Small Enterprises' Contribution to National Income—An Alternative Approach,' *The Economic Weekly*, Vol. 15, September.

Maleanson, James M. 1981. 'Unemployment and the Efficiency Wage Hypothesis,' *Economic Journal*, Vol. 91, December.

Mazumdar, D. 1983. 'The Role of Small-Scale Enterprises in the Indian Economy,' World Bank mimeo, June.

——————. 1984. 'The Issue of Small Versus Large in the Indian Textile Industry: An Analytical and Historical Survey,' *World Bank Staff Working Paper*, No. 645.

McBain, B.S. 1977. *The Choice of Techniques in Footwear Manufacturing for Developing Countries*, London, Ministry of Overseas Development, HMSP.

Mehta, B.V. 1969. 'Size and Capital Intensity in Indian Inaustry,' *Oxford Bulletin of Economics and Statistics*, August.

Mellor, J. 1976. *The New Economics of Growth—A Strategy for India and the Developing World*, Cornell University Press.

Mitra, L.K. 1967. *Employment and Output in Small Enterprises of India*, Calcutta.

Morawetz, D. 1974. 'Employment Implications of Industrialisation in Developing Countries,' *Economic Journal*, September.

National Council of Applied Economic Research. 1963. *Small-Scale Industries of Mysore*, New Delhi, June.
—————. 1972. *Study of Selected Small Industrial Units*, New Delhi.

Nayudamma, Y. (coord.). 1980. Development Alternatives, Production of Leather-goods: A Case Study, Madras, Centre for Development Alternatives, Central Leather Research Institute.

Nayudamma, Y.K., **Sarjuna Rao**, and **K. Seshagiri Rao**. 1980. *Development Alternatives, Manufacture of Footwear—Pitchaiah's Model, A Case Study*, Madras, CDA, CLRI.

Ohkawa, K., and **M. Tajima**. 1978. 'Small-Medium Scale Manufacturing Industry: A Comparative Study of Japan and Developing Nations,' International Development Centre of Japan, March.

Ojha, P.D. 1982. 'Finance for Small-Scale Enterprise in India,' *Reserve Bank of India Bulletin*, November.

Page, J.M. 1979. 'Small Enterprises in African Development: A Survey,' *World Bank Staff Working Paper*, No. 363.
—————. 1984. 'Firm size and Technical Efficiency: Applications of Production Frontiers to Indian Survey Data,' *Journal of Development Economics*, September-October.

Papola, T.S. 1978. 'Small Scale Industries in Uttar Pradesh,' *Occasional Paper*, No. 2, Lucknow, The Giri Institute of Development Studies.
—————. 1981a. 'Industrialization, Technological Choice and Urban Labour Markets,' in A.K. Bagchi & N. Banerjee, (eds.).
—————. 1981b. *Spatial Diversification of Industries* (A Study of Uttar Pradesh), New Delhi, Allied Publishers.
—————. 1982. *Rural Industrialisation—Approaches and Potentials*, Bombay, Himalaya Publishing House.

Papola, T.S., and **V.N. Misra**. 1980. 'Some Aspects of Rural Industrialisation,' *Economic and Political Weekly*, October.

Pathak, H.N. 1970. 'Small Scale Industries in Ludhiana,' *Economic and Political Weekly*, No. 5.

Pillai, P.P. 1978. 'Scale and Efficiency of Small Scale Industries in India, *Asian Economic Review*, 8 April.

Prakash, Prem. 1961. 'Relationship Between Size and Productivity in Selected Indian Industries,' *Asian Economic Review*, Vol. 11, May.

Raj, K.N. 1956. 'Small-Scale Industries—Problems of Technological Change,' Parts 1 and 2, *The Economic Weekly*, Vol. 8, April.

Rangarajan, C. 1980. 'Innovations in Banking: The Indian Experience, Impact Deposits and Credit,' *Domestic Finance Studies*, No. 63, World Bank, June.

Rangarajan, C. *et al.*, 1981. *Strategy for Industrial Development in the 80s*, New Delhi, Oxford and IBM Publications.

Ramakrishna, K.T. 1962. *Finances for Small-Scale Industry in India*, Bombay.

Rao, C.H., Hanumantha, and **P.C. Joshi** (eds.). 1979. *Reflections on Economic Development and Social Change: Essays in Honour of Professor V.K.R.V. Rao*, New Delhi, Allied Publications.

Rao, M.V. 1959. 'Small Units in the Capital Goods Sector—Their Role in a Developing Economy,' *The Economic Weekly*, Vol. 10, March, pp. 441–74.

Reserve Bank of India. 1979. 'Survey of Small Industrial Units 1977,' *Statistical Report*, Vols. 1 and 2, Bombay, Department of Statistics.

Saito, K.A., and **D.R. Villaneuva**, 1980. 'Transaction Cost of Credit to the Small-Scale Sector in Philippines,' *Domestic Finance Studies*, No. 53, World Bank, Public and Private Finance Division, December.

Sandesara, J.C. 1966. 'Scale and Technology in Indian Industry,' *Oxford Bulletin of Economics and Statistics*, August

—————. 1969. *Size and Capital Intensity in Indian Industry*, Bombay, University of Bombay.

—————. 1981a. 'The Small Industry Questions: Issues, Evidence and Suggestions,' in A.K. Bagchi & N. Banerjee (eds.).

—————. 1981b. 'Small Industry in India: Evidence and Interpretation,' *Indian Planning and Economic Policies*, Ahmedabad, Gujarat Economic Association.

—————. 1982. *Efficiency of Incentives for Small Industry*, Bombay, Industrial Development Bank of India.

Sharma, S.L. 1963. 'Small-Scale Industries in India—Case for Modernization,' *Small Industries Bulletin for Asia and the Far East*, No. 1, January.

Singh, Baljit. 1961. *The Economics of Small Industries—A Case Study of Small-Scale Industrial Establishments of Moradabad*, New Delhi, Asia Publishing House.

Spengler J.J. 1956–57. 'Cottage Industries: A Comment,' *Economic Development and Cultural Change*, Vol. 5.

Squire, I. 1979. 'Labour Force, Employment and Labour Markets in the Course of Economic Development,' *World Bank Staff Working Paper*, No. 336, June.

Srivastava, D.B. 1979. *The Province of Agra, Its History and Administration*, New Delhi.

Stiglitz, J.E. 1974. 'Alternative Theories of Wage Determination and Unemployment in LDCs: The Labor Turnover Model,' *Quarterly Journal of Economics*, Vol. 88.

Suri, K.B. 1983. 'Quality and Marketing of Laundry Soap,' Development Economics Department, World Bank mimeo, June.

Tajima, M. 1978. 'Small-Medium Scale Manufacturing Industry: Further Discussion in a Comparative Study of Japan and Developing Nations,' International Development Center of Japan, March.

Tambunlerchai, Somsak, and **Chesada Loohawenchit**. 1981. 'Labour Intensive and Small-Scale Manufacturing in Thailand,' in Rashid Amjad (ed.), *The Development of Labour Intensive Industry in ASEAN Countries*, ILO, ARTEP.

Thomas, T. 1978. 'Relationship between Small-Scale and Large-Scale Industry—A Different View,' *Economic and Political Weekly*, 3 March.

Tinbergen, J. 1957. 'Mill Versus Cottage Industries,' *The Economic Weekly*, Vol. 9, January.

Tyabji, N. 1980. 'Capitalism in India and the Small Industries Policy,' *Economic and Political Weekly*, October.

Uttar Pradesh Industrial Consultants (UPICO). 1981. 'Leather Footwear Artisans in Uttar Pradesh,' Report for the Uttar Pradesh Leather Development and Marketing Organisation (UPLDMC).

Uttar Pradesh Leather Development and Marketing Corporation. 1976. 'Survey of Footwear Industry in Agra,' mimeographed, Agra.

Uppal, J.S. (ed.) 1978. *India's Economic Problems, An Analytical Approach* (2nd. ed.), New Delhi, Tata McGraw-Hill.

Van der Veen, J.H. 1973. 'A Study of Small Industries in Gujarat State, India,' *Occasional Paper*, No. 65, Cornell University, Department of Agricultural Economics, May.

Varma, R. 1980. 'Employment and Production in Small Scale Industries: Some Findings of the Reserve Bank of India Survey,' Reserve Bank of India *Occasional Papers*, Bombay.

Virmani, Arvind. 1982. 'The Nature of Credit Markets in Developing Countries: A Framework for Policy Analysis,' *World Bank Staff Working Paper*, No. 524.

White, L.J. 1978. 'Appropriate Factor Proportions for Manufacturing in Less Developed Countries: A Survey of the Evidence,' *Economic Development and Cultural Change*, Vol. 27, No. 1.

——————. 1981. *Measuring the Importance of Small Business in the American Economy*, Solomon Brothers Centre for the Study of Financial Institutions, and Graduate School of Business Administration, New York University.

Appendix

List of Participants at the Conference

Shankara N. Acharya,
Department of Economic Affairs,
Ministry of Finance,
Government of India,
NEW DELHI.

Isher J. Ahluwalia,
Centre for Policy Research,
NEW DELHI.

Y.K. Alagh,
Bureau of Industrial Costs and Prices,
Ministry of Industry and
    Company Affairs,
Government of India,
NEW DELHI.

Amaresh Bagchi,
Department of Economic Affairs,
Ministry of Finance,
Government of India,
NEW DELHI.

Nirmala Banerjee,
Centre for Studies in Social Sciences,
CALCUTTA.

Adi Bhavani,
Institute of Economic Growth,
DELHI.

Suleiman I. Cohen,
Netherlands School of Economics,
Rotterdam,
THE NETHERLANDS.

Mrinal Datta-Chaudhury,
Delhi School of Economics,
DELHI.

Nitin Desai,
World Commission on Environment
    and Development,
GENEVA.

Lalit K. Deshpande,
Department of Economics,
University of Bombay,
BOMBAY.

Bishwanath Goldar,
Institute of Economic Growth,
DELHI.

Roger Grawe,
The Word Bank,
WASHINGTON D.C.

D.B. Gupta,
Faculty of Management Studies,
University of Delhi,
DELHI.

H.H. de Haan,
Centre for Development Planning,
University of Erasmus,
Rotterdam,
THE NETHERLANDS.

S.R. Hashim,
Planning Commission,
Government of India,
NEW DELHI.

John R. Hansen
The World Bank,
NEW DELHI.

S.P. Kashyap,
Sardar Patel Institute of Economic and
    Social Research,
AHMEDABAD.

K.L. Krishna,
Delhi School of Economics,
DELHI.

J. Krishnamurty,
Institute of Economic Growth,
DELHI.

M.R. Kulkarni,
Planning Commission,
Government of India,
NEW DELHI.

I.M.D. Little,
Nuffield College, Oxford,
ENGLAND.

Dipak Mazumdar,
Department of Economics,
University of Toronto,
CANADA.

V.G. Patel,
Indian Institute of
    Entrepreneurship Development,
AHMEDABAD.

V.S. Patvardhan,
Gokhale Institute of Politics and
    Economics,
PUNE.

G.N. Pradhan,
National Institute of Public Finance
    and Policy,
NEW DELHI.

G. Pursell,
The World Bank,
NEW DELHI.

G. Ramachandran,
Central Statistical Organisation,
Ministry of Planning,
Government of India,
NEW DELHI.

M.R. Saluja,
Indian Statistical Institute,
NEW DELHI.

J.C. Sandesara,
Department of Economics,
University of Bombay,
BOMBAY.

M.G. Sardana,
Central Statistical Organisation,
Ministry of Planning,
Government of India,
NEW DELHI.

Atul Sarma,
Indian Statistical Institute,
NEW DELHI.

D.U. Sastry,
Institute of Economic Growth,
DELHI.

Ramprasad Sengupta,
Jawaharlal Nehru University,
NEW DELHI.

Nitish K. Sengupta,
Ministry of Tourism and Civil Aviation,
Government of India,
NEW DELHI.

Sunanda Sengupta,
The World Bank,
NEW DELHI.

K. Sundaram,
Delhi School of Economics,
DELHI.

K.B. Suri,
School of Planning and Architecture,
NEW DELHI.

S.D. Tendulkar,
Delhi School of Economics,
DELHI.

R.S. Tiwari,
Sardar Patel Institute of Economic and
    Social Research,
AHMEDABAD.

J. George Waardenburg,
Centre for Development Planning,
University of Erasmus, Rotterdam,
THE NETHERLANDS.

E. Bevan Waide,
The World Bank,
NEW DELHI.

About the Contributors

Nirmala Banerjee is a Fellow in economics at the Centre for Studies in Social Sciences, Calcutta. She had earlier worked as a fiscal scientist at the Calcutta Metropolitan Planning Organisation. Her current work focuses mainly on the urban unorganised sector and its workforce. She is also deeply involved in research on gender issues in economic development. In these fields, she has published a number of articles as well as several books both as author and co-editor.

H.H. de Haan is an Assistant Professor in development planning at the Centre of Development Planning, Erasmus University, Rotterdam, where he teaches agricultural and industrial development, and econometrics. He has carried out research on employment and income distribution, human resources, small scale industries and rural transformation, with field work experience in Mexico, Colombia and India.

Arun Ghosh is an economist who has been associated with the government in various capacities, as Alternate Executive Director for India on the World Bank and the IMF, as economic adviser to the Ministry of Industry, as Chairman of the Bureau of Industrial Costs and Prices, and as Vice-Chairman of the West Bengal State Planning Board. His publications include a monograph entitled

Prices and Economic Fluctuations in India: 1861–1947. He is President of the Indian Association for Research in National Income and Wealth.

Bishwanath Goldar is a Reader at the Institute of Economic Growth, Delhi. He has published several papers on different aspects of Indian industry and is the author of *Productivity Growth in Indian Industry*.

S.R. Hashim is Professor of economics at the M.S. University of Baroda and is presently serving as Adviser, Perspective Planning, Planning Commission, Government of India. He earlier served as Consultant, Ministry of Planning, Government of Iraq and as Member, Narmada Planning Group, Government of Gujarat. He has published several articles in technical journals. He has authored several reports and monographs and has co-authored *Capital Output Relations in Indian Industries*.

I.M.D. Little is an Emeritus Fellow of Nuffield College, Oxford, and formerly Professor of economics of underdeveloped countries at the University of Oxford. He has also been Vice-President of the Development Centre of the OECD, and an Adviser at the World Bank. He is the author of many articles and books, the most recent being *Economic Development—Theory, Policy and International Relations*.

Dipak Mazumdar, a Senior Economist in the Development Research Department of the World Bank, is at present Professor of economics at the University of Toronto on leave of absence from the Bank. He taught at the London School of Economics before joining the Bank in 1976. He is the author of *Urban Labour Markets and Income Distribution: Case Study of Malaysia* and *Wages and Employment in Indonesia*, and has co-authored the forthcoming book on *Small-Scale Enterprise Development*. He has contributed to professional journals in the fields of development and labour economics.

V.S. Patvardhan has been a Reader in economics at the Gokhale Institute of Politics and Economics, Pune, since 1977. Prior to this, he was Deputy Chief in the Maharashtra State Financial Corporation, Bombay. He has published several research articles and his research publications include *Role of Small Scale Industries in the Process of Industrialization*. He has co-authored *Impact of PL 480 on Indian Economy*.

G. Ramachandran is a statistician who has been associated with the Government of India in the Central Statistical Organisation, the MRTP Commission, the Department of Company Affairs and has been, for a long period of twenty-four years, in the field of small industries under the Ministry of Industry. He planned, organised and conducted the country's first census survey of small industrial units in 1973–74.

M.R. Saluja is an Associate Professor at the Indian Statistical Institute, Delhi. He has published several articles on input-output analysis and planning models in technical journals. His books include *Indian Official Statistical System* and *Input-Output Tables for India: Concepts, Construction and Applications*. He has been a Consultant to various state governments on the formulation of planning models. He has also served as a Consultant to the World Bank. His current interests include planning models and data base of the Indian economy.

J.C. Sandesara is a Professor of industrial economics at the Centre of Advanced Study in the Department of Economics, University of Bombay. Earlier, he was at the M.S. University of Baroda. He has published books and papers on theory and policy largely in the area of industrial economics. He is a Member of the governing bodies of a number of research and training institutes. He has worked or is presently working as Chairman/Member of various panels of the central government, state governments, Planning Commission, Reserve Bank of India, Indian Council of Social Science Research and as member of the Board of Directors of public and private sector companies in India.

K. Sundaram is a Reader in economics at the Delhi School of Economics, University of Delhi. He has served as a member of the Expert Committee on Population Projections and of the Working Groups set up by the National Sample Survey Organisation in respect of the surveys on population, industry, employment, un-employment and consumer expenditure. He has published several articles in the area of poverty, unemployment, tax evasion and black money, tax reform, resource mobilisation and demography-development interrelations. His current work extends to issues of migration and productivity in Indian agriculture.

K.B. Suri is a Professor of economics and Head of the Humanities unit at the School of Planning and Architecture, New Delhi. Earlier, he taught at the International Institute of Population Sciences, Bombay, and worked at the Institute of Economic Growth, Delhi. He has been a Consultant to the World Bank on the Small Scale Enterprise Project. He has contributed to professional journals and edited the book *Environment, Shelter and Networks*.

Suresh D. Tendulkar is a Professor of economics at the Delhi School of Economics, University of Delhi. Earlier, he was with the Indian Statistical Institute, Delhi and the Gokhale Institute of Politics and Economics, Pune. He has been working in the field of economic development and planning in India.

J. George Waardenburg is Professor in development planning at the Centre for Development Planning at the Erasmus University, Rotterdam. He has co-authored the book *The Element of Space in Development Planning*. He has been researching and publishing on aspects of development in India and in China, in particular on small scale industries, rural capital formation and rural transformation.

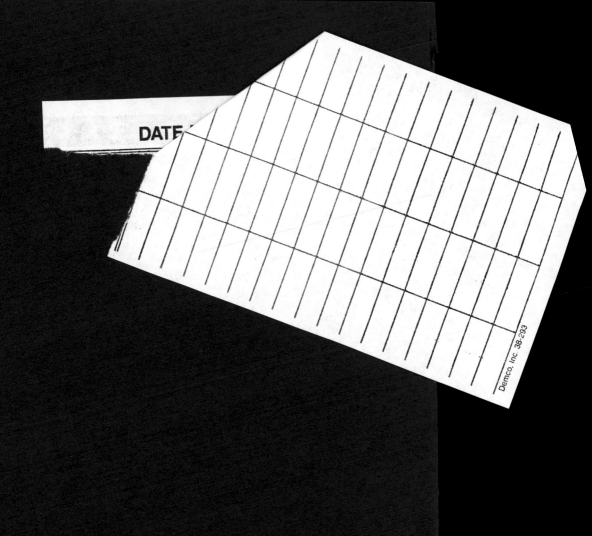

DATE

Demco, Inc. 38-293